COMMUNICATION AND CONTROL

THE GUILFORD COMMUNICATION SERIES

edited by

Theodore L. Glasser
Stanford University

Howard E. Sypher
University of Kansas

COMMUNICATION AND CONTROL: NETWORKS AND THE
NEW ECONOMIES OF COMMUNICATION
G. J. Mulgan

CASE STUDIES IN ORGANIZATIONAL COMMUNICATION
Beverly Davenport-Sypher, Editor

Forthcoming
VOICES OF CHINA: THE INTERPLAY OF POLITICS AND
JOURNALISM
Chin-Chuan Lee, Editor

STUDYING INTERPERSONAL INTERACTION
Barbara M. Montgomery and Steve Duck, Editors

COMMUNICATION AND CONTROL
Networks and the New Economies of Communication

G. J. MULGAN

THE GUILFORD PRESS

New York   London

© 1991 Geoff Mulgan
Published in the United States of America and Canada by
The Guilford Press
A Division of Guilford Publications, Inc.
72 Spring Street, New York, NY 10012

This book is printed on acid-free paper.

Last digit is print number: 9 8 7 6 5 4 3 2 1

Library of Congress Cataloging-in-Publication Data
Mulgan, G. J. (Geoffrey J.)
    Communication and control: networks and the new economies of
communication / G.J. Mulgan.
        p.   cm.   — (The Guilford communication series)
    Includes bibliographical references and index.
    ISBN 0–89862–311–1
    1.Computer networks — Social aspects.   2. Computer networks —
Political aspects. 3. Computer networks — Economic aspects.
I. Title.   II. Series.
TK5105.5.M85   1990
384 — dc20   90-40759
                                                       CIP

#21971212

64044

Printed in Great Britain

+K
5105.5
M85
1991

Contents

Introduction

The late twentieth-century world is covered by a lattice of networks. Public and private, civil and military, open and closed, the networks carry an unimaginable volume of messages, conversations, images and commands. By the early 1990s the world's population of over 600 million telephones and 600 million television sets will have been joined by over 100 million computer workstations, tens of millions of home computers, fax machines, cellular phones and pagers. Costs of transmission and processing will continue their precipitate fall.[1]

As networks and terminals spread, the story of how they have evolved, and of how computers and networks are being used to reshape the nature of culture and social life, war and work, is being told in a vast range of books, reports, articles and programmes, reflecting the full range from naive optimism to unmitigated pessimism. This study is concerned with just part of the story, with the changing relationship between control and communication and with the organization of the 'economies' of communications, the social structures governing networks, the allocation of the resources needed for communication, and the conditions of access and use.

Central to the argument advanced here is a set of ideas about control. We have become used to the idea that communications systems can carry conversations, films or sounds, but it is their nature as control infrastructures that generally pre-dates their role as media in the modern sense. The early postal networks of the Persian, Roman, Mongol and Chinese Empires, were tools of administration, under the direct control of military and politicial authorities. The first modern global network based on electricity, the British Empire's cable network, was also a tool of extensive control as well as a medium for trade and personal communication. The very first telegraph networks were designed to control the movements of trains along tracks, the radio to control the movement of ships; today's computer networks are primarily used to control flows of aircraft, missiles, goods, ideas and money. At the close of the twentieth century, too, it is the nature of communications networks as control technologies, as the means for coordinating the production, distribution and exchange of commodities, the logistical organization of armies and missiles or the effective governance of civil populations, that is proving most decisive in shaping the direction of technological development.

Most of the central questions of the information or post-industrial society are about control. They concern how information is to be controlled, whether through censorship, copyright, or privacy laws; they are about control over processes and flows of information at work and in the home; about the relationships between information and democratic control; and about state control over complex industries.

The bumpy evolution of techniques of control is one of the basic features of the modern world. The modern bureaucracy, a creation of the second half of the nineteenth century, the modern corporation, the plan, the forecast, the abstraction of information into statistics and cases, the replacement of judgement by decision-making rules, are all creatures of this evolution. All are now commonplace, but all are also very recent both in their practice and in the theoretical perspectives they implicitly carry. This economy of control is part of what Habermas describes as the systems world, made up of the abstract systems (primarily those of money and power) that shape human interaction with rules and structures, a world whose development of systems is a defining feature of industrial civilization. It is a world that contrasts with and stands against the 'life-world' of human experience that periodically bursts through and challenges its ordered regularities.

The crucial point for the argument made here is that it is into the history of the systems world and its economies of control that the new technologies are inserted. Placing technologies within this larger movement towards bringing predictability and order to the human and natural world, the argument suggests some of the tensions inherent to any application of technology.

One is the problem of complexity. As institutions, economies and societies grow and become more complex, their costs of coordination and control tend to rise faster than their material capacities. If the scale of a system doubles, the number of possible permutations is squared. This phenomenon, which was experienced in a very stark way in the early railways and telephone networks, gives rise to a permanent pressure to reorganize the way things are done. Reorganization turns out to be the only way to lower costs. It can be achieved through the use of information technology or through new relations of work and authority. The growing complexity of a more interconnected world, gives rise to a permanent crisis of control.

Usually there is more than one way to solve the crisis. The application of new methods of control engenders a tension between order and change: technologies can be used to tighten control and eliminate uncertainties, but unless there is some space for experiment, for risk and creativity, adaptation and evolution cease. This lesson from the world of biology applies throughout the social world. It is the first of the many limits to control.

Other limits arise from the distinctive characteristics of a world held together by the instant links of electronic communication. Interdependence (for good or ill) replaces independence and autarky, making it much harder to exercise control within a closed system. The operation of communications networks and of their industries, and of parallel sectors such as broadcasting and finance, begins to take on a quite different character. The kinds of control used in the past lose their efficacy. Speed replaces distance, so that the centres of two cities are often for practical purposes closer to each other than they are to their own peripheries. Equally characteristic of the networked world are the new forms of chaotic behaviour that have emerged, new vulnerabilities to sabotage or internal collapse. A larger quantitity of communication also makes for greater visibility, whether through imaging satellites or flows of financial data: in parallel, secrecy and invisibility take on a higher premium.

A world built on networks challenges traditional categories and intellectual structures on many fronts. It calls into question older conceptions of space and power. Where the early market economies grew out of the temporal and spatial regularities of city life, today's are built on the logical or 'virtual' regularities of electronic communication, a new geography of nodes and hubs, processing and control centres. The nineteenth century's physical infrastructures of railways, canals and roads are now overshadowed by the networks of computers, cables and radio links that govern where things go, how they are paid for, and who has access to what. The physical manifestations of power, walls, boundaries, highways and cities, are overlaid with a 'virtual' world of information hubs, data bases and networks. Buildings are redefined in terms of their position in networks as the electronic office and the automated factory are joined by the 'smart house', and as national boundaries are bypassed by flows of data and television images. In some cities the value of the electronic component of new buildings is reaching a third of the total value, a proportion almost as high as that prevailing in the case of machine tools. Meanwhile war, too, is redefined by the logic of speed and instant response, by electronic boundaries and surveillance, and by the rules of artificial intelligence programs that run weapons systems and robots. In war, as elsewhere, it is not that new forms of virtual power displace the older forms of power based on physical control, on monopolies of violence and coercion, but rather that they come to overlay the older forms, providing the space for new kinds of strategy and counterstrategy.

This book is an attempt to analyse the dynamics of these networks, and to suggest some of the keys to the life of societies increasingly dependent on flows of information and knowledge. Running through it is a story about control: the paradoxical fact that communications technologies simultaneously bring enormous enhancements of control to governments, corporations, consumers and voters, and a quite new order of chaos and uncontrollability which brings, in turn, a sense that control is unachievable.

Control has a double nature. Throughout human history two conceptions have coexisted, implicitly and explicitly. One is the notion of control as exogenous, imposed, abstracted and rationalized. The second is the notion of control as endogenous, as communicative and shared. Their twin histories, the one that of tools, weapons, techniques and structures, the second that of language, of commonality, of self-regulation and nurture, run in parallel. The tension between the two ideas of control forms a dramatic fault line at the heart of all information technologies which simultaneously offer massive enhancements of both types of control. It is a tension with implications far beyond the organization of the economies of communication, concerning as it does the ability of individuals and societies to determine their own fate, to learn collectively and to master the structures they create.

New technologies have served to highlight the extent to which control is never simple or one-dimensional. Just as more information can often mean less knowledge (one of the many paradoxes of an 'information age'), more control can also often mean less. More intensive control fosters a more intensive search for ways to avoid it, whether by dissidents, computer hackers and thieves, or disaffected workers. The proliferation of media can diminish their role as warning systems in relation to war or ecological catastrophe, thus lessening people's ability to control their own destiny. As Baudrillard has written in his typically extravagant style, 'instead of facilitating communication, it [information, message-in-circuit] exhausts itself in the staging of communication ... this is the gigantic simulation process'.[2]

Control technologies create their own limits, their own characteristic forms of volatility and unpredictability. The instantaneous nature of modern warfare or finance, a consequence of the marriage of computers and communications, takes many decisions beyond direct human control. Defense and safety systems demonstrate perverse behaviours when confronted with unforeseen events. Instantaneous global markets bring their own tendencies to sudden crisis, the value of currencies or commodities being highly dependent on networked perceptions and perceptions of perceptions. In the words of an official report on 1987's Black Monday, 'at no time did the risk of linking computers and telecommunications networks become more apparent'.[3] The same networking that is essential for extensive control brings with it new threats to security, strange phenomena such as the computer virus, and the erosion of familiar property rights evolved for a world in which goods could be bounded in space and time.

Two fundamental distinctions are used in the analysis of control in the communications economy. The first, already mentioned, is that between organic and imposed, or endogenous and exogenous, forms of control. Complexity is shown to be favouring a long-term shift towards more endogenous means of organizing control, cellular, decentralized, and less amenable to centralized pyramidal control. The second distinction that runs throughout the analysis is that between cybernetic, instrumental or purposive control, and positional control. The former concerns control towards given ends, the maximization of profit, or the solution of logistical coordination problems. The second is concerned with power and position in situations of uncertainty: what is valuable is the ability to exercise control and choice in the future. Together these pairs form a thread running through the book.

A number of other themes also run through the analysis. One is the relationship between openness and closure. Openness is a concept used both in the technical organization of networks (such as the open systems standards for computer communication and open network regulations for telecommunications networks) and in talk about economies and political systems. Openness is generally held to be a good thing, a guarantee of liberty and the free flow of ideas, of competition and efficiency in the economy and of transparency in the network. It appears to bring liberation and creativity. The argument developed here, however, suggests that openness in systems is not inherently superior to closure, but rather that they evolve in tandem. The human tendency to close, to create including and excluding groups, is paralleled in economic organization where institutions seek to create boundaries, and in technology where trends towards openness meet equally strong trends towards limiting it. Closure in its many forms is a necessary defence against uncertainty, danger and chaos. The complex dynamics of openness and closure derive from the overall increase in control capacities: because more control is available to all, the relative impacts of this on the balance between different social classes, professions or institutions are inherently hard to predict.

Another set of themes arises from economic theory which still finds it hard to theorize the nature of the values that circulate in a communications network or that are stored in a CD-ROM (compact-disc read only memory). All networks function in an environment in which values behave quite differently to those of material production and distribution.

Networks are nothing if not social; their usefulness and value are dependent on the numbers connected, their rules of inclusion and exclusion. Communication is never a simple transmission from one point to another, akin to the transport of a car or a loaf of bread. Instead, communications involves channels and systems in which the receiver and user plays as active a part as the provider or sender; for communications to work there must be shared languages, shared formats and shared assumptions about what is important or irrelevant. Gregory Bateson's definition of information as a difference that makes another difference, is a reminder that the second difference is actively made by the receiver.[4]

The subtitle – 'the new economies of communication' – refers to a further theme that runs through the analysis. In its older senses an economy is a household, farm or enterprise, rather than its more modern meaning of a structure of systematically interacting elements. In Friedrich Hayek's useful definition, an economy is a 'complex of activities by which a given set of means is allocated in accordance with a unitary plan among the competing ends according to their relative important'.[5] The national or international economy is thus better described as a 'network of interlaced economies'. This older sense of the economy is useful for understanding the dynamics of communications. Much of the story of recent years is of the convergence of different economies onto the same technologies and networks. Narrowly economic goals mingle with cultural and social ones, collective ones with individual ones. A monetary economy driven by profit maximization meets systems driven by very different ends. Disentangling these, and recognizing that different types of end must necessarily coexist in any system of communication is important if communication is not to be crudely reduced to a single economy, a single system of profit maximization or consumer sovereignty.

The analysis is also concerned with issues in economic theory. Modern neoclassical economics grew up to describe the world of the emerging industrial economies. Factories were seen to use inputs of raw material, labour and capital to produce goods which were then sold to consumers. The shift towards economies based on information has thrown up profound problems for this metaphoric world of scarcity and equilibria, of marginal quantities and equations of cost and price, a world of physical inputs and outputs. The situation echoes that faced by the Physiocrats of the eighteenth century, who confronted an embryonic industrial world that called into question the very essence of their theories. Twentieth-century economics faces an equally unsettling experience. It is extremely hard, if not impossible, usefully to define the value of creativity, of a mathematical theorem, or an artificial intelligence program. The value of any informational product bears little relation to the costs and conditions of production. Marginal costs of reproduction and dissemination are generally close to zero. In place of the relatively simple world of physical goods, of definable inputs and outputs, the information economy is bound up with strategy, with the organization of repertoires of products and the creation of markets, and with short and unstable half-lives as information becomes worthless. Most fundamental of all, where economics is the study of scarcity and of how naturally scarce resources are produced and exchanged, the fundamental problem facing those involved in making and selling information is the need to constrain the natural fluidity of information by creating artificial forms of scarcity with copyrights, patents, and encryption codes. In the broadband fibre-optic networks being built in the major cities and laid beneath the world's oceans there is almost unlimited potential capacity for communication; their problems too will be those of abundance rather than scarcity.

Communications technologies also challenge the political motifs of Western thought. We are beginning to understand that flows of information and communicational competences are crucial to making ideas of representation, of citizenship or of democracy meaningful. According to some commentators the personalization offered by new generations of technology bypasses problems of representation and mediation, returning politics to a simpler and more direct world of one-to-one communication. A more measured response recognizes that what is happening is not an end to mediation, but rather the emergence of more complex structures of mediation through which the world is seen and comprehended (and systematically misrecognized). The greater flows of communication sustained by new technologies can never be expected to promote enlightenment or the triumph of the true over the false. Knowledge is rarely equivalent to power in any simple sense. It is worth recalling Umberto Eco's definition of semiotics as the study of whatever can be used to lie with. The age of Bell, Zworkin and Baird may also be by definition the age of Goebbels and Zhdanov, Saatchi and Saatchi and Ronald Reagan. Techniques of swamping, spin control, the unattributable leak and the unanswerable lie develop in tandem with the technologies which carry them. Walter Benjamin's critique of the equation of knowledge and power is also worth recalling: certain kinds of knowledge can be disabling unless they have a place in practice.[6]

Underlying the arguments made here is a claim about the emerging societies of the industrialized world: rather than being information societies these are better understood as structured around ever more pervasive and complex systems of control. The notion of the controlled society (the 'Kanri Shakai' in Japanese), where control is conceived as something that weighs down on people from above, is fairly widespread: what takes the argument a step further is the recognition that control is not simply a burden. Control can be liberating as well as oppressive. Even as societies become more systematic and controlled, freedom and control pass to individuals and groups to be used in non-rational, anti-systemic ways. Control is neither inherently good nor evil but rather a basic resource of advanced societies that needs to be understood both as to its potential and as to its limits. Like power and reason, it demands neither an excessive love nor an excessive fear.

The focus on control represents a move away from the use of the concept of power as a dominant political metaphor. Where power is a physical, energizing and mechanical metaphor, control is a concept more appropriate to a world aware of the importance of information. Control includes within itself the principles of feedback, command, strategy and surveillance. As a concept of cybernetics it moves the focus from questions of 'control over' to those of 'control within' a system or environment. The virtue of an analysis of control is, in other words, its recognition of process and structure, and its recognition that effective 'power', influence and achievement depend on the ability to formulate strategies and understandings, on channels of command, feedback and surveillance. The aim is not to deny the deep roots of social power, but rather to suggest a complementary perspective.

Through the course of the book the argument develops from general observations about the nature of networks and control to more focused analyses. Each chapter is written to stand alone as a self-contained essay. Chapter 1 is concerned with the nature of the information or post-industrial society and the place of control; it emphasizes the importance of understanding information as a derived demand, that is to say an intermediate good and service in the wider economy of control. It then proceeds to discuss the nature of networks, both social and economic, and the emergence of network utopias and dystopias. Chapter 2 describes the role of electronic networks in the advanced economies, the trends towards fragmentation and integration, complexity and convergence. Chapter 3 develops the distinctions between organic and imposed, purposive and positional control, and the contexts within which control networks are being implemented: the control of households and consumers, of governments and firms, war and democracy. Chapter 4 discusses the changing nature of control in economic life and the history of the emergence of corporate forms and automation, placing current generations of technology within the historical context of changing forms of control in economic life. Chapter 5 provides an overview of the evolution of network technologies – in particular the Integrated Services Digital Network, the Intelligent Network and broadband networks – and the peculiar nature of control as a commodity within electronic networks. Chapter 6 brings together analysis of free flow and control in ideas and in the cultural industries, covering questions of intellectual property, piracy, security and censorship, and the ways in which network technologies undermine older structures of control. Chapter 7 offers an analysis of the changing forms of state regulation and control over networks, suggesting that deregulation is better understood as a change in the nature of control rather than its dissolution, a change that is a response to the paramountcy of economic considerations. Chapter 8 develops a critique of unified value theories and suggests how an analysis of value in communication reveals the heterogeneous spheres or economies that make up economic life. Chapter 9 discusses the nature of standards in communication, and the relationship between standardization and flexibility, and chapter 10 the role of markets and bureaucracies in the allocation of electromagnetic spectrum. Both seek to show the limits of classically conceived markets, and to demonstrate that complex institutional structures are essential to the effective organization of communication. Chapter 11 analyses private corporate networks and the relationships between communications systems and organizational structure in transnational corporations. Finally, chapter 12 addresses the issue of how public control has been defined and deformed during the course of the twentieth century, and how it might be rethought to guide the evolution of networks in the twenty-first.

1

Networks and Post-industrial Societies

Electronic communications networks transmit, manipulate and process electronic information. Radio waves radiate through space. Electrons and photons travel along cables and around semiconductors forming complex patterns of ons and offs. Process and transmission, input and output, and the storage of wave patterns and bits represent the sum of what these networks can do. Why then are they so important and why have electronic communications networks come to be seen as the essential infrastructure of advanced societies?

The communications revolution, familiar from a thousand television programmes, articles and books, is generally conceived as a revolution in the production and dissemination of information and knowledge. Both are seen as things that are created and disseminated. Data, literally the given, are formed into information which, through the application of intelligence and experience, produces knowledge. The information revolution is seen to bring a transformation in the ways in which information is produced, formatted, packaged, processed and distributed. Vastly more can be stored, disseminated and cross-referenced than ever before. Knowledge becomes increasingly exterior to its producers and to the trained minds which use it. It takes on the characteristics of a commodity that is priced and exchanged in markets, while culture takes on the form of flows of electronic information.

The focus on flows and stocks of information, culture and knowledge brings with it a series of economic and political implications. The economic ones parallel those of other industries, concerning how production is to be made competitive, how trade is to be organized, and how the nature of information as a commodity is to be controlled. The political questions also come to concern access and flows – who has access to information, who is information rich or information poor.

Unfortunately, this common-sense approach, which sees the information revolution as primarily about information, is misleading. Information only gains meaning within a particular context. Otherwise information is meaningless; it is indistinguishable from noise. A starting point for understanding why this is the case is the use of information in machines. Very diverse activities and technologies are lumped together as examples of information technology. Both automated factories and compact discs manipulate symbols, but this observation does not help us understand the dynamics of why and how they are produced or the purposes for which they are used. What they do share with all other information technologies, however, is a common control capacity: in the one case ordering flows of inputs and outputs, in the other recreating the integrity of an original recording and eliminating interference and errors.

No machine requires information or knowledge except as a means to control, in a context of decision rules and purposes defined by the maker or programmer. It is this capacity which unites the cluster of technologies that use and manipulate electronic information – the transistor and semiconductor, the fibre-optic cable and microwave transmitter – and which has helped them become 'heartland' technologies that have an impact on and are integrated with all other goods and services from cars to healthcare, household appliances, sensors and mobile telephones to production systems. The names generally used to describe this cluster of technologies, information technology, telematique and informatics are in this sense inappropriate. All refer to the content or form rather than its underlying purpose, which is the systematic and pervasive enhancement of capacities to control things and people. From the early applications of Hollerith's machines to the censuses of the late nineteenth century, to the aircraft tracking algorithms of the first ENIAC computer and the software problems of the USA's Strategic Defense Initiative (SDI), the trend of change has been towards more efficient, comprehensive and rapid means of coordinating and controlling objects and events dispersed in time and space.

As systems become more complex their control needs expand disproportionately. The early railways experienced this dramatically. As lines spread across the US and Europe, the railway companies found that, far from experiencing returns to scale, costs per ton-mile rose. The 'basic reason was the lack of proper internal organization'. One part of the solution was the invention of much of the machinery of the modern corporation; the problem was solved through organization.[1] A few decades later, the first telephone operators experienced a similar phenomenon. As more subscribers joined the networks, switchboards grew out of hand and labour costs mushroomed. Again, costs-per-line rose as the networks grew. According to one early operator 'all we had to do was get enough subscribers and the company would go bust'.[2] Again, the solution was organizational, involving new management structures and the use of the new Strowger automatic switches.[3]

Though particularly acute in the case of networks the experience is general. A more complex, interconnecting society or economy demands a higher order of control. The needs of a global system are distinct from those of a national one. This underlying pressure of complexity explains much about the information society, and why the incessant revolutionization of the means of production described by Marx has given way to an incessant revolutionization of control itself: a permanent revolution in organizational structures, of risk, error and innovation. It also explains why there is nothing particularly revolutionary about current generations of computers and networks. Problems of control are eternal and ubiquitous in all economic systems, military enterprises and political structures. The revolutionizing of control in accounting; in continuous-flow production processes; in distribution, marketing and finance; in bureaucracies, governments and intelligence has been an essential response to the growth of modern industrial societies.

What is distinctive about the present era is the changing nature of the techniques and technologies of control that are used to cope with complexity: the intelligent machines of the late twentieth century not only carry out control tasks but also produce information about themselves, enlarging by an order of magnitude both the scope for surveillance and control, and the realm of choice and strategy. In the word used by Shoshanna Zuboff, they 'informate'.[4]

The emphasis on information as a means to control carries its own economic and political implications. The economic focus shifts away from information as a commodity towards its use within structures of control. The emphasis shifts from information as a discrete commodity towards flows and systems of communications, and towards the problems of controlling flows. At the same time the political issues of the 'information society' come to be concerned less with access to information (as if it were a resource analogous to housing or energy), than with the distribution of control capacities within a society, and with the availability of competence and time to use control technologies or to participate in decisions. Access to quantities of information becomes less important than the structures within which information becomes meaningful and usable. What turns out to be scarce is the capacity to use information rather than information as such.

Post-industrial Societies

The emphasis on control offers a different explanation of the post-industrial society to those which focus on higher needs or the end of work. In many contexts the deployment of new technologies is less a transcendence of the industrial age than an extension of its principles to knowledge, culture and control. Societies are becoming super-industrial rather than post-industrial.[5] Most labour is still directed in regimented and standardized ways towards the output of goods and services and towards the more intensive and extensive movement from inputs to outputs. Information technologies continue to be most revolutionary not in creating the new out of nothing but rather in restructuring the way old things are done. Industry remains a dominant social, political and ideological force while leisure is, paradoxically, downgraded (not least because of its association with the enforced leisure of the unemployed victims of restructuring) at the very moment when the post-industrial age comes in sight.

Much of the world, too, is only just experiencing the fruits of an industrial revolution: the heady brew of mobility and social disruption, consumer durables, cars and industrial pollution. Elsewhere there is a full-scale retreat from even the most modest economic progress. Uneven development across the globe, within countries and cities, is more marked than ever before, in communications as in every field. Over a hundred years after it was invented between a third and a half of the world's population still lives more than two hours' travel away from the nearest telephone and, even in an advanced country like the UK, a sixth of all households and about half of those on low incomes do not have a telephone.

Uneven and uncertain though its realization may be, the idea of a rapid transition to a post-industrial or information society or economy has become an accepted common sense, particularly amongst political and economic decision makers. Ideas of modernity and of progress towards the new society have been profoundly shaped by perceptions of how communications technologies could work. In the plethora of writings about the near future the post-industrial or information society is often described as having a cluster of related characteristics which flow from the properties of communications technologies. The definitions of Yoneji Masuda, President of the Institute for the Information Society in Japan, ranging through economic, political and social life, and outlined in his book *The Information Society*,[6] are typical. Information and computing power are held to be the key resources of this society, its essential function the amplification of mental labour and its leading industries the knowledge industries. Its basic unit is the voluntary community, its governmental form the participatory democracy. Work is to be dispersed in electronic cottages and flexible, small-scale units, the media 'demassified' and awareness heightened as the global flow of messages accelerates. The information society is nothing if not desirable, seen as consonant with the true values of civilizations both East and West, values which had had to be suppressed to serve the crude demands of industrial society. In the work of others, notably Daniel Bell, Tom Stonier, James

Martin and Christopher Evans, the changing place of information is explicitly linked to changing structures of control, above all to its devolution from traditional concentrations in government, office, factory, television network and newspaper.[7]

Underlying all ideas of a new stage of civilization based on information is the older one of a unilinear course of social development, or at the very least an assumption that even if the paths of change are different their destinations will be the same. Few commentators believe that there might be fundamentally different lines of development and fundamentally different destinations. Widespread acceptance of the unilinear analyses of the information society has led many countries to compete in the struggle to expedite the transition from agricultural societies, through industrialism to the post-industrial society. For the advanced countries the important questions concern when and how this transition can be effected rather than whether it is either desirable or possible. The European Commission, for example, has estimated (albeit on very doubtful premises) that by the year 2000 telecommunications will be its single largest industry, accounting for 7 per cent of Gross Domestic Product compared to 2 per cent in 1984, and indirectly supporting 60 per cent of all employment. Numerous programmes of research and investment are justified by the need to speed up the informatization of European economies, the better to compete with the US, Japan and the newly industrialized countries. Change is conceived as discontinuous, a profound break with the past, and described as a new industrial revolution that demands rapid changes in institutions, everyday processes and attitudes.

The unilinear course is sometimes understood as a march through the sectors: from agriculture, arms and construction through consumer durables to the cultural industries and information services. A parallel heirarchy (associated with Maslow) describes human needs, passing from the need for food, shelter and security, through possessions to self-value, belonging and self-realization.[8] In one version, the information society is an inevitable consequence of prosperity: once basic needs are satisfied, time and resources can be devoted to higher psychic and cultural needs. According to this view the rapid growth of new industries in computing and communications is essentially a reflection of changing patterns in final demand. As such it is to be welcomed, for it reflects the maturity of societies that can now devote resources to the full panoply of human needs.

Nearly all the information society projections contain an implicit link between human needs and industrial outcomes. But the foundations for this link are tenuous. Even the most cursory study of history or anthropology reveals the surprising scale of resources devoted to religion and meaning in materially poor societies, and the complex ways in which meanings are bound up with the making and use of material objects. But the most striking weakness of theories that link human needs to changing industrial structures is their failure to explain the present. Far from originating in final demand and human needs, the most urgent demands for the new communications technologies have come from within industry and from state and military organization.[9] They reflect the need for information only as a means to control. New and higher human needs are rarely reflected in home consumption patterns.

The point was clearly made by one commentator in an analysis of the US economy: the 'output of the information sector is used primarily by industry rather than directly by consumers. Whereas final consumption of such information items as the media and printed matter had reached $84 bn by 1972 this figure is dwarfed by the $806 bn flow of information sector services required by the production sector.'[10] A similar point was made in relation to employment by Gershuny and Miles:

during the 1960s and 1970s changes in the occupational distribution of employment have resulted more from changes in occupational structure within economic sectors than from changes in demand patterns between them. Increased demand for professional, technical, clerical and other specialised service occupations relative to other employment within each sector accounts for much more of the increase of employment in these sorts of occupation than does the increase in demand for the products of service industries.[11]

The transformation of services and manufacturing, and their interpenetration, have arisen from changes in organization and technology rather than in final demand. In one study,[12] over three-quarters of information technology investment in both the UK and US was found to be in services, as services became industrialized and less bound by time and space and by the need for face-to-face interaction.

Consumer demand for culture and information services as a proportion of overall spending has in fact risen only very slowly, if at all, over the last century. Its stability is such that within communications studies there is a famous 'law of relative constancy' derived from time-series analyses of consumer spending. Where change has occurred it has been in the composition of this spending, mainly in the shift away from services towards the domestic capital of television sets, video recorders, personal computers and hi-fi systems. There is little evidence that the material watched on new television sets meets higher needs than the plays or films of the past. What evidence there is shows how limited is the capacity of consumers to use information, not least because cultural consumption takes place within real time. It is extremely hard, and scarcely rewarding, to read two books or watch two television programmes at the same time. Where demand has increased it has been in the most utilitarian forms of information. In the United States the proportion of consumer spending on books, newspapers and magazines, radio, television, records and cassettes actually fell between 1947 and 1983 from 2.3 to 1.7 per cent of GNP. Relative constancy had turned into relative decline. During the same period consumption of information such as legal or medical advice, financial services and private education almost doubled, from 3.4 to 6.6 per cent.[13]

Where the demands of the home are limited, the demands of the economy appear at first sight to be almost limitless, especially when technologies are being used to integrate planning, control, production and distribution into a total system. Some see this 'derived' demand as a simple reflection of complexity: firms and governments are faced with ever more complex tasks of coordination and information-gathering. Their demand for information is not constrained by the time economy of home consumption, especially when it can be consumed and processed by computers. But the idea that complexity demands more information provides only a partial explanation. Complexity only has an impact on demand because of its context. Again what is being described is the what and how rather than the why. The demand for the hardware and software of information technologies can be better conceived as reflecting a need for control that goes beyond coordination. What is needed is a capacity to cope with unpredictable and volatile environments and 'noisier' information environments, and to bring order and responsiveness to variables within the organization. This wider conception helps explain why spending on communications technologies has risen so fast during periods of economic crisis, intensified international competition and intensified struggle between labour and management.

The Control Economy

Only one major recent work has analysed the origins of the 'information revolution' in terms of control. James Beniger has traced the causes of change 'back to the middle and late nineteenth century, to a set of problems, in effect a crisis of control generated by the industrial revolution in manufacturing and transportation', arguing that the turn of the century brought 'a revolution in societal control'.[14] From this perspective Beniger sees the modern bureaucracy as in many ways more revolutionary than the computer. He also emphasizes the striking speed with which the key communications technologies, ranging from the typewriter to the radio, the telephone to the television, all emerged within the span of a single lifetime between 1860 and 1925. Despite Beniger's overly simple conception of control he is to be credited for focusing attention on the crucial importance of what I term the control economy: the set of techniques, institutions and people concerned with coordination, decision-making and command.

The emergence of control as an organizing principle in modern societies brought with it new values, now professions and new centres of power. Although control never depended solely on technology (extremely complex collective projects involving huge numbers of calculations such as the Manhattan Project, Wall Street and the London Stock Exchange, were organized without computers and high-capacity networks) it has nevertheless been shaped by the available means of organizing knowledge, commands and surveillance. This emerging control economy has proved extremely hard to map or model. Those variables that can be quantified and defined are rarely the ones that determine the practice of control, which depends rather on authority and legitimacy, informal networks and oral relationships. Unlike manual and clerical work, the work of management has always proved extremely resistant to systematization. More generally the 'softening' of the economy, as non-material functions contribute an ever larger share of value, has proved hard to capture in theoretical analysis.

Such estimates as have been made, notably Marc Uri Porat's research suggesting that the decision-making and control apparatus of the US economy represented 21 per cent of GNP in 1967, can offer only limited insight.[15] Even Porat's basic distinction between the knowledge economy of research, broadcasting and education, and the control economy of transactions, accountancy and management is less than clear cut, when much of the output of the knowledge economy is ephemeral, structured economic information used within everyday control tasks. Statistical rigour requires that information-processing tasks are abstracted from other tasks. Thus the program stored in a robot is judged to be informational, while the craft knowledge that it replaces is not. The different categories of information work, involving producers, processors, distributors and infrastructure workers, are only loosely defined. The general impression given by the work of Porat and his predecessor, Machlup,[16] is of a steadily growing demand for various forms of information, but the evidence remains ambiguous.

Lumping tasks together into an information economy has some value as a crude way of pointing to the importance of information in economic life. But it fails to explain the underlying dynamics or why different kinds of information usage are growing or declining. A more fruitful approach has been taken by economists drawing on the theories of Joseph Schumpeter who have analysed the spread of information technologies as one of a succession of structural technological revolutions. Change is understood in terms of the diffusion of a set of techniques associated with core technologies such as the steam engine, electricity or microelectronics.[17] Historical analysis highlights the cycles whereby swarms of inventions emerge around new technologies, bringing incompatible standards, overinvestment, and a subsequent wave of technical and commercial rationalization.[18] The focus on technologies rather than information in its widest sense brings the analysis down to earth: what is occurring is a spread of control technologies, centred on the programmability and processing power of microelectronics, together with a set of new techniques for organization.

The emphasis on technologies avoids the danger of abstracting control functions from other ones: the worker, the manager, the teacher and the media worker all combine control functions with other roles.

Their productivity remains a central problem for advanced societies. Studies of informational work and productivity have consistently shown that while employment in the control economy, or the wider information sector, has grown substantially, its productivity has grown much less rapidly than that of the rest of the economy. In the advanced industrial countries since 1900 blue-collar productivity has risen sevenfold while white-collar productivity has been roughly constant. As the information sector has grown it has correspondingly served to slow down overall productivity growth in the economy as a whole. In the US, its contribution to GNP has stabilized at around 34 per cent, the proportion of employment at around 41 per cent. The role of the informational sector as a drag on productivity can also be explained in terms of the relative efficiency with which information is used in industry.[19]

During the 1970s and 1980s there were marked shifts in spending patterns as consumers used domestic capital to solve the productivity problem on their own behalf. Between 1970 and 1980, spending on informational machines rose from 2.3 of GNP to 3.2 per cent, on information services from 6.7 to 8.4 per cent. At the same time spending on education fell from 14.8 to 12.5 per cent. This is one of many examples where the spread of communications capacities, an apparently socializing trend, can coincide with the privatization of collective consumption. It is a shift analogous to that from the telegraph to the telephone (expenditure on the telephone first exceeded that on the telegraph in the US in 1890) and that from public transport to the car (expenditure on the car first exceeded that on public transport in 1930). A similar shift occurred in the 1980s as the video sector overtook cinema exhibition.

Differences in productivity growth between and within sectors often go a long way in explaining the origin of crises. As productivity rises in manufacturing sectors similar crises are faced by welfare states and information services, neither of which can easily increase productivity.

The state seeks to improve efficiency of provision, moving labour costs onto the informal and voluntary sector and narrowing the terms of provision. Informational services have to strive all the harder to achieve economies of scale or a unique specialization. The result of differential productivity growth is a shift in value. According to the French communications theorist Jean Voge, the added value of information, representing essentially the costs of organization, has grown (in constant money terms and for the average American worker) twice as fast as its global productivity, multiplying 14 times in 83 years.[20] This added value involves a shift in value and profit from the industrial sector towards information and financial sectors, which, paradoxically, become the beneficiaries of enhanced industrial productivity.[21]

Drawing on analogies from other fields, including the work of the ecologist Howard Odum, Voge has argued that there is a general limit, around 50 per cent, to the amount of resources or energies which can be devoted to control rather than primary productive activity. As the resources devoted to control have neared 50 per cent the control economy has become a fetter on the development of production as a whole. The added value left to the 'material sector' barely increases once the information sector exceeds 40 per cent of the economy and begins to fall once it reaches 50 per cent. Most advanced economies have come near to this point, as each worker supports roughly one non-worker, each white-collar worker one manual worker. Although Voge's argument may not have the wide applicability it claims, it does at least suggest why massive investments in control technologies have not had the predicted effects on productivity (Robert Solow has pointed out that the computer age can be seen everywhere but in the productivity statistics) and why the organization of control is likely to remain a pressing problem for any advanced economy.

The Idea of the Network

If the classic structure for exercising control is the pyramid, the classic structure within which information is distributed is the network. Networks have come to be seen as the quintessential organizational form of the post-industrial or information society.

A network is a system of nodes and links that can be described by its topology and architecture. It has both a physical form and a logical one in so far as it is governed both by physical interconnections and by sets of rules that govern exchanges of energy or information. The spread of electronic networks has been matched by a widespread use of the network as a logical device or metaphor, something that is good to think with. As a metaphor the word fills many different roles, describing grids of fibre, copper cable and radio, links of personal friendship and informal relationships in political organizations, to mention just a few. So widely used is it that the word sometimes seems to lose its original meaning, of an object in which threads or wires are arranged in the form of a net: a sense that came to include systems of rivers, canals and railways. This underlying meaning, of a set of lines and crossing points, of nodes and links, gives the idea of a network broad applicability in complex, dense and highly interactive societies. Few areas of human life do not involve connecting webs of this kind.

The network also serves as a suitable image for the computer age for another reason. Computers have done much to spread familiarity with the idea of logical rather than physical space, with their topological representations of flow diagrams, branching trees and other patterns. In a culture based more on images and less on the linear logic of texts there seems to be a need for topographical and visual metaphors to replace older metaphorical systems based on such concepts as equilibrium and order, hydraulics, repression and entropy. Just as the physical machinery of networks and computers creates new logical spaces of configuration, this visual, metaphoric language transforms how the world is seen. Examples of this change include systems theories of society and cognitive psychology both of which model systems in logical space. And whereas in the eighteenth and nineteenth centuries the workings of the brain or of societies were conceived as analogous to those of the loom or the steam engine, both are today conceived as complex networked systems for producing and processing information.

The communications networks that give complex systems their coherence sometimes appear as the 'entire nervous system of social organisation',[22] the primary means for linking an advanced society's senses, thoughts, and actions. This theme is not new. It echoes a long tradition that has analysed society as an organism. An earlier writer described commerce as the lifeblood of Britain, and the roads, railways and waterways as 'the arteries through which this blood is conducted, while the telegraph and telephone may be compared to the nerves which feel out and determine the course of that circulation'.[23] Sociobiologists and functionalists have drawn on these metaphors to incorporate the study of communications networks into their field. James Beniger's work on control treats biological organisms, computers and societies as essentially analogous, guided by control structures and programs towards clearly defined goals. In a similar vein some evolutionary theories of economic life see the economy as a single organism evolving to higher levels of complexity. The evolution of control technologies is simply part of the long-term movement towards greater complexity and differentiation, an unambiguous progress.

This widely used analogy between societies and living creatures is deceptive. What it fails to explain satisfactorily are the purposes that underlie both the spread of networks and the actual uses of communication. Networks are not simply systems for coordinating resources towards clear goals. The goal of survival or reproduction that guides the behaviour of an animal's nervous system has no clear parallel in complex human societies. Instead all purposes and all controls are contested. There are no universal ends. The networks which humans create exist in a world of power and conflict, of positional advantage and struggle over surpluses. The same is true of the information and knowledge that is distributed over networks. The greatest value of information appears in situations of conflict and competition, where exclusive or superior knowledge confers leverage. Networks are created not just to communicate but also to gain position, to outcommunicate. This basic truth applies equally to informal social networks of kinship, ethnicity or shared education, and to private corporate networks used to enhance control over labour and to maximize competitive advantage over rivals.

The social nature of networks is double-edged. The value of a network grows in proportion to the number of possible interconnections rather than the number of those linked to the network. But the value of networks is also bound up with the demand for exclusivities and restraints on communication. Information often takes the properties of what economics describes as club or quasi-public goods. In the earliest days of the telephone rich customers complained that if penetration rates grew they would be subject to unsolicited disturbance by members of other classes. Today, digital technologies offer the possibility of screening incoming calls, and of creating entirely closed user-group networks within institutions or between groups of individuals. Each is a response to the double-edged communality of the network.

The world of the sociobiologists and systems theorists is mirrored in an alternative view of the network that has spread with surprising rapidity in recent years. According to this view evolving network structures are a natural repository of cooperation, equality and harmony. Networks are systems of exchange and integration rather than violence and coercion. The pacific reciprocity inherent in the network lends it a benign, harmonious image. In principle any node can communicate with any other as an equal. Many writers have drawn on these associations. In the early nineteenth century the Saint-Simonians wrote of the network as the means to the universal association. Lenin wrote of the postal network as prefiguring communist society, and made explicit the relationship between electricity networks and socialism in one of the most famous slogans of the revolutionary period.[24] The writers of the 1980s have argued that the 'information float' that preserved elites in the past are set to disappear as networks make information universally available. Because networks use endlessly reproducible information, concentrations of power become impossible to sustain: 'the new power is not money in the hands of the few but information in the hands of the many'.[25]

Networks also become agents of decentralization, dissolving the pyramid structures of the traditional bureaucracy or corporation. Toffler wrote of a 'fundamental decentralization of communications as the power of the central network wanes',[26] Nora and Minc of telematics allowing 'decentralization or even autonomy of basic units' multiplying the areas in which the small organization would be superior to the large. 'The workshop will replace the factory, the branch office will replace the conglomerate.'[27] The rise of distributed processing, rapid reductions in the cost of processing power symbolized by the spread of the personal computer and experiments with interactive cable systems all seemed to portend a technologically led restructuring of power. Interconnectivity would have spiritual as well as social effects. When 'such systems become widespread, potentially intense communications networks among geographically dispersed persons will become actualized. We will become a network nation, exchanging vast amounts of information and social and emotional communications with colleagues, friends and "strangers" who share similar interests, who are spread all over the nation'.[28] 'The vast, vibrant, still-inchoate metanetwork of people and organisations we call the Invisible Planet is coalescing in every area of personal and social life.'[29]

Writers such as Toffler, Naisbitt, Masuda, Hayashi, Lippnack, Hine and Nora have argued that there is an historic transformation away from hierarchical, pyramid-like structures towards more complex, decentralized, interactive and egalitarian structures. The era of the one-way television network, of the bureaucracy, the centralized state and the pyramidal corporation is seen to be evolving towards one based on reciprocal relationships and participation, in which knowledge and creativity are the key resources and the free flow of information erodes traditional authority and concentrations of power. Echoing the earlier writings of Thomas More, Gerard Winstanley and Marx, they make the claim that greater material abundance can begin to release energy for innovation and creativity. Utopia begins with a heap of gadgets, carrying on the long tradition (ably described by Stuart Ewen) of symbiosis between consumerism and utopianism.[30]

The claim is that control can be dispersed throughout a society on the back, as it were, of the communications system. The communications society is conceived as self-regulating and self-controlling. The vision, which has spread through sociology and radical movements, business theory and futurology, is a hopeful one of greater openness and fluidity, whether in organizations or in the physical architecture of communications networks. It is tied to the idea that all advanced industrial societies are undergoing a fundamental and revolutionary transformation, a third revolution involving information and knowledge that will prove as profound as the industrial and agricultural revolutions before it. Within this revolution the network, open, horizontal and interactive, has emerged both as a dominant organizing principle and as the main infrastructure for economic activity.

Faith in the redeeming power of technology has a long history. Kropotkin believed that electricity would help to break down previously centralized organizations dependent on inflexible, concentrated sources of energy, while the rifle was seen as a democratizing technology. Once in the hands of the people it would render tyranny obsolete. Control over physical violence would cease to be a monopoly of the state. In the mid-nineteenth century writers seriously discussed a future in which steam would come to replace all work. Railways were expected to eliminate wars, uniting Europe and the Americas, and radio was to act as an unstoppable force for cultural elevation. It is not hard to appreciate the attractions of the vision of a technology as *deus ex machina*, come to end problems of domination, inequality and alienation.

What is striking about the 'network utopians' of the late twentieth century, however, is the new nature of the link made between technological forms and social ones. The horizontal and open network is emerging as a technical reality, based on small computers, on open systems standards and open network type regulations, at the same time as it emerges as a political vision of a self-organizing society. Within networks control in a technical sense can be devolved in ways that were not possible in the past. Ideas, slogans and metaphors slip from the writings of futurologists into network planning committees and out again into political debate. This often brings conceptual confusion. Technical openness in a network is very different from true openness in communication and widespread access to the competences needed to communicate effectively. Just as the rifle could be used in the most tyrannical armies, so can liberating technologies and networks organizational forms be used within structures that remain deeply authoritarian. But the power of network utopias remains resistant to qualifications of this kind. Like any modern revolutionary ideology its attraction stems from its ability to combine the 'is' of existing transformations and the 'ought' of a better world.

Transparency and Remote Control

Alongside the vision of the pacific, harmoniously communicating community the technical capabilities of communications technologies have also fostered a parallel theme, with very different social and political implications. This is 'transparency': communication without noise or impediment in real time throughout the globe. It is a goal with origins in the military sphere: the enemy's movements and purposes become transparent through the use of high-resolution satellites and remotely powered spy planes and the plethora of techniques now used to 'vacuum the electromagnetic spectrum' for voices and data. This notion of transparent control was present in the earliest networks. The optical telegraph of Chappe in France was designed as a means of territorial surveillance, the communicational glue of the modern nation state. Like the famous panopticon it guaranteed the ability of the centre to monitor the periphery.

In the military sphere transparent control affords the central command instantaneous access to monitor and command every plane, missile, tank or company. An assault on a hill village or the firing of Inter-continental Ballistic Missiles (ICBMs) can be controlled from a headquarters in Washington or Moscow, with every action and reaction continuously monitored. The goal is a system of total control and flexibility, in which human frailty is banished. A very similar ideal has gathered momentum in economic life. The imaging satellites of the military are now matched by commercial satellites such as SPOT which sell pictures showing objects less than 10 metres across.[31] The military communications networks are paralleled by the private networks of transnational firms pursuing a vision of real-time control over distant factories, offices, research laboratories and warehouses. As for the military, the continuous gathering and processing of information, in this case about changing markets, prices, technologies and political conditions, is inseparable from the use of command structures. Their application of 'transparent' technologies has prompted a fundamental restructuring of organizations as layers of middle management are removed. Used in the past as relayers of information, these are now seen as unnecessary and costly, neither directly productive nor able to make decisions. The general result, seen in armies, firms and bureaucracies, has been the simultaneous spread of 'responsible autonomy' for those at the bottom and enhanced control capacities at the top. The pyramid flattens, yet those at the top are able to exercise power more extensively.

The potential of transparent control suggests the dystopian mirror image of the benign network: instead the network becomes the agent of centralized oversight and control. The panopticon of Bentham and Foucault, the means of surveillance that denies horizontal communication, finds it apotheosis in the digital network. There is now nowhere to hide. Satellites can view troop movements, major constructions or the interior of a nuclear plant (as was the case in the Chernobyl accident). For the individual each transaction on an advanced network leaves a trace, and each trace compiled in lists relating to bank accounts, social security, school and criminal records, can be cross-referenced, bought and sold.

These two very different conceptions of the social use of technologies, the one optimistic the other pessimistic, have the same origin: both are responses to the ability of technology to enhance control. One emphasizes decentralized access to control, the other its potential use by existing institutions and powers. The same heartland technologies that permit people to publish from the home also allow a government to maintain and cross-reference hundreds of millions of files on its citizens. As a result the effects of a general increase in the availability of control as a resource are inherently unpredictable. They are similar to the effects of a radical downwards shift in the cost of a production process. At first sight this lowers barriers to entry, favouring greater openness. But the same change can also be exploited by incumbents who can use their added surplus to consolidate power and exclude competitors in some other part of the productive cycle. Benefits spread unevenly, setting in motion unpredictable dynamics that depend as much on strategy and tactics, on the relative abilities of small and large corporations, governments and campaigning groups to exploit new technologies, as they do on any underlying technological or social logic.

Social and Economic Networks

In the real world, transparency and communality overlap. Formal structures intersect with informal ones. In science and technology, for example, studies of diffusion patterns have highlighted the role of the informal networks linking producers and users, governments and research organizations that work in parallel with the formal structures for disseminating information and transferring technology. The role of these networks is crucial both to accessible technologies such as the radio and personal computer around which formed innumerable amateur groups, journals, and conferences, and to the higher reaches of technology. Within the firm, the informal networks of 'who's who, what's what and why's why' are as important as formal structures.

Social networks long pre-date even the most rudimentary information technologies. Networks of kindship, of influence and gossip, of espionage or credit, cliques and cronies, are apparent in all known societies. The networks whereby people come together informally outside formal hierarchies, to share and spread information, are equally ubiquitous: the Saudi *diwanniyas*, Chinese *guanxi*, Western clubs, lodges, bars and cafes, Japanese bathing houses and Polish churches all have this common characteristic. Some are power networks, clubs and societies which provide the personal bindings for a ruling class; others spread on the underside of power. The Manicheans of the fourth and fifth century, Gnostics, Cathars, Buddhists, Sufis, all in their different ways used network forms, bound together by common belief rather than hierarchy, linked horizontally in polycephalous structures.

Drawing on the work of Georg Simmel and Jacob Moreno, sociology has developed the study of human networks of this kind, now a fully formed subdiscipline with an established body of literature and journals. The work of Stanley Milgram, Barry Wellman, Lipnack and Stamps, Bavelas and Leavitt, and Everett Rogers and Lawrence Kincaid on everything from voting behaviour to the pivotal significance of mothers' clubs in Korea have shown how illuminating this kind of network analysis can be. Network analysis focuses on flows of communication and on the extent of connectedness, integration and diversity of units in a system.[32] Equally important is the analysis of the relative powers associated with different positions in networks, showing features common to networks that link retailers and consumers, auctioneers and bidders, or promiscuous teenagers.[33] The power to exclude people from networks often turns out to be crucial to their operation. Mapping human interconnections reveals informal, shadow power structures as important as their visible and formal counterparts. Silicon Valley in California, source of many of the basic technologies of communications networks, is described 'not as just a geographical area but as a network'.[34] Daniel Shon and the Hungarian economist Janos Kornai have written about the shadow networks that make formally hierarchical systems function in centrally planned Eastern Europe, and about the negotiation and brokerage that takes place in the interstices of rule bound bureaucracy.[35] The telephone, ostensibly a tool of hierarchy and centralized control, is instead used to forge informal reciprocal relationships which can 'deliver' in ways the formal system cannot. The American psychologist Stanley Milgram illuminated the extensive nature of informal networks in industrialized societies by mapping out the chains of acquaintance which linked the people of the US, showing that between four and seven links joined any one person with any other, a reflection of the dense relations of a 'civil society' of voluntary and professional associations, trade unions, churches and corporations spread across the country.

Infrastructures of energy, transport and communication are also organized as networks, a set of network industries with common problems of organizing peaks, buffers, and interconnection rules. Transportation networks based on human backs, camels, railroads and steamships that act as material infrastructures for flows of goods and values have emerged and decayed over millenia. In the work of historians such as Fernand Braudel the economy itself is conceived as a series of overlapping and interacting networks of exchange. The economic history of the last five hundred years is read as the spread of the overlapping networks of different forms of market economy, reaching into new regions, into new areas of everyday life, and interacting with the institutions of the state, of finance and of the international corporation. The communal and informal networks of family, locality and friends remain the base on which the market economy is built: when the market contracts, informal networks expand providing goods and services in a spirit of sympathy and loyalty that helps the recovery of the market. Before the emergence of modern company structures the basic commercial unit was frequently not the simple partnership but often a chain of mutually supporting partnerships based on a kinship network.[36]

Early markets were dependent on cities and towns, and governed by rules as to prices, conditions of access and taxation. At the end of the medieval period the close, local and dense networks of the 'material economy' were to provide a foundation for the spread of market economies which in turn provided an indispensable foundation for the birth of capitalism,[37] a word Braudel uses to describe the relatively footloose concentrations of capital associated with the commanding heights of trade, finance and later industry. According to Braudel, until the eighteenth century the mass of people even in the most developed countries were 'encapsulated within the vast domain of material life', unaffected by the webs of trade and exchange of the money economy.[38] Yet at the same time truly global markets were forming, evidenced by the 'dominolike variation in market prices' across the world from Europe to India and China. Integration within more extensive networks of exchange began to change its character. The transparent exchanges of the traditional face-to-face public market located in a single place were being joined in the fifteenth century by what English historians have called the private market: the activity of dealers and merchants seeking to free themselves from the constraints of the public market, creating longer chains between production and consumption so that they alone could know market conditions at both ends of the chain creating scope for greater leverage and profit. The merchants created more dispersed networks, at one remove from the denser networks of the city or region, and from the regulations which tended to define them. Under the names of *tayir*, *mercador*, *sogador* and *négociant* they were to prefigure many of the strategic struggles of our own time, struggles over choice and control in economic life. Their achievement points to one of the consistent themes in the history of networks.

Scale and Control

By creating more extensive networks, the merchants engineered a leap forward in the scale of economic life, an increase in the number of participants that undermined the dense, local control of the traditional market network. As trade spread 'economic life escaped the control of the municipalities'.[39] By re-defining the terrain of economic life they carved out for themselves a position of advantage, a higher ground from which they could dominate the lower levels of the market and material economy. Similar patterns occur in the use of modern communications networks: the satellite network can be used to create a new and larger terrain with which the transnational bank or television channel can outmanoeuvre its domestic counterpart. In part this is a question of what happens to the surpluses generated in economic exchange. Where the economic and social networks of a region are dense, where most exchanges take place within the local economy, there will be a tendency to recycle surpluses in local markets and local institutions. The aim of the embryonic capitalist is to break from this pattern, to extract a surplus away from the local circulation of goods and services so that it can be applied to the most profitable uses wherever they may be. Ultimately the power of the early capitalist and the transnational firm rests on the same base, the ability to choose. Having won choice over the dispersal of surpluses capitalism can exercise leverage. When market conditions change, or when a prince's of government's regulations become unacceptable, ships and investments are simply redirected to more congenial shores.

Networks, whether those of economic exchange or of communication, change the scale of affairs and break its limits. Durkheim wrote of industrial societies that the 'producer can no longer embrace the market in a glance nor even in thought. He can no longer see limits since it is, so to speak, limitless,'[40] When scale changes, the nature of human relationships and institutions changes too.[41] An increase in the number of actors and interactions tends to bring an increase in volatility and uncertainty. There is also the phenomenon familiar to students of democratic organization, the 'risky shift': when larger numbers of people are involved in making a collective decision there is a tendency to opt for more risky choices, perhaps because responsibility has become nebulous and diffuse.

Volatility has become highly visible within the increasingly interdependent world economy. It may be no coincidence that accelerating trends towards globalization of production and distribution have coincided with deep instability in exchange and commodities markets, stock markets and interest rates. The sheer scale of transactions is partly to blame. The average daily volume of messages carried by SWIFT, the world banking network, which links 1,460 institutions in sixty-eight countries, rose from 77,000 in 1977 to 950,000 in 1987. As technologies allow value to flow more freely, predictability, regulation and control become harder to impose. The paradox of scale and control is most visible in the financial sector where heavy investment in technologies designed to enhance predictability and responsiveness has been blamed for exacerbating instability: when a multitude of different and competing actors seek to improve their control capacities, the result at the level of the system is a breakdown of control. What is rational at the micro level becomes highly irrational at the macro level.

Scale and Cooperation

An increase in scale and in the degree of interconnectedness will tend to make relationships, particularly economic ones, less transparent and more opaque. The face-to-face market is replaced by automated dealing on a terminal, in which the buyer and seller are largely unaware of each other. Within organizations an oral culture is replaced by a more formal, written one. Although continuing relationships, and the reciprocity they foster, survive even in the most global markets, they tend to be replaced by continually changing patterns of exchange in which reciprocity must be the exception rather than the rule. As exchange becomes more opaque, its rules must become more rigorous. The contract replaces trust, and penalty clauses replace the implicit threat of not doing business in the future. Insurance industries prosper, as uncertainty is transformed through the prism of a commodity form into calculable risk. Yet there are clear limits to this trend. As Kenneth Arrow and others have pointed out, all economic exchange depends on trust, simply because no contract can foresee all possible outcomes and because action to remedy a breach is costly in itself.[42] In the same vein Niklas Luhmann described trust as a 'blending of knowledge and ignorance', something unavoidable in a world 'being dissipated into uncontrollable complexity'.[43]

The structural contexts of cooperation and reciprocity were described by Robert Axelrod in his well-known study of the limits to cooperation.[44] Axelrod based his work on the famous prisoner's dilemma in which two players interact with a choice between antagonistic or cooperative actions. The benefits accruing from use of an antagonistic play against a cooperative one exceed those from mutual cooperation. This in turn benefits both more than mutually antagonistic plays. Both therefore benefit in the long run from cooperation. As Axelrod demonstrated in extensive computer simulations the 'tit for tat' strategy which begins with cooperation and then simply emulates each move the other player makes 'beats' any other strategy in the long run by forcing the other player to cooperate. In the short run, or in an isolated interaction, however, more aggressive strategies are more effective since the other player's cooperative behaviour can be exploited. Axelrod concluded that cooperation, whether between friends or enemies, depends on frequent interaction and the expectation of future interaction.

There are many more subtle ways of explaining the pervasive existence of cooperation and altruism. Axelrod's argument benefits, however, from its clear simplicity. As a common-sense observation it helps to explain much of the everyday cooperation that takes place within an institution or locality. Rousseau was making a similar point when he wrote that the only moral society would be a small one. By the same token, the model suggests that as networks spread and the extensiveness of interactions increases the structural support for cooperation is weakened. Only when networks can be used to create stable, small groups continuously engaged in exchange will the optimistic vision of a cooperating, interconnected world be credible.

Networks as Markets

In ancient Sumerian, the ideogram for market is a 'Y', defining the market as a junction of traffic routes, a node in networks of exchange. Early markets, placed in a central square, a street or in the precincts of a temple, were situated at the point where communications routes intersected. Centuries of development gradually replaced the traditional face-to-face, public market with more dispersed, 'virtual' markets. The modern electronic market which links buyers and sellers on different sides of the world is a natural development. The essential role of the market in bringing together buyers and sellers with common prices and information, remains intact when it takes the form of an electronic network: the network provides instant and common access to prices and a means for transferring funds.

The existence of interconnecting networks enables markets to become more extensive and limits traditional forms of monopoly. Adam Smith believed that faster transport would help to erode local monopolies and favoured public spending on the roads to this end. More recently the spread of communications networks has eroded local monopolies in broadcasting, telecommunications services and banking. While markets have taken the form of networks, communications networks have taken on the characteristics of markets. The same physical machinery that permits the interactive exchange of information can accommodate the exchange and circulation of values. Reuters, originally an international news agency, evolved from the provision of financial information to service every aspect of a transaction, from insurance and trade itself, to settlements. A Stock Exchange based on an information system like SEAQ (Stock Exchange Automatic Quotation) in London can easily evolve into a system of automated dealing where supply and demand are matched electronically. Informational networks regularly turn into transactional markets. This was the experience of British Telecom's Prestel videotex network. Conceived as a means of disseminating information to the general public, it was soon transformed into a medium for organizing transactions in travel, freight, home banking and shopping. Instead of creating a channel of packaged information Prestel created a market. Similarly, the French Minitel/Télétel videotex network created a virtual marketplace within which several thousand information service providers could sell their wares.[45] Like a medieval prince the network operator regulates the rules of access to the market and the prices charged, in the French case offering high potential profits to service providers to speed the growth of the market.

The electronic, networked market appears to be close to the ideal market of economic theory, in the sense that it is driven by price and by perfect information. In practice, however, almost all network markets have been characterized by systematic manipulation, particularly of the terms of access and interconnection. A well-known example is the case of airline reservation systems, which have given priority to information about flights from the airlines which sponsored the network, a substantial advantage as users (in this case travel agents) scan only the first few entries offered in response to a request. Similar phenomena have been encountered in freight networks and banking. Overcoming discrimination of this kind depends on external or internal regulation to agree standardized and fair procedures for accessing and distributing information. Similar questions about the terms of access to and interconnection of networks have arisen in telecommunications as regulators attempt to guarantee fair access to the physical infrastructure of cables and switches for competing service providers.

Economics treats markets as price systems. In the pure theoretical model of general equilibrium the market is a system for equalizing large numbers of marginal quantities, prices acting as information signals to investors, workers and consumers. The electronic, networked market is seen as a vast computer for instantaneously equalizing prices without the need for market makers, brokers and other intermediaries.

Yet the traditional market had many more dimensions than the familiar picture of economic theory. The marketplace was also a site for exchanging knowledge and gossip, for sharing experience and building up relationships of trust. This is one reason why the word 'marketplace' summons up images of community that bear little relationship to electronic stock-selling systems. In the marketplace price is only one of many items of information to be exchanged. As the price functions of markets are taken over by electronic networks, other networks also play a role in forming other kinds of 'market' relationship. Value added networks that link designers in supplier and user companies, or that link federations of enterprises or groups of professionals are all examples of non-price market networks. The modern industrial districts of Palo Alto and Route 128 in the US, or Sophia Antipolis in France, often based around educational institutions, depend for their economic success on informal links that foster cooperation alongside the familiar competitiveness of the marketplace. In them 'the university campus is like the corner cafe where Italian artisans solve one anothers problems and share – or steal – one anothers ideas: a place where Proudhon might have taken Marx to show him where cooperation and competition meet'.[46] These informal links are now as likely to take place on a videotex or computer network (such as JANET, Britain's Joint Academic Network) as in a restaurant or bar.

In financial markets electronic and informal networks interact in surprising ways. Although technologies can replace the functions of physically concentrated markets, most financial centres remain intensely concentrated in small areas: a handful of streets in London, New York, Tokyo and Hong Kong. Informal interaction is as important as electronic communication, and it is informal interaction that fuels the characteristic crime of modern financial markets, the use of privileged inside information. The rise of insider trading, particularly during the bull market of the 1980s, raised major problems for those responsible for regulating markets. In principle, the transparent technologies of transaction make it easier to detect suspicious behaviour that indicates access to inside knowledge, since apparently inexplicable purchases can be instantly detected by regulators. In practice, proof of criminal behaviour is hard to establish. The sheer volume of rumour and gossip circulating on the informal networks of a financial centre make it easy to construct a rational and innocent explanation for any action. As a result convictions for insider trading tend to depend on confession. Two alternatives remain for those responsible for maintaining the integrity of the financial marketplace. One is to develop more intensive policing methods, to monitor more exchanges, and to eavesdrop on more telephone conversations. The alternative, perhaps more appropriate to an age of open networks, is to use communications technology further to increase the distribution and transparent availability of information, thus reducing the scope for secret actions to take advantage of secret information. The powers of open electronic networks can thus be used to counter the tendency of human beings to exploit closure.

2

The Dynamics of Electronic Networks

Sophisticated communications networks long preceded the development of electricity and electronics. The early Chinese Chou dynasty operated message services. The Mongol Yuan dynasty in the fourteenth century operated five routes with 1,600 post stations staffed by 70,000 men and 40,000 horses. One of the most extensive pre-electric networks was the French optical telegraph network, developed by Claude Chappe in the 1790s and based on the use of telescopes and visual signalling devices. By 1842 the War Department was responsible for a network with links totalling 3,000 miles and 534 stations. In eighteenth-century Russia semaphore messages could reputedly travel 1,000 miles in two hours.

It was electricity which transformed the potential scale and capacity of communication. Electricity, and later electronics, could deliver messages at speeds far higher than any previous delivery medium, while also controlling their flow. Electricity freed communication from the constraints of space and from the limits of physical transport. The telegraph was in this sense the decisive invention from which all other communications networks flowed. It was 'the first product – really the foundation – of the electrical goods industry and thus the first of the science and engineering based industries'.[1]

Numerous telegraphic devices using electricity were experimented with in the early nineteenth century, usually sponsored by armies. The first to gain widespread use was Edward Cooke and Charles Wheatstone's system, patented in Britain 1837. The British telegraph used first five and later two lines to transmit any message. The US adopted what came to be the standard solution after Samuel Morse's invention of a code which enabled messages to be sent along a single wire. In this way the telegraph focused attention for the first time on what has become a predominant concern of communications engineering: the economy of signals, that is to say the economy of using bandwidth to convey information.

Since the first telegraph systems spread alongside railway tracks after 1844, an apparently endless succession of new electric and electronic networks formed on top of each other, rarely displacing old ones and always increasing the volume and number of communications. The telegraph systems soon set a pattern for future developments. They established the precedent of communications networks growing up around spectacular events: telegraphy linked Washington to the 1844 Democratic National Convention in Baltimore; later radio would be boosted by its ability to cover the Americas Cup, television by its coverage of the 1936 Olympics and the coronation of Queen Elizabeth II. Satellite communication would benefit from its association with later Olympics, the Moon landing and more recently, fund-raising events such as Live Aid. Great events were one side of the coin. The other was the communication of an endless stream of news about financial and commodity markets. Telegraphy established the tradition of an intimate relationship between communications networks and finance: the earliest large-scale commercial use of the telegraph was by stockbrokers serving the New York and Philadelphia stock exchanges.

Telegraphy also set a pattern in other ways: 'virtually all subsequent developments in telecommunications can be seen, in latent form, in the conversion of telegraphic technology into a commodity bought and sold for profit and saved from the "wastes of competition" by collective actions that preserved monopoly prerogatives within the industry and shielded their beneficiaries from public accountability.'[2]

The very high fixed costs and low variable costs of cable networks like the telegraph have tended to make competition unstable. Competition threatens to reduce prices to variable costs, thus undermining revenues and the prospect of new investment. Monopoly, cartels and tight forms of regulation have all been used to limit this tendency. The US telegraph industry was a near monopoly by 1866, swallowed into the Western union conglomerate, which was one of the largest companies in US history and arguably the world's first great industrial monopoly. Two years later the British Telegraph Act authorized the Post Office to buy and run all the private telegraph companies in Britain, which had in any case already formed themselves into various market-sharing arrangements, just as the independent telephone companies had formed themselves into a near monopoly by the time of nationalization in 1912. Transoceanic cables were dominated by a group of British companies, providing a model which Marconi tried to replicate in cable's competitor technology, radio. Telegraphy set precedents in other ways too: Morse's first line between Washington and Baltimore was financed by a $30,000 Congressional appropriation in 1843. Morse offered the US Government his telegraph patent, although it was refused because of the apparent unprofitability of the new industry. Later, companies like Western Union depended heavily on railway rights of way which were in turn dependent on the federal land grant policy. Ever since, communications networks have depended on government aid, either direct or indirect. Whether under a rhetoric of regulation or deregulation, governments have consistently acted to sponsor stable monopoly, duopoly or oligopoly structures in communication, and to subsidize the leading edge of research, usually through military budgets.

The telegraph companies, like the telephone companies, immediately broke records. Along with the railway companies they were the largest of their time, needing unprecedented sums of money to sink in the ground or string in the air. American Telegraph and Telephones (AT&T) became the world's largest company in the twentieth century, and Japan's Nippon Telegraph and Telephone Corporation (NTT) became the world's most highly capitalized company in the 1980s.[3] In Europe Siemens is the largest private sector employer, the Deutsches Bundespost (DBP) the largest public sector employer. In the early days of the networks huge workforces were needed to lay lines and to operate exchanges. These were also among the first genuinely transnational enterprises; the British cable companies and others like the Danish Great Northern company which laid cables across Siberia and Japan had to devise new ways of working and deploying resources. In their pyramidal structure, their precise division of labour and responsibility, and their production of a wholly standardized service they were quintessential examples of the new era of corporate capitalism, held up as models of efficiency.

Telephony was originally developed as a means of multiplexing telegraph and in some cases developed as an adjunct to the telegraph. Telephone networks were introduced into the US in the late 1870s, and spread there much faster than in Europe. By 1914, 70 per cent of the world's telephones were in the US.[4] In Germany telephone services were in use in the early 1880s, not only in Berlin and the large cities, but also to link villages too small to support a telegraph office. It was soon clear that the technology could be used in many different ways. Some were used to broadcast news, concerts and religious services before the use of the telephone as a point-to-point medium displaced all alternatives. The most famous example of broadcasting on the telephone was the Telefon Hirmondo (the 'telephonic town crier') in Budapest, created by Tivadar Puskas (who had earlier helped to invent the telephone switchboard) as a medium for the Magyar elite. Telephony in the US was quickly consolidated into AT&T's near-monopoly, while in other countries it was generally run by government departments. In Britain, private companies operated under Post Office licence with little or no government support (though long-distance routes were taken over in 1892),[5] before being fully nationalized in 1912.[6] Sweden soon established a tradition of wide availability of communications networks, helped by intense competition between a Bell subsidiary and its local counterpart, and by 1895 had a telephone penetration rate nearly double that of the US.[7] In most countries the telephone made a slow but steady progress towards becoming a universal good: household penetration rates were by the late 1980s well over 90 per cent in the USA, over 100 per cent in much of Sweden, and between 70 and 100 per cent in most of Western Europe.

Unlike the electricity industry, which was riven by the conflict between AC and DC technologies, telephone networks all across the world used the same basic principles that had been established in Bell's patents. Radio, too, was initially developed under the tight control of its inventor, Marconi. Radio links for military and shipping uses emerged in the 1900s, and offered a means to bypass British cables. Not until Westinghouse's 'KDKA' in Pittsburgh began broadcasting in 1920 as a promotional gimmick to sell sets was it fully realized that radio is also effective as a medium for communication from one point to many. Radio broadcasting networks under commercial or state control, which general- ly used telephone land lines to connect their transmitters, sprang up in the 1920s. In the Soviet Union, more audio receivers were linked by wire than by radio until as late as 1964. Television networks were launched in most Western countries in the 1940s after a false start in the 1930s. Some attempts were made to broadcast to large communal screens (as in Germany in the 1930s and rural France in the 1940s). Television and radio have now reached almost 100 per cent penetration in most of the industrialized countries. Cable networks built first for the improved delivery of broadcast signals, and later providing their own material, became widespread in the 1960s and 1970s, reaching 60 per cent penetration in the US by the late 1980s and 80–90 per cent in some of the smaller European countries.

Computer networks originally linked terminals to mainframes for timesharing, but gradually evolved into distributed structures during the 1970s and 1980s. Microwave networks for computer data and telephony have been available since the 1950s. Local Area Networks (LANs) providing high-speed data communication within a site, company or institution spread rapidly in the 1980s and have been developed into Metropolitan Area Networks (MANs) covering part of a city (and often associated with a 'teleport' of satellite dishes) and Wide Area Networks (WANs) which may cover several continents. Satellite networks first emerged in the 1960s in the wake of Sputnik, and have been used for broadcasting, for military espionage (two-thirds of all satellites launched have had a military function), for observing minerals or crop patterns, and for transmitting long-distance data and telephone conversations. Very Small Aperture Terminals (VSATs) and mobile receivers are now beginning to extend the scope of satellite-based networks. Mobile and cellular radio networks have begun to transform the principle of communicating from one building to another into that of communicating from one person to another, unconstrained by location. Videotex networks like Prestel and Minitel, Lexis, Compuserve and The Source overlay the telephone network to provide information and messages on screens.

Amidst this burgeoning chaos of new, overlapping networks, technologies continued to be developed at great speed, often beyond the capacities of industry or regulators to respond. Each brings predictions that it will bring untold wonders, that it will render all existing technologies obsolete, and that it will irreparably destroy all existing industry and regulatory structures. Optical fibres, optical storage systems and switches and new transmission techniques are the 1990s prime candidates, expected to replace the electron with the photon as the raw material of communications. Ranged against them are a set of radio technologies, using various cellular and microcellular techniques, and advanced satellite technologies. Fast packet techniques based on self-routeing electronic information that can turn voices and images into bursts of information have suggested entirely new models for organizing and linking networks. Advances in superconductive materials for use in switches and aerials point the way to rapid advances in the capacities and speeds of communication, while the supercomputer, neural networks and parallel processing techniques are dramatically increasing the range and depth of expertise and intelligence that can be made available over networks.

During the 1970s and 1980s new electronic networks spread, interconnected, overlapped and competed with a ferocious dynamism. Telegraph and telephone networks, FM, medium and long-wave radio, VHF and UHF, cable and satellite television, cellular and cordless telephones and mobile radio, computer local area networks, 'neural networks' that mimic the workings of the human brian, videotex networks like Prestel and Minitel, payment networks for cash dispensers or international banks and retailer ordering networks continue to pile up on top of each other without apparent limit. New kinds of terminal, whether personal computers or fax machines, use older networks in new ways. Just as the invention of writing complemented rather than displaced the spoken word, so has each new form of communication accumulated on top of the old, bringing with it a new logical structure of connection, dependency and control.

Beneath the apparently expanding diversity of new networks, most new technologies have been incorporated within traditional structures. Older corporations and regulatory structures have proved proficient at adapting to new technologies. As Raymond Williams argued in relation to broadcasting, their history 'shows very clearly that the institutions and social policies which get established in a formative, innovative stage – often ad hoc and piecemeal in a confused and seemingly marginal area – have extraordinary persistence into late periods, if only because they accumulate techniques, experience, capital of what come to seem prescriptive rights'.[8] In telecommunications most of the dominant companies of the 1980s were also dominant in the 1920s; AT&T, IBM, Siemens, Philips and Ericsson are obvious examples. There is also a continuity in terms of control structures. Probably the most important are those of licensed common carriage whose origins date back to the sixteenth century and beyond and which are now being redefined to set conditions for the interconnection of networks. A common carrier is given rights to run a communications system, using a monopoly, on the condition that access is open to all and that communications are not interfered with. The most famous early common carrier was the Tassis (later Taxis) family which organized a postal system for the fifteenth-century Emperor Frederick III. Telegraphy, telephony and more recent services like videotex and the ISDN (Integrated Services Digital Network) have been dominated by common-carrier Postal, Telegraph and Telephone administrations, collectively known as the PTTs,[9] whether as government departments, as public corporations, as state-owned private corporations (such as NTT in Japan after 1949) or, as in the case of AT&T in the USA, in the form of a regulated private corporation.[10] In Britain state control was organized through the Post Office, bringing with it relatively weak accounting systems and annual parliamentary approval of budgets. In the communist countries telecommunication was run directly by ministries (often alongside transport and construction), a large proportion of profits being siphoned off for other areas of state spending.[11] Broadcasting, too, was soon organized in state or quasi-state monopolies, based originally in Britain on a consortium of equipment manufacturers. Most satellite communication has been run by Intelsat, the strange phenomenon of a US-sponsored international nationalized industry, jointly owned by 112 of the world's state telephone monopolies, alongside its regional counterparts such as Eutelsat and Arabsat, and Intersputnik, which used Soviet space technology to provide satellite communication for the communist world.

As will become clear this history of close links between states and networks, symbolized by the fact that the military networks of both East and West are more advanced than their civilian counterparts, shapes much of the politics of communications and control. In practice, the exercise of control over networks has taken many forms. Influence over cable networks depended on physical control. The British global network would have been impossible without Britain's dominion over innumerable islands, ports and islets such as Ascension or Gibraltar. Radio by contrast was more flexible, allowing competing empires such as that of the French to construct their own short-wave networks, no longer reliant on British cables. Control also depends on terms of interconnection. When the Pacific Cable Board (a consortium of governments in the British Empire) built a cable between Australia and Canada it ensured that it did not pass any non-British islands. Within the US, AT&T dominated telephony by owning the long-distance network and using its control over interconnection as a lever on local telephone companies.

Generic Strategies

In competitive communications markets a number of generic control strategies have been pursued since the early days of telegraphy. Though all firms are different in detail, the patterns are remarkably consistent throughout the history of the communications industries. For large firms the ability to control the development of networks and ultimate profits has depended on three elements: interconnection strategies, patents strategies and vertical integration. Their aim is to restrict entry and to maximize market share. The means is the maintenance of control over a system of communication, rather as transport and energy companies have often sought control over a system in which they retain discretion over pricing and the lines of technical change. Since communication depends on the interworking of a system of receivers and transmitters, shared formats and the languages, some degree of systemic control is essential.

For smaller companies and entrants, success often depends on an opposite strategy, the ability to 'disintermediate', through bypassing established networks and creating a direct link to users. Where the systemic strategy offers a complete packaged service (such as the provision of a telephone set, access to local and long distance, maintenance and specialized services), the counterstrategy offers either a specialized service or a module or component. Alternatively the smaller company can offer a gateway between two systems: a physical link between different networks, or a means of converting from one computer language to another. In both cases systemic control is undermined.

AT&T, which until its 1983 divestiture was the world's largest corporation, provides a classic example. Initially AT&T licensed local telephone companies to operate their own networks, while using its long-distance network and control of interconnection to guarantee position and profits, which were consistently higher than those of the local companies. Later regulation was used to legitimize the monopoly and bar entry. Regulation shored up systemic control by banning unauthorized attachments to the network. At the same time the company made strategic use of patents and standards to control the terms on which networks and equipment could be interconnected: when its telephone patents ran out in the 1890s, the company actively accumulated other patents and inventions and sought to 'occupy the field' through the researches of Bell Labs and the systematic purchase of others' inventions. Later, patent pools were the key to the monopoly agreements on broadcasting made between RCA, Westinghouse, General Electric and AT&T. IBM, too, has used its domination of computing standards to limit the scope for interconnection of machines, to limit entry to the industry and thus control pricing.

The third element of AT&T's strategy involved vertically integrating to incorporate manufacturing so as to increase costs of entry and exercise full control over standards. Again this route has also been followed by many other companies, ranging from IBM to the Japanese electronics giants such as NEC, Fujitsu and Toshiba, which operate in a vertically integrated fashion from components manufacture to computers, communications and consumer electronics.

The alternative, disintermediating, route has been consistently used to weaken the systemic grip of companies like AT&T. Competing companies have sought to sell telephone handsets; they have built microwave networks that bypass long-distance routes; they have used satellites directly to reach large business customers and they have offered gateways (such as the modem) that allow the network to be used for other purposes. IBM has faced a similar series of inroads: PC clones, IBM compatible softwares and conversion devices to aid communication with other manufacturers' machines. All seek to make the system more modular and thus less amenable to central control.

The battles between these strategies have been echoed in technology. The technologies and architectures used in networks have been organized in structures which reflect pre-existing patterns of power. Telephone networks were traditionally organized in switching hierarchies, reaching from the home through local to central switches and organized in the form of a pyramid or tree and branch structure under the central control of the PTT. The first international radio networks were built on the same, star-shaped model, until it was understood that they could support many more horizontal links. The earliest computer networks were also hierarchical, tying relatively dumb terminals to a centrally controlled mainframe in star-shaped networks. Broadcasting has traditionally branched downwards from sources of central control and programming in the major cities.

With more recent generations of technology the incorporation of the new within old structures has become more turbulent and unpredictable. Disintermediation strategies have become more prevalent and more successful, taking advantage of the blurring of industry boundaries.

Monopolies have faced competition within their traditional markets from competitors using substitute technologies and from erstwhile customers operating their own networks. During the 1980s AT&T entered computing (accumulating losses of $3 bn), IBM entered telecommunications (through its interests in Rolm, SBS and MCI), British Telecom, France Telecom and the Deutsches Bundespost all invested in satellite and cable broadcasting, and the BBC began a data transmission service. In the cultural industries distribution technologies proliferated with ever greater speed: cable and satellite appeared alongside telephone networks, in competition with videos, CD-videos and digital tapes. Turbulence has been accentuated by the properties of open technologies (like the compact or personal computer) able to carry and control a wide range of types of communication. In telecommunications, competition has been deliberately introduced by governments (primarily the US, UK and Japanese) in the provision of services, in long distance and, indirectly, through the spread of private corporate networks. By the late 1980s the US had half a dozen major long-distance companies, Britain two and Japan three. In addition the UK had two cellular radio operators, and seven holders of licences for new mobile services, while Japan had over thirty new local public network operators in competition with NTT. All had highly competitive value added sectors, offering services over the public network. Where previously a single telephone network carried all voice or data signals, most advanced countries moved to a complex web of overlapping networks, ranging from videoconferencing to packet-switching, only some of which are open to the public. The history of ISDN (Integrated Services Digital Network) exemplified the change. Initially conceived as a universal, standardized service, ISDN was instead marketed to target groups as one of a number of specialized services.

The fragmentation of the unitary network was aided both by trends in technology and by changes in the structure of regulation. Microwave and satellite technologies made it much cheaper to create long-distance networks to duplicate older, cable-based ones. More intelligent switching permits specialized logical networks to be created and reconfigured, and tailored to special needs even where the physical network remains under monopoly control.[12] Packet switched networks based on the 'x.25' standard sustain transactional networks and VANs for such things as automated teller machines (ATMs) and hospital ordering systems. Private leased lines with ever higher transmission rates can be used by companies to link their own private exchanges, aggregating and circulating information about such things as stock turnover, physical output, fault levels and cashflow.

As the replacement of analogue techniques by digital ones gives networks a new degree of freedom, they have also become more important to the smooth working of other economic sectors. Financial institutions, car manufacturers and traders have taken on some of the characteristics of communications companies. As much as 50 per cent of the cost of a car and 60 per cent of the cost of a jet are accounted for by electronics. Each industry now has heavy fixed investments in communications technologies, and an almost total dependence on rapid and transparent communication. In this, they reflect fundamental pressures towards greater flexibility which arise from the changing nature of capitalist economy, the rapid growth of an intermediate service economy, and the move away from standardized mass production towards greater specialization, customization and shorter product cycles. Communication between different stages in the production process is under pressure to become as transparent as possible so as to speed up the circulation of goods, money and ideas, and to eliminate waste and downtimes.

While communication becomes central to the workings of economic life, the growing significance of communications costs and needs has raised the political profile of communications, prompting large corporate users such as General Motors, Mitsubishi, Hitachi, General Electric and Citicorp to lobby for lower costs and more suitable services, to develop their own systems, and to use communications as a tool of competitive strategy and positional advantage. Public networks are now overlaid with a myriad of private and exclusive networks, mainly built out of lines leased from PTTs. General Motors, in collaboration with Electronic Data Systems (EDS), is constructing what is probably the largest private network linking 500,000 terminals (roughly half voice and half data) in a private global network that will reputedly cost over $500 m. Half of all international information flows now take place within transnational corporations.

The fragmentation of a once unified network can be understood as a response to the growing communications and control needs of industry. But it also reflects intensified competition to share in the rewards of the rapidly growing field of computing and communications. Equipment manufacturers effectively created new services through the sale of terminals, such as PCs and fax machines. Deregulation allowed companies in sectors ranging from finance and utilities to publishing trading or railways to build their own networks. In the US $17 bn was spent on private networks in 1987, more than the infrastructure spending of all the regional operating companies.[13] Companies like IBM, General Electric and General Motors have intruded on the domain that was once exclusive to AT&T; in Japan, Mitsubishi and Mitsui have entered the closed world of NTT and the DenDen family; in Britain erstwhile subsidiaries of BP (Scicon), the Midland Bank (Fastrak) and British Leyland (Istel) are among the beneficiaries of deregulation. In each case deregulation is less a means for small companies to overthrow large ones than a restructuring in the relations and terms of competition at the summits of economic power.

If any set of technological changes can be credited with assisting in the transformation of communications it is the cluster of technologies developed after the invention of the transistor in the late 1940s. Semiconductors and microprocessors brought miniaturization and with it the dispersal of intelligence into car engines, hand-held calculators, and portable terminals. Because semiconductors can be cheaply replicated the industry has experienced spectacular falls in the cost of computing capacity. Until the year 2000 it is anticipated that the number of components placed on a chip will continue to double every eighteen months, continuing the trend that has led from the semiconductor to the Large-Scale and Very Large-Scale Integrated Circuit (LSI and VLSI). Whether the result of a technical logic or of huge infusions of state support through the Pentagon and the US space programme, the effect has been to render the power to manipulate, route or store information both cheap and ubiquitous.

Just as De Forest's vacuum tube was used both as a signal repeater to improve the efficiency of telephone networks and as a core technology of competing radio networks, so has the microchip had a double-edged impact on modern telecommunications networks. Computerization has massively increased the power and flexibility of networks. Chip-based switches can carry much larger volumes of communication at lower costs than their electromechanical predecessors.[14] The rising demand for data communications has allowed PTTs to grow while lowering prices and raising productivity faster than almost any other sector. Cheap processing power, however, has also served to erode traditional structures of control. As costs of processing and switching fell more rapidly than the cost of transmitting signals, fundamentally different network topologies became viable, more like a mesh or grid than the traditional pyramid, with multiple points of access and interconnection.

The theoretical foundation for more flexible, distributed network architectures of this kind came from computing. As computers began to migrate from their mysterious air-conditioned rooms into every office or workshop, and as machines which had previously stood alone came to be linked together, entirely new principles of networking were needed. While the earliest networks passed signals up a hierarchy to a central mainframe, more distributed systems began to emerge during the 1960s, allowing for a decentralization of computing power. As more intelligence is dispersed into terminals or towards more autonomous workers in branches and distant offices, new topologies and architectures have been evolved. One is the token ring used for Local Area Networks. Instead of passing a signal up and down a hierarchy of switches, signals are effectively broadcast around the ring, 'stopping' only at the nodes they are intended to reach. In place of a multiplicity of branching connections, the token ring is a single, horizontal link in which each node is also a switch, the diametrical opposite of the hierarchical structures favoured in traditional telephony.

This technical restructuring was reflected organizationally. In the 1960s most medium- and small-sized firms would use computer bureaux to perform their irregular, 'batch-processing' tasks such as the payroll. Information would be fed in with punch cards or paper tapes. Later, telecommunications links could be used to input data into large computers able to work simultaneously on several different jobs. Computing came to resemble telecommunications. During the 1970s this trend was partially reversed as falling prices of mini- and microcomputers returned processing tasks to within the firm. The growing importance of data communications, and the spread of formally structured information, coincided with new opportunities to decentralize and 'privatize' control over voice traffic. Equipment such as the PBX (Private Branch Exchange or switchboard), now used in most offices, performs many of the functions of public switches. Intelligent terminal equipment allows users to develop their own specialized local networks which substitute for the functions of the public network. For large firms with extensive internal networks, the long-term goal is to gain access to the very heart of the network, the signalling and control capacities which determine where and how signals are transmitted.

The Politics of Change

No technical developments could alone restructure the shape of the communications network. The trend towards the liberalization of markets and the fragmentation of networks has instead involved a continuing interplay between technology, economics and politics. Deregulation of telecommunications has gone alongside deregulation in banking, airlines and freight in the US, privatization of electricity, gas and airlines in the UK. In some cases older monopolies have been able to extend their privileges to new technologies such as cable and mobile radio, while in others technologies have been used as levers to prise open the public monopoly. The technologies that in some countries appear as unstopable bringers of competition and fragmentation can serve in other environments as the means of extending the existing order.

As important as technical change has been the erosion of the traditional political base on the centralized network. This base, described by Eli Noam as the 'postal-industrial complex', brought together PTTs, equipment manufacturers, rural and residential users, trade unions and parties of the centre and left, around a political programme built on regulation, universal service, cross-subsidy of domestic telephony, and de facto domestic protection.[15] Much of the power of this coalition reflected the sheer size of telephone companies. AT&T was much the largest company in the world, and by all accounts the one with the most extensive body of lobbyists and the most comprehensive and effective political skills. In Germany today the Bundespost remains the largest single employer. Within the EC one million people are employed by the telecommunications arms of PTTs, and another 350,000 in equipment manufacture.

The political and economic successes of this coalition are now widely questioned. For all the rhetoric of social benefit, the cherished goal of universal service has never been met in most Western European countries, where between 10 and 30 per cent of all households remain unconnected to the telephone network. In countries like Britain the telephone network was systematically starved of investment, initially to protect state investment in the telegraph, and later to provide funds for other areas of public spending. The close relationship between PTTs and equipment manufacturers sustained high prices and profits at the expense of users, particularly in Europe where, according to the Organization for Economic Co-operation and Development (OECD), protectionist policies kept prices around 50 per cent higher than in the more competitive US market. The coalition which sustained public service has now been eroded both from within and without. PTTs themselves, their workers and unions, have been tempted by the prospects of a new, more flexible and competitive regime, and by the higher wages possible in privatized companies. This was a key factor behind the support of the Japanese union Zendentsu for the privatization of NTT, and has made full-scale renationalization of British Telecom highly unlikely in the UK. The largest users of telecommunications, particularly in the financial sector, have learned to mobilize in collaboration with computer companies like IBM and DEC, and with advanced electronics companies like GEISCO and EDS, through bodies such as INTUG, the International Chamber of Commerce, and the Committee of Corporate Telecom Users (CCTU) in the US. Their goals include greater choice and openness in equipment markets and network operation and policies that orient PTTs more towards their needs. This emergent 'telematics' coalition, which has been particularly strong in the UK and US, argues that PTTs are structurally ill-equipped to respond to the burgeoning demand for specialized VANS-type services and that the growth of precisely this kind of service is essential for economic growth.

The politics of deregulation fit uneasily into traditional political categories, particularly in Europe. For some it is simply an arm of US foreign policy, a means of breaking the autonomy and public accountability that was possible when telecommunications and broadcasting networks were under unitary state control. The new coalitions, dominated by US transnationals and US computer companies, appear to confirm this view. Yet the most obvious political divisions over the extent and speed of deregulation are not between left and right or between pro-American and anti-American interests, but rather between modernizing, technocratic forces and more conservative and traditional interests. The divisions cut across both left and right. In the US deregulation in all industries was backed by an alliance between radical consumer groups and Democrat politicians opposed to the capture of regulatory bodies by corporations like AT&T, and anti-statist conservatives and business groups. This is one of the reasons why deregulation proved most successful in the industry-specific regulatory bodies like the Federal Communications Commission (FCC), precisely the bodies which were least hostile to business. Social regulators such as the EPA (Environmental Protection Agency) and OSHA (Occupational Safety and Health Agency) survived the deregulation movement relatively intact. In Europe the Swedish Social Democrats and French Parti Socialiste have favoured the rapid modernization of networks and some degree of liberalization, against a shifting coalition of Conservative, Communist and Green parties favouring the status quo. Arguably the most deregulatory regime in the world has been that of the New Zealand Labour Party. In power, Southern European socialist parties have become notorious for deregulating in order to favour 'their' conglomerates against those of the right. Nor are the Japanese conflicts between the more nationally orientated Ministry of Post and Telecommunications (MPT) and the more internationally orientated Ministry of International Trade and Industry (MITI) easily cast in terms of a traditional political spectrum, particularly when most conflicts are settled within the LDP.

Integration and Common Standards

The fragmentation of the network and of its political base has evolved alongside new pressures towards integration. The vision of the mosaic of competing customized networks stands in stark opposition to that of a global integrated network based on common standards. The struggles between these alternatives, and the many gradations that lie between them, come up repeatedly during the course of this book. They can be said to adhere to the poles of a whole range of long-standing conflicts: between rational planning and the market, certainty and uncertainty, between a social consciousness and a narrowly economic one, between the sovereignty of producers and of consumers. While the interests behind both visions fight it out in the political, economic and regulatory arenas, a striking gap persists between a vision of unified, interconnecting networks and a reality of fragmentation and difference.

More than ten years after the campaign of the United Nations Educational, Scientific and Cultural Organization (UNESCO) for a New World Information Order of more balanced flows of information, the gap between the most advanced networks and the least developed has substantially widened. Uneven development between countries and between different regions within the same country is one of the most striking features of this phase in the spread of networks. A strange informational geography is emerging around key hubs, pockets of skills, universities, data havens like Liechtenstein and Bermuda and havens of deregulation like the UK and Singapore. That the benefits of advanced communications are not restricted to the First World is demonstrated by the experience of Singapore, which is probably unique in that its mix of strong central coordination and massive investment in infrastructure and training, has produced one of the world's first ISDNs. Elsewhere, however, uneven development tends to feed on itself. Those areas with the most advanced networks attract the most advanced sectors of manufacturing, finance or services which in turn do most to generate new demands for communication. As new global transoceanic fibre-optic networks are built (Cable and Wireless's Global Digital Highway) in competition with those run by the PTTs, they tend further to enhance the relative weight of key hubs such as Tokyo, Singapore, Seoul, Hong Kong, London, New York, Chicago and Los Angeles. Advanced producer services follow the transnationals, located near the main highways of the global network.

Throughout the world the networks are in turmoil even as they expand. The Soviet Union has committed itself to doubling the number of telephones by the year 2000 (from current penetration rates of around 12 per cent), and a similar target has been adopted by China. At the same time the ministry structures which traditionally ran the networks have experienced the same pressures as the wider economy: pressures to become more commercial, to replace planning according to principles of need with planning informed by financial considerations. In Hungary there are glimpses of one possible future in the proposals to privatize telecommunications, a result of the same necessity to attract foreign capital which has forced many Third World countries to pass their networks over to private, Western companies. In both East and West unprecedented spending on the hardware and software of networks combines with great uncertainty about the durability of institutional firms. For it remains unclear whether the current fragmentation of networks in terms of both ownership and function will prove transitory, to be replaced by a new order based on broadband networks under some form of public control; or whether communication is being irreversibly drawn into the logic of an intensively competitive, chaotic and near-sighted system which will fatally undermine the control of public institutions and nation states. The speed of technological change also undermines any long-term policy, encouraging rapid depreciation of equipment and maximum flexibility.

This then is the state of the networks 150 years after the first telegraphs came into use: a state of almost manic progress in some parts of the world and of stagnation in others. While much of the world suffers from ten-year waiting lists for a telephone, in the cities of the First World innumerable experiments attempt to discern the patterns of communication of the twenty-first century: the usability of videophones (whether for conversation, security or a hundred other unforeseen uses), of personal, mobile communicators and personal televisions, all part of an extraordinary and excessive feast that has left no time for the digestion of the last innovation.

3

Communication and the Limits of Control

The word 'control' is part of the distinctive vocabulary of the modern world, equally at home in everyday conversation, in psychology, engineering, politics and computing. Its meanings range from a loose sense of influence towards some goal, to a stronger sense of direct command over things or processes. All points along the continuum retain the crucial idea that control depends on channels of communication for commands and on channels of feedback to monitor effects and changes. Because of this relationship between control and communication, structures of control are circular in nature, rather than sequences of causes and effects, systemic rather than linear.

Any channel of communication can also serve as a channel of control. This is true in both a narrow and a broad sense: the technical operation of a computer or network depends on the tight control of flows of information between memories and buffers and input/output devices. Within the network infrastructure too, signal control channels function alongside the channels used to deliver messages. Communications networks can also be understood as control infrastructures in a more general sense. Historically they were constructed as tools of administrative direction and as the means for coordinating flows of goods, services and money. Control and communication are also inseparable for another reason, summed up in Gregory Bateson's famous definition of information: both concern differences that make other differences.[1]

This chapter examines some of the contexts within which technologies can be used to enhance control. Each time a control technology is put into place in a real social context it forces a reappraisal of how control is organized and of people's capacities to exercise control. The opportunity can be used for malign or benign ends, as a way of rationalizing tight and authoritarian structures or as a means of devolving responsibility. As a result technologies throw into new relief much older questions about the nature of control, its cultural and psychological contexts, and its meaning for the structures of public control, oligarchy or democracy.

Concepts of Control

The concern for control has deep roots. Some notion of personal control, or mental and physical discipline, is present in many cultures. The peculiarly modern, Western and rationalist conception of control is different. It is part of a tradition that has analysed the world as made up of machine-like laws, a tradition that is inseparable from the belief that humans, separate from nature, can exercise mastery over it. Ideas of this kind, tying a belief in the machine like regularities of nature to the possibility of systematic mastery, can be found in Descartes, Locke, Newton and Bacon. Bacon's utopia, the New Atlantis, had a research scientist for king, whose purpose was the 'knowledge of laws and the secret motions of things . . . the enlarging of the bounds of human empire to the effecting of all things possible.'[2] Knowledge and mastery are two sides of the same coin. Paradoxically, even theories that emphasize chaos and the random are best understood as attempts to tame chance and uncertainty.

The sociological origins of a culture based around control lie perhaps with the influence of the artisans, artist-engineers and architects of the Renaissance, believers in the inseparability of theory and practice and the solubility of all problems.[3] Faith in language and reason were also important: from the belief that anything can be comprehended flows a belief in the controllability of the world. In Bacon's words, 'a true model of the world . . . cannot be done without a very diligent dissection and anatomy of the world'.

In the age of the computer, too, anything that can be defined and specified can be automated and simulated. Abstraction is in this sense the first step towards control. A language, a set of numbers or a diagram, can serve to map the real world without acting on it.[4] Each abstracts, simplifies and preprocesses in order to make the representation usable. Their use then combines the attributes of a description, a tool for exploration and a type of social organization, structured in institutions and ways of thinking. The concern for control is thus bound up with the practices that make things simple and classifiable. The urge to preprocess, to break things down, to label and reconstruct, links the earliest scientific thought to the most modern digital techniques. Abstraction and control are also tied to the imposition of universals. The abstract time of the clock imposed a universal time in place of the different rhythms of each activity, that of historians and record-keepers a linear and cumulative time in place of myriad subjective times.

This concern for control as the means to understanding and mastery has been shadowed by its critique, the long-standing assault on instrumentality, narrow reason and the imposition of apparently universal principles. Weber, who pioneered the study of control structures, feared the erosion of primacy of purpose in rational actions and the loss of moral meaning and freedom that would come in the world of the iron cage. One of the most cogent recent exponents has been the French Protestant writer Jacques Ellul, for whom the critique of technique, those methods which are designed to control, is essential to the affirmation of the true values of a human society.[5] Control, far from guaranteeing the mastery of humanity, would condemn it to servitude at the hands of its own tools and machines and to the instrumental rationality they bear. All technologies of control are thus inherently suspect. From this perspective increasing control is seen to erode the human spirit and feed domination even as it promises liberation. The abstraction of decisions into impersonal rules, decision rules, cost-benefit analyses, or the demands of the market, is seen to erode human judgement and responsibility. It is an argument that shows no signs of losing its potency as networked defence systems and financial markets either leave their creators dependent and literally out of control or become tools for domination by the handful of institutions that can command them.

Norbert Wiener, founder of cybernetics, the science of communications and control, which he defined as the 'study of messages as a means of controlling machinery and society', recognized the danger of letting 'his inventions go to the wrong hands', those of the military and of industrialists who would use cybernetics to dominate and destroy labour.[6] His personal solution was to work as a consultant to the American labour movement, but in his work he never solved the problem of how an increase in the capacity to control, which can at first sight be liberating and decentralizing, could erode rather than shore up domination. Wiener wrote of the 'hope that the good of a better understanding of man and society which is offered by this new field of work may anticipate and outweigh the incidental contribution we are making to the concentration of power (which is always concentrated, by its very conditions of existence, in the hands of the most unscrupulous)'. The problem with this statement is, perhaps, its assumption that a better understanding can exist in abstract, away from the purposes of those who can use such an understanding.

Control as mastery has often been seen as a peculiarly male concern, a product of patriarchal societies that can be contrasted with the nurturing, more ecological forms of control associated with childcare, agriculture and animal-rearing. In these cases control seeks to set the parameters of organic change rather asserting a direct domination. Gregory Bateson summarized one of the ecologist's arguments against the idea of total control that is associated with Western scientific rationality when he wrote that 'man is only a part of larger systems and . . . the part can never control the whole'. An alternative approach sees control as immanent order, as part of the structural relations of a system. This sense is loosely captured in everyday speech when things are 'under control', or at least not 'out of control'. In non-Western traditions its purest form is possibly to be found in the Chinese concept of 'li', described by Joseph Needham as the 'invisible organising fields of forces existing at all levels within the natural world',[7] a concept analogous to pattern, order or information (and one which contrasts with the Western idea of natural laws, an idea dependent on the existence of a lawmaker or deity). In other traditions too, the traditional idea that a natural harmony can provide for human needs stands in contrast to the idea that mastery is essential for a 'sense of control'.

In everyday usage the words 'power' and 'control' are often used interchangeably. A closer analysis reveals crucial differences. The word 'power' tends to refer to a property, the ability to do something; it can be possessed and stored. Like a mechanical energy it can be harnessed and directed. The word 'control' by contrast carries with it the sense of an informational environment, of a system of influences, commands and feedback. Where power often seems a static concept, control is clearly situated in time.

These meanings are directly derived from the words' roots. As a political and psychological concept 'control' is unusual in having a technological etymology. The Latin *contra rotulare* refers to the practice of comparing something 'against the rolls' (it is claimed that the Roman Empire was the first to be based on a sound filing system). This meaning is retained in the modern word comptroller (misspelt because of an early etymological error), the one who keeps the counterroll. Control thus refers to the practice of keeping records over time, and of using them to balance the power of the treasurer, so that actions can be called to account. It also includes a sense of what is now known as feedback and points to the fact that control is impossible without communication so that effects can be monitored and actions adjusted.

The general problems of bringing together the activities of looking, interpreting and acting are common to many spheres of life, common to human bodies, steam engines and nations. The human body can be understood as being controlled by the brain and nervous system, by genetic and cultural programming and by the systems of homeostasis that maintain blood temperature and sugar levels. The steam engine is controlled by a mechanical governor which 'communicates' to the engine when a certain speed has been reached. The apotheosis of the idea of control in nations was probably first reached in English utilitarianism, whose formula consisted of 'inquiry, legislation, execution, inspection and report', the familiar cycle of action and feedback, in this case executed in the name of the calculus of pleasures. Statistics, the medium of feedback, became 'part of the technology of power in a modern state'.[8] The various types of control structures, genetic codes, cultural conditioning and the decision rules of organizations, all share some of the properties of the computer program, a set of rules embedded in software or hardware that directs responses to a changing environment. Complex control structures also have a property shared by only the most advanced computer software. This is the capacity to select and replicate, changing the program itself in response to changes in the environment. Most enduring structures can be explained in terms of their evolutionary ability to maintain themselves through constant adaptation of internal states to changes in environment, a process that tends towards greater diversity and complexity.

Analogies between electronic or biological systems and social ones soon become very problematic. As soon as control enters the field of social life it becomes contested. Whereas in the machine or body the ends of control are self-evident, in any human society they are bound to be disputed, to benefit some at the expense of others. Utilitarianism for example explicitly pitted itself against the unproductive poor. Questions of purpose, and of who or what is the subject of control, are inherently political and contestable, however much utilitarianism and its modern counterparts aspire to a universal calculus. To restate a theme mentioned in the Introduction, any society is in effect a network of distinct economies each with its own hierarchy of ends. The question of determining these ends concerns what Max Weber referred to as a substantive rationality, which judges means and ends against a set of values open to reflection, a rationality which is clearly different from the formal rationality of industrialism which loses the ability to question ends and which, according to Weber, runs the risk of degenerating into a narrow calculus, a parody of reason.

The social organization of control is substantially dependent on available communications technologies. Without direct and rapid communication, control must depend on the use of agents: this was the case before the arrival of developed communications links. Instead of direct control, indirect methods had to be used, such as trust in family members and personal friends or the threat of violent punishment in the future. It is often easy to forget just how little central control was in practice exercised the empires of the past, in large part because of the absence of transport and communication. Michael Mann has distinguished between the differing spheres of control of pre-modern states:[9] the sphere of military control determined by the speed and resources of armies, the sphere within which a looser control can be exercised through local rulers, and the broader spheres of economic or cultural domination. As the work of Harold Innis demonstrated,[10] empires and nations evolved on the backs of their means of communication and transportation, and were shaped by their properties. Equally, large corporations evolved alongside the telegraph and the railway, multinationals alongside the jet and the satellite. With the advent of rapid postal systems, telegraphs and telephones control could become more direct, instantaneous and operational. The capital could command the colonial governor, and the central office could control the branch or, with a Wide Area Network or ISDN, monitor in detail the output of a factory or the flows of stock in a warehouse. In warfare the situation room, a centre of control and communications, emerged in the twentieth century as the key hub of power, able to maintain direct contact with a distant warship or batallion. Rather than being dispersed among satraps, governors, managers and officers, control could be consolidated at the centre and imposed on the periphery.

As will become clear, apparent centralizations of control do not solve the problems inherent in its exercise. At this stage, it is simply worth noting that the two basic types of control, the one exogenous and imposed on a system, the other endogenous, are both strongly shaped by the nature of their means of communication. One depends on vertical flows of information, the other on horizontal flows. Exogenous control depends on a centralized capacity to process information and knowledge so that the most appropriate commands are given and the most effective strategies followed. It requires reciprocal communication with the thing being controlled, while endogenous systems distribute this capacity. In machines, this reciprocal communication is generally described as feedback or feedforward. Within the computer, control and communication can be organized either on hierarchical, serial principles or through the simultaneous communication of many processors as in parallel processing structures. In human systems, the forms of reporting, accounting, discussion, conflict and negotiation, can be organized either vertically or horizontally. Within the market, the signalling that takes place through the price system can either be dominated by oligopolies engaging in forms of cost-plus pricing or, alternatively, can arise from the interaction of many different agents. Nearly all societies and structures in practice combine elements of both types of control: bonds of trust, loyalty and charismatic authority combine with more formal structures, vertical links with horizontal ones.

In addition to this distinction between the exogenous and endogenous a second distinction is also needed. Institutions and individuals struggle not only to achieve given ends, such as to gain hold of scarce resources: they also struggle to achieve control itself. At one level control is sought so that ends can be met in the future: in this sense the second meaning of control is compatible with the narrow, cybernetic or purposive sense of control being orientated to given ends. But it also means something more: being in a position of sufficient positional advantage that unexpected changes and threats can be dealt with. Control is thus bound up with the inherently dangerous and uncertain nature of life. In this second sense control ceases to be extrinsic, aimed towards other ends, and becomes an end itself.

A communicational analysis of the British Empire might, for example, point out that the Pax Britannica was based not only on dominant sea power but also on a near-monopoly of undersea cables linking every continent, a positional power. As a result of this monopoly the key nodes of the world's communication were based in British colonies, enabling the Reuters news service to steal a march on all its rivals and allowing Britain to impose a 'communications blockade' on Germany during World War I which, among other things, cut Germany off from potential sources of finance in the New York Stock Exchange. Communicational control allowed the British Empire a flexibility of response that was not open to its enemies.

The two types of control, purposive and positional, reflect different informational environments. The first is compatible with perfect information and with a calculus of ends and means. The second, by contrast, reflects a world of noisy information and unforeseen shocks.

The Cost of Control

Control is never without cost. It requires investment of time, materials and energy. This is what is meant by the economy of control. The desire to exercise control faces limits: limits on the intellectual resources available to develop strategies and tactics, limits on the more narrowly technical ability to process information, limits on information available without options or projects underway, and limits on communication. The nature of this economy shapes what forms of control are feasible. Whether in the case of a machine, personal life or an institution, choices have to be made as to the optimum or most appropriate degree of control. Henry Ford wrote of his dream of being able to control the whole process of producing cars through owning all the rubber plantations, steelworks and retail outlets that participated in the car industry. When Ford's moves into steel and glass-making proved disastrous (as Chrysler and General Motors had expected), Ford came to understand that there are strict limits to vertical integration: distant mines and rubber plantations would be extremely hard to manage, demanding new skills and knowhow. They would become a fixed burden when change demanded flexibility. The costs of control would outweigh the possible benefits. More recently, many of the larger conglomerates contracted during the late 1970s and early 1980s, in parallel with the attempts of numerous governments to reduce their sphere of operation because of their inability effectively to monitor or control departments and subsidiaries.

Similar considerations apply in political and personal life, where control is equally limited by an economy of time. The idea of a strictly autonomous, free and choosing individual belongs to mythology. No one has the time or resources to evaluate all possible choices or to maintain active reciprocal links in every sphere. If such individuals did exist they would have no time for food, work, love and play. Formally, democracy is a means by which the subjects of power exercise control over how that power is used. The extent of control can vary from a five-yearly choice between two opposing programmes, to the near-permanent politicization of all decisions which takes place during periods of revolutionary upheaval. These periods tend to be brief for a simple reason. The cost of total democracy is that no one has any time to make food, look after children or guard the frontiers. The result of trying to exercise too much control is that there is nothing left to control. This is also one of the limits to the hope for an electronic democracy in which all participate in all decisions. Even though it is technically feasible, few would have the time to participate genuinely in weighing up choices and making decisions.

Engineers distinguish between mechanical or energizing systems based on strong power engineering and weak power engineering. The former use large quantities of energy relative to the processes they control, the latter relatively little. The human brain or the CPU (central processing unit) of an automated factory or computer are examples of weak power control, using very little energy relative to the processes they control.[11] Much of the machinery of the late twentieth century is also weak power in this sense, controlled by highly efficient electronic devices. Most human institutions by contrast depend on strong power controls, organized in hierarchies. The mechanical machinery of industrial societies was matched by its strong power, pyramidal organizations. Perhaps the greatest economic weakness of political or socialized control in human societies is their dependence on strong power techniques. The most advanced forms of democracy require that people come together physically and spend long periods discussing options. Bureaucracies, the pre-eminent control mechanisms of the twentieth century, use most of their energies simply reproducing and servicing themselves. Much the same is true of the modern army, the corporation, the political party and the trade union. All of these adopted similar ideas of organization in the late nineteenth century, centred around pyramidal hierarchy, explicit rules, fixed authorities and structures, single lines of accountability and a strict division of labour.

The inefficiency of strong power structures is arguably one of the more intractable problems of the late twentieth century, and one that has become more acute as societies attempt to restructure around greater flows of information and more sophisticated control technologies. Information technologies have usually been introduced within bureaucracies to shore up older strong power structures, tightening the power of the pyramid, enhancing centralized supervision and command, and furthering the division of labour. This is always problematic. Within an authoritarian pyramidal structure, those lower down tend systematically to distort the information going up. Manipulating information to highlight successes, hide failures and bid for resources is about the only way of negotiating control with superiors when power is not dispersed.

Other things being equal, within any structure greater complexity makes it harder effectively to impose control from above. Technologies may improve the effectiveness of formal downward controls and vertical communications but on their own they can neither foster the kinds of creativity that are central to the production of value in more advanced, knowledge-based economies nor provide the variety needed to respond to unforeseen situations. W. Ross Ashby provided an elegant formulation of this idea in the 'law of requisite variety' which states that the variety of a controlling system must be at least equal to that of the activity being controlled.[12] A similar conclusion was reached by Jan Tinbergen in relation to economics, when he argued that the number of economic policy instruments must be greater than or equal to the number of policy targets.[13] The principle turns out to be important in understanding the regulation of communications networks, where the attempts to control through a single parameter (such as price or profit) lead to distortions of other parameters.

The point can also be understood in terms of positional control: to cope with disruption an open system must contain sufficient variety to cope with unforeseen variations in its environment. These lessons are beginning to be understood within organizations, as weak power structures based on networks, flows of horizontal communication and greater flexibility in the definition of roles come to be used. In human and biological systems efficient weak power controls use more decentralized and cellular structures with a stress on horizontal rather than vertical communications. Control ceases to be a resource that is held by some and exercised over others but becomes embedded within the structure, as a means of adapting and of meeting goals. Exogenous or imposed control is replaced by endogenous and organic forms of control. Small units are encouraged and kept relatively closed to foster intense internal communication; autonomy combines with incentives for creativity and fluidity of structure. Control in a narrow managerial sense is ceded to the control needs of the institution.

Many of the new communications technologies encourage a greater flow of information. It becomes much easier to copy and multiply reports, memoranda or television programmes. Within organizations, however, more rapid flows of information bring costs as well as benefits. Less vertical duplication, greater coordination and horizontal links are fostered at the cost of diluting originality and innovation. Although it assists the short-term control tasks of organizing formal processing and decision rules, excessive information flow can undermine the long-term need that any control system has for replication and selection. Creativity and change seem to depend on intense and enclosed forms of communication, on the ability to think in uncontrolled and even irrational ways at one remove from the rational rule orientation of larger organizations. The Belgian biologist Ilya Prigogine made a similar point, writing about fluctuations in chemical and biological processes:

the fluctuation that leads from one regime to the other cannot possibly overrun the initial state in a single move. It must first establish itself in a limited region and then invade the whole space ... depending on whether the size of the initial fluctuating region lies below or above some critical value, the fluctuation either regresses or else spreads to the whole system ... the faster communication takes place within a system, the greater the percentage of unsuccessful fluctuations and thus the more stable the system ... this means that in such situations the 'outside world', the environment of the fluctuating region, always tends to damp fluctuations. These will be destroyed or amplified according to the effectiveness of the communication between the fluctuating region and the outside world.[14]

Visible and Invisible Hands

The contrast between an organic and a dominating control is familiar in economic theory. Adam Smith's 'invisible hand' was a highly influential invocation of the idea of control emerging out of structural relations, the aggregate of a multitude of individual actions. Bernard Mandeville's *Fable of the Bees* is another example of order and cohesion arising out of the self-seeking activities of its parts.[15] In the 200 years since Smith wrote, the market has been repeatedly invoked as an efficient information-processing and decision-making system, inherently superior to central planning because of its decentralization. Fritz Machlup and Friedrich Hayek, who described the market as a spontaneous order, are among those who have argued that the market can often be more democratic than democracy itself, a more efficient mechanism for registering preferences than an infrequent choice between two or three alternatives. The market is efficient precisely because it is a weak power structure effortlessly producing information about aggregate wants through the workings of the price system. Planning by the state, by contrast, is relatively inefficient, a strong power form of control that must explicitly gather information and process it through centralized and therefore inefficient mechanisms.

At first glance the technical ability of digital systems to manipulate and monitor information transmitted seems to make them ideally suited to market forms of exchange, enhancing the weak power character of the market, as they produce information at the same time as they support exchange. This ability to produce information can be read in more than one way, as creating a more perfect and competitive market or as a new tool of producer control over consumers.[16] The same networks which transmit and receive information can become transactional networks, buying and selling goods and services. Money becomes increasingly shaped by its nature as a form of information, processed and transmitted alongside all others. Once money becomes fully electronic it takes on the flexibility and the speed of all digital communications. The trend to remove commodities from their representations (which are then traded, discounted and pre-sold in futures markets) gains a new tool. In the case of informational services each transaction can, in principle, be endlessly broken down, and priced appropriately. The 'lumpiness' of traditional market exchange can be left behind, leaving an approximation to neoclassical economics' perfect and continuous supply and demand curves. The very act of exchange can be closely monitored and controlled. One example of this is the addressable converter, rapidly spreading in the world's cable and satellite industries. Addressable converters enable a broadcaster to encrypt signals, to monitor viewers' credit, and thus control whether an individual subscriber is able to decrypt, and so view, any signals. With such a system, 'pay-per-view', whereby programmes are priced and sold individually, becomes viable.

Intelligent networks can also target markets much more accurately than mass media advertising: messages can be shaped to a variety of audiences, which can in turn be monitored for their responses. Database marketing, which shapes marketing material to customer profiles and previous spending patterns is already beginning to transform areas like mail-order shopping. The same techniques can be used as commercial or political aids, or to shape educational materials to different cognitive styles. Digital networks can also provide almost perfect information both for the consumer, who can instantaneously access information about market conditions, and for the supplier, who can monitor each transaction and purchase detailed information about each consumer's purchasing habits and lifestyle. Effective control within the market, both for consumer and producer, can be massively enhanced. As in Hayek's catallaxy,[17] all interhuman transactions can take the form of market transactions, while all information about markets and conditions of supply and demand can be turned into commodity form.

As Marx showed, however, the crucial question in any market is the real balance of control that lies behind the formal equalities of exchange.[18] In practice consumers have little control over how information collected about their consumption or financial behaviour is used and traded. Equally workers have little control over how information is used by employers in the labour market.[19] It is precisely because of these imbalances of control that legal remedies are needed: laws against discrimination in employment or insurance, laws upholding individual rights of control over information. In each case the law is used to constrain the transparency of the informational marketplace.

Many of the same technical functions that support a market mechanism can also be deployed by organizations as overt coordination tools within a single hierarchy of given ends. Such a contrast between visible and invisible coordination mechanisms provided the central theme for Alfred Chandler's famous accounts of the birth of the modern corporation,[20] which tell the story of the replacement of market mechanisms by bureaucratic ones towards the end of the nineteenth century, as corporations internalized control functions. The demands of efficient coordination (what Weber described as imperative coordination) led the hierarchy to replace the market. A similar argument is made by Oliver Williamson, who emphasized the imperative of lowering all forms of transaction cost.[21] A 'governance hierarchy' of putting-out, contracting, peer groups, federations and industrial relations, of unitary, holding company and multidivisional forms, can be analysed in terms of the calculus of cost and control.[22] Both are concerned with coordination in an environment in which the ends of profit and efficiency are paramount. Both are more interested in purposive than positional control, discounting the alternative view of the firm as a form of closure against uncertainties.

Control in the Home: Culture and Interactivity

Despite the plethora of utopian writings about the role of networks in dispersing control, far more resources have been spent on using technologies to enhance consumer sovereignty than on alternatives which express control through the communication of views within public or voluntary bodies, local services or assemblies. This relative underdevelopment of technologies for upwards control outside economic life is one factor behind the potency of the politics of consumerism, autonomy and freedom: the real, albeit highly restricted, control of the consumer can be contrasted to the largely theoretical control which is exercised over large bureaucratic public institutions. Disillusion with the large, standardized and remote institution is reflected in the utopian visions of future networks in which control is returned from the state and corporations to the individual or family based in the home.

In the network utopias of Toffler, Masuda and others, communications technologies allow the individual or family in the home to choose the parameters of work, politics and leisure. Dependence on mass-produced goods and services is replaced by prosumption – production for use within the home. In the 'self-service' economy,[23] in which the dish-washer, the food processor, the microwave oven and the video recorder provide services currently bought externally through the market, domes-tic life is transformed by a revolution in control. Networked information technologies are anticipated to further this trend, providing the home with access to storage, information and control technologies with the potential to transform entertainment, education, medicine and the every-day life of the home.

The vision often begins with the television set, the dominant image of passive manipulation in an industrial society and, with the car, its classic commodity. Culture will be transformed as viewers are linked to interactive television networks and videotex channels with instant access to the cultural heritage of the whole world. People will learn 'to play with the television set, to talk back to it and to interact with it ... changing from passive receivers to message senders as well ... they are manipulat-ing the set rather than merely letting the set manipulate them'.[24] Media will be 'demassified' and the means of cultural production, the video camera and recording studio, made universally available. The same control capabilities that allow a network to be used to support a market or a surveillance system will allow the user at home to scan, select, record or reject. The user will be able to exercise discrimination over what services are used and when and how they are configured; he or she can also pay only for what is needed, and can manipulate information without being subject to a centrally determined flow.

The utopian aspirations have spawned numerous applications. Interac-tive forms of video and television can mitigate the pure passivity of existing film and broadcasting: in one model, for example, the viewer can choose which items of news to follow up in more detail, or participate in determining the narrative structure of a drama. Programs can sift information according to the revealed interests of the user. 'Cybernetic' and interactive forms of video art are emerging which claim to breach the traditional relationship between artist and audience and to dissolve the identity and integrity of the work of art.[25] The creators of 'virtual realities' offer an equally radical unification of the production and consumption of art and experience.[26] Meanwhile the digital sampling and scratch techniques that are already playing havoc with ownership rights in recorded music or television news can be used to create personal cultures.[27]

How far these capacities can reach into the home is not clear. Interactive experiments in television have been strikingly unsuccessful. The dream of millions of people producing and distributing their own audiovisual material remains precisely that, a dream that is unlikely to be realized because of the nature of audiences reared on highly edited and structured forms of entertainment. The utopian hopes have also been matched by dystopias of atomized family life, seen as increasingly cut off from public interaction and imprisoned behind the television. If neither view is wholly satisfactory it is in part because they assume that technologies have an impact on home life, rather than being absorbed and redefined within the complex interactions of family life.

The history of communications technologies in the home is not a simple one. As they have brought information and communication into the home (through radio, television, cable and videotex), automated domestic machinery (meters, 'smart houses'), and stored large quantities of information on tapes and discs,[28] they have brought out some of the underlying relationships of control and identity in the home. The early radio, for example, was resisted by women as an unwelcome intrusion;[29] later the television set came to be seen as disruptive of child-rearing and marital relations, distracting women from their proper tasks. Both contributed to reinforcing the 'pleasures of the hearth' and of home life, while women came to use the telephone more intensively than men for the opposite reason – to relieve the isolation of home life.

Simultaneously private and social, communications technologies such as the telephone, the answering machine, and the videorecorder (which fits broadcast television into domestic time) allow the individual and family to control the terms of interaction with the outside world. But the problem, which belies the simplistic utopias, is that technologies sometimes offer too much control. They allow the child to bypass the parent: in the case of computer games, bypassing their accumulated knowledge; in the case of video nasties bypassing their moral control; and in the case of telephone services bypassing their control over escalating bills.[30] This double edge becomes more pronounced as home technologies have taken on the character of other communications devices, becoming more easily controlled through remote controls and touch-sensitive switches, more programmable, even if this is usually within narrow parameters, more integrated, and more likely to be linked to networks. These new capabilities create a tension over who is to exercise them: the remote control switch for the television, the automated home security system and other innovations all generate new conflicts.

Problems arise whenever control demands too much of the user. Greater user control paradoxically combines with the emergence of more programmed devices which relieve the user of choices: examples include cameras, microwave cookers and cars which automatically provide the appropriate response to a given situation. Excessively complex devices seem to bring an inappropriate economy of control.

The more ambitious experiments with the networked home have also come up against the resistance to excessive control. The Japanese experiments probably represent the boldest attempts to create a practice out of the theory of home-based utopias. The Hi-Ovis interactive cable experiment in Ikoma linked households to community information, educational services and video on demand. The later INS (Information Network System) experiments in Mitaka and Musashino offered videotex, digital fax, videophones and sketch phones to suburban households in Tokyo.[31] Similar experiments have been carried out in Biarritz in France and Project Victoria in California. Each sought to determine if there really was a demand for home shopping, for home-based medical diagnosis, for video telephony, for home commuting, for new forms of neighbourhood and new forms of democracy. In each case the experiments revealed complex social barriers to new uses of technology, along with unforeseen demands (such as Japanese housewives' use of videocommunication). The apparent promise of individualized control seemed to rub against barriers of confidence and competence.

One additional reason for these failures was the unsatisfactory nature of the technologies as symbols. All consumer goods function within a symbolic economy: as Mary Douglas and Baron Isherwood wrote, goods, 'in being accepted or refused ... either reinforce or undermine existing boundaries. The goods are both the hardware and the software, so to speak, of an information system whose principal concern is to monitor its own performance'.[32] Their value as control technologies depends not just on their practical usefulness, but also on their value in giving an appropriate sense of control and meaning.

Work in the Home

Telework or telecommuting has played a part in all of the network experiments. The practical need to reduce the time spent in commuting converged with visionary hopes for a wholesale 'demassification' of work using communications technologies. The office and factory are centralized sites which serve to concentrate productive machinery and labour. With high capacity networks and cheap computing power, mental labour can be removed to the home, reviving the old integration of work and home life that existed before the industrial revolution. The promise is that in place of the discipline of the workplace, the individual can again be able to choose the timing and pace of work. According to Alvin Toffler, there will be a 'return to cottage industry on a new, higher, electronic basis, and with it a new emphasis on the home as the centre of society'.[33]

Contrary to the wilder predictions, home-based electronic work has established only a limited role in North America, Japan and Europe. British examples include ICL's remote software and technical authorship unit and Rank Xerox's experiments with networking; in the USA Blue Cross/Blue Shield and Aetna Life have both run fairly substantial schemes. By the mid-1980s many companies were encouraging executives to work from home, motivated at least in part by the hype surrounding telework. The more immediate incentive was to save the costs of overheads and the costs of staff needed to service management. Productivity seemed to increase, by between 15 and 25 per cent.[34] Executives were encouraged to become quasi-independent consultants, selling their services back to the company, still in place on organizational charts but no longer a long-term commitment for the company. For the worker the reward is to be relieved of commuting and of working in a stressful environment. Other pockets of telework formed in occupations such as journalism, editing and relatively sophisticated data processing.

The other side of telework has been its application to low-grade wordprocessing and data entry work. This tends to draw on much older traditions of home work, where distance from the concentrated environment of the office or factory is used to weaken labour, to sweat it, to remove rights to health insurance or pension rights. Again, as at the top of the hierarchy, the aim is to pass costs of overheads and security back onto labour and to enhance management flexibility.

Despite high expectations the reality of telework remains modest. Studies in the early 1970s[35] estimated that as much as 85 per cent of all white-collar work could be done remotely. In the UK in 1987, however, only 15,000 people were judged to be working from the home in this way,[36] and around 100,00 in the USA.[37] The very benefits of work from home, freedom from the direct disciplines and interactions of the workplace, seemed to make it unacceptable to managers. Robert Kraut has written that 'in large organisations some coordination is accomplished by adherence to common rules and regulations ... or through traditional hierarchical reporting relationships ... but in the face of novelty, uncertainty and unstructured environmental conditions, informal communication is needed to gain new information, clarify values, evaluate alternative and make decisions'.[38] It is for this reason that physical proximity is so crucial, and for this reason, too, that it is tasks with little need for coordination which are most amenable to home work.

The chance to spend all day at home is also a mixed blessing for the worker. For many teleworkers the greatest advantage of working at home, being able to spend more time with their children, turned out to be its greatest disadvantage. Home work is also, of course, limited by the nature of the home. Few people live in homes with enough space and variety to accommodate the working day.

By the early 1990s telework was beginning to take a range of forms. Sweden experimented with train carriages designed as mobile offices and remote work centres. British Telecom set up work centres where remote workers could rent space and facilities in a compromise between the home and the remote office, while in Japan NEC developed technologies for the 'satellite office'. In both countries the role of these halfway houses as means of enabling women to participate in the workforce also led to criticisms that they further locked women into the double obligations of work at home and in the office. The ambivalent nature of telework also became apparent in the USA, where prison inmates were used to process hotel bookings, part of a new economy of remote processing in which India, China and Barbados all competed for processing work. Just as technologies like the telephone and television were adapted into the complex dynamics of domestic life,[39] and the imbalances of an international division of labour, so have systems of telework been fitted into the structures of the office and the wider global economy in ways that bear little relation to the utopian hopes of earlier writers.

Smart Houses

The uncertain spread of telework has gone in parallel with the much more confident transformation of the fabric of the home. During the 1980s intelligent domestic systems rapidly emerged as an integral part of the construction industry, offering the means to control heating, lighting, cooking and security, room by room, sometimes with machinery that can recognize spoken commands. In most conceptions of the intelligent building (NTT claim that the phrase first came into use in Japan in 1984[40]) internal control and external communication overlap. The smart building systems, known as building management systems or building automation systems, range from energy management and security through to Local Area Networks, electronic mail and internal video networks. Like office buildings, the homes of the affluent classes of the industrialized countries are being transformed into a sophisticated control system, with the same link between internal control and external communication. The electrical networks inside a house are overlaid with communications and control networks, programmed to individual needs. The house can then be programmed to activate or adjust heating levels, ovens, videorecorders, to switch lights on and off, and to regulate sprinklers or security sensors. In principle, parents can program the house to prevent their children from watching certain channels or spending too much time playing computer games. Control can be exercised from a distance using the telephone, and the smart house can itself 'contact' the owner in the event of a crisis.

Programmable controllers have emerged as the core technology for smart buildings, replacing the less flexible 'hard-wired' approaches. The use of controllers of this kind makes it possible continually to collect data about the building's environment; the building can learn to diagnose its own faults, while also being controlled remotely through the telephone network. As in other fields of computing and communications, alternative topologies have been developed. In some control is centralized in a single computer, while in others semi-autonomous control points operate in a network allowing for greater flexibility in the case of breakdowns. As with domestic machinery, smart homes offer no technical answer to the problem of access to programming and control: conflicts between parents and children, husbands and wives, tenants and landlords are almost inevitable concomitants of enhanced domestic control.

Electronic Democracies

The fourth field that promises to use networks to transfer control into the home is politics. Electronic democracy offers the removal of control from parliaments and governments into the home. Instantaneous referenda, and on-line accountability replace the loose accountability of existing representative systems. Control may be applied to local government, to the governing bodies of local schools and hospitals or to decisions on planning permission for a new road or shopping centre. Supervision, accountability and the direct expression of opinions can all be exercised from the living-room. The personalization of politics, and the bypass of intermediaries echo the consistent theme of the network utopias, the idea that the only authentic control is direct and unmediated.

For the proponents of electronic democracy direct legislation by the people would accelerate the long-term decline of political parties. If representation was to continue, representatives would be immediately and publicly accountable to their constituents. A range of technologies are seen as ushering in this age of sovereign public opinion. The opinion poll, or television and radio call-in, are now joined by interactive cable, videoconferencing, computer conferencing and electronic mail, permitting debate and voting over electronic systems. Exponents of a technologically driven move towards more direct participation include Toffler and Naisbitt, Frederick Williams and T. L. Becker. In the writings of Benjamin Barber,[41] lottery elections and civic videotex systems help to transform democratic institutions, teaching citizens about responsibility and involvement in decision making. A common assumption is that access to the tools of participation will generate its own interest. Ideas of this kind raise enormous and probably unanswerable questions about implementation, about the framing of questions and about how governments would cope with inconsistent decision, indeed with most of the basic questions of public policy that are at least formally solved in representative systems. Implicitly they seem to assume that the world is moving towards the ideal of Saint-Simon, Marx and Engels, that of the 'administration of things', in which the implementation of policy decisions is a purely technical matter, untouched by the threat that a state and its employees can become a political force in their own right.

Several small-scale experiments in the USA have been conducted to test the potential of this idea, though none even approaches the ideal of electronic democracy. In the Televote Project in Hawaii, packets of information and argument were sent out prior to telephone votes which were in turn publicized in existing media; the Honolulu electronic town meetings combined television discussions with viewers calling in or casting votes. On the 'QUBE' cable system in Columbus, Ohio, local leaders debated issues while viewers periodically registered agreement or disagreement. In Massachussets, Representative Edward Markey used the Compuserve network to create an 'Electure', setting off discussions on the computer network of his position papers on the nuclear freeze in such a way that participants could interact with each other's contributions.[42] The Special Interest Group (SIG) networks allow home computer owners to debate with each other or form campaigning groups through networks such as Compuserve and The Source. California's assembly and senate allow citizens to access a database about current debates and register comments or questions.

A study by Christopher Arterton at the Roosevelt Center in Washington of thirteen experiments of this kind concluded that, although on occasions activists and authorities did benefit from the experience, there was no evidence that the technologies actually changed the political psychology of those participating or prompted participation from people who would not otherwise participate in policies.[43] The most successful depended on substantial resources of time and money. Moreover, experiments have remained just that, almost never becoming embedded in political life. The few exceptions have used computer networks to access representatives where what has changed is a means of communicating complaints or ideas rather than a decision-making process as such.

To understand the limits of electronic democracy it is necessary to think with some rigour about the nature of democratic participation and control. Participation can be understood as a form of communication, bounded by access to time and competences. The effective exercise of control through democratic structures depends on much more than formal rights. Whether we choose to communicate depends very much on whether we believe we have a right to communicate. This sense of a right is in many ways more important than formal rights of free speech and political participation. Participation in daily politics depends on feelings of competence, judged by socially shaped criteria, on whether it seems legitimate to see an issue as one's own business. The indifference towards politics that electronic means seek to overcome can perhaps be better understood if it is recognized that the propensity to use a political power or a formal right, the right to vote, to talk politics or get involved in politics, is usually commensurate with the reality of this power. By and large, the capacity to think about power and about political strategies is something that is taught, and taught only to those for whom it will be a relevant knowledge. The other side of this coin is that indifference is often only a manifestation of impotence.

There are many ways of countering structural imbalances in political participation, of spreading competences, of guaranteeing spare time away from obligations of work, childcare and domestic labour to devote to learning the means to exercise the broadest possible control over one's own life. Democratic politics always rests on a material base that provides the time and resources for participation. The important point is that such a material base is likely to prove much more significant than the technologies involved.

In the absence of a serious discussion of the structural foundations of democracy, the claims for an electronic agora are deceptive. They fail to ask how agendas of political discussion will be formed and how the network will bring people together rather than isolating them in their own homes, defined as a lone consumer rather than as a member of a class, religion, ethnic group or gender. Democracy depends also on media for argument, information and debate, mediations that sustain a public sphere of communication. Unmediated relationships between the individual citizen and the state will tend to be unbalanced and unequal. Where the proponents of electronic democracy fail to address questions of this kind, the need for diverse flows of information, for political education and an active, argumentative civil society, prophets of the electronic democracy run the risk described by Pierre Bourdieu, of succumbing to that 'indulgent populism which credits the common people with innate knowledge of politics [and] . . . helps disguise and so consecrate the "concentration in a few individuals" of the capacity to produce discourse about the social world, and, through this, the capacity for consciously changing that world'.[44]. It is access to this kind of knowledge that allows people to play a role in shaping the choices that are then offered to them. Otherwise in the course of driving the user is also driven.

Barriers to Control in the Home

The deceptions of electronic democracy amplify the evidence of the 'wired city' experiments that there is deep resistance to electronic interactivity beyond a small number of enthusiasts. In most spheres of life there seems to be resistance to an excess of choice and control. This may be the mark of a transitional period. In the long run the move away from one-way mass communications systems towards more interactive forms may seem as natural as the spread of the telephone, an interactive technology for which few people could initially imagine much demand. It is worth recalling the predictions made at the beginning of the twentieth century that the motor industry faced an upper bound of around one million cars worldwide, constrained by the shortage of chauffeurs and by people's unwillingness to drive themselves. Several decades after its invention the car remained a luxury, awaiting lower costs and the creation of infrastructures of roads and fuel. What the example of the car shows, however, is that a movement from centralized provision to self-activity and self-control depends on there being an appropriate economy of control. The amount of time and energy required to master driving was seen by enough people as commensurate with the added utility offered by the car.

There are also more fundamental social barriers to the removal of control into the household. Each new use of communications technology tends to create frictions with older ways of doing things. These may be the etiquettes of conversation and invitation into the home (a particularly severe problem in the case of the videophone). Smart homes may cause new frictions over who has access to the control pad. Frictions also arise over who has access to information. Doctors will tend to resist home-based medical diagnostic systems if these threaten their authority and material rewards, just as schools will tend to resist changes that give easier access to pupils and parents. In all cases people rarely take advantage of rights and opportunities unless they have the competence and confidence to do so.

Many also have valid doubts about the psychological and social viability and desirability of these visions of control situation in the home. Control often seems to be won at the cost of community. Conviviality seems to have little place in their image of decentralized control; instead the individual and the family unit are defined by their electronic interactions, as community and solidarity are mediated through the network. This is certainly the weakness of home work. The home can be as lonely and alienating as any workplace. Yet it is too early to judge the viability or desirability of these models. There is some evidence that networks like the Minitel in France and Compuserve in the USA have created new and active social networks,[45] 'virtual' friendhips and associations particularly for those living outside large cities. Given that the architecture and geography of cities and suburbs has dissolved older ties of community, electronic networks may indeed become tools of conviviality within cities as well. The Japanese INS (Information Network System) is advertised as a means to recreate the sense of community ruptured by rapid urbanization, AT&T's advanced networks as a new 'telecommunity' for a highly mobile society.

The various transformations in home life remain possible social innovations and have yet to make a decisive move from the margins of social life. But even as possibilities they suggest the extent to which the pursuit of control is becoming pervasive. Control over body and mind, image and identity is widely taken to be the ideal of modern life. Even the computer hacker, at first glance a playful subversive, is perhaps better understood as an exemplar of a culture which greatly honours those who master technique and control. The historian of the hackers, Steven Levy, gave one of the clearest descriptions of this feature of information technology when he wrote of his realization that the computer was just 'a dumb beast . . . You could control it. You could be God.'[46]

State Controls and the Transparent Network

The benign image of individual or domestic autonomy stands in sharp contrast to the many traditions of state control over the economy and everyday life. These lend credence to the alternative vision of future networks, a vision of the consolidation of coercive controls. States and empires were traditionally bound together with the strongest forms of strong power control: nearly all their energies were devoted to sustaining power, crushing dissent and preserving or extending territorial power. There is a sense in which all states remain 'monopolies of violence' whose first priority is survival.

The exercise of control depends on both the individual technologies of control – the records, policing systems, mental institutions, prisons and bureaucracies – and the means whereby these are linked to each other – the networks of runners and couriers, telephones and satellites and most recently the 'open systems' computer communications networks. Carolyn Marvin quotes W. E. H. Lecky writing about the impact of communications technologies in the 1890s, that 'the telegram . . . has greatly strengthened the central Government in repressing insurrections, protecting property and punishing crime', and in meddling with local administrations.[47] The peculiar technical power of the modern state derives from this extensive capacity: the ability to establish instantaneous links to the most remote regions and to deny such links to the opposition.

The centre of power in a time of crisis is the situation room, in essence a communications hub providing real-time surveillance. Just as the first targets of modern revolutionaries are the broadcasting stations and the telephone exchange, so the first step in the imposition of martial law in Poland in 1981 was the closure of the public telephone network. Bismarck is reputed to have been the first political leader to recognize the importance of the telephone and in 1877 ran a 230-mile line from his palace in Berlin to his farm in Varzin (prompting Tolstoy to speculate on what would have happened if Genghis Khan had had a telephone).

Extensive control of this kind is sometimes described as panoptical. Jeremy Bentham's famous panopticon was a prison (or a school or factory) so designed that the eyes of the centre could continuously survey activity anywhere in the building. In its most developed form each cell could be monitored and observed from the centre, while sideways contact was impossible. Bentham also envisaged a system of pipes for aural surveillance but failed to devise a system that would guarantee asymmetry, preventing those being listened to from being able to listen to the surveyor. At least, one predecessor had managed to overcome this problem. Denis I, the fourth-century BC tyrant of Syracuse, reportedly built a network of acoustic horns throughout his court to monitor all conversations, and used a similar system for distributing commands on boats.[48]

Though digital networks can be used for horizontal communication, they also bear many of the attributes of the panopticon: every purchase or communication leaves a digital footprint, visible from the centre.[49] When stored program control switches are used it becomes theoretically feasible to copy and record every transaction without the sender or receiver having any knowledge of interception.[50] Digital enhancement techniques and digital cameras (CCDs) have also greatly improved the quality of satellite surveillance, and the ability to sift through confusing mixes of sounds and data.

These capacities of digital technologies are only one part of a wider movement towards the systematic gathering and commodification of information and intelligence, designed to bring predictability and control. The permanent monitoring of markets, competitors and consumers has become a major industry in its own right. William Colby, a former director of the CIA, has written of 'the maturation of the intelligence function from its origins as a Government spy service to full growth as an intellectual discipline serving the public and private sector alike ... today's proliferation of information banks and analytical centres for investment counselling, political risk assessments and "futures" estimates are witness to the growth of the intelligence discipline outside traditional government circles'.[51]

Alongside the spread of intelligence as a discipline, techniques for managing, collecting and cross-referencing large quantities of data have given a powerful tool to governments.[52] The state's capacity to operate or intervene in networks has led to a widespread fear that the computers and data bases managed by different arms of the state, health, education, police, tax and those run by banks, credit and insurance companies, can be linked, providing each with a comprehensive picture of any individual's life.[53] According to one survey there were 3.5 billion separate government records on US citizens by the mid-1980s.[54] Open systems models have been actively promoted in government,[55] to allow government networks to interconnect, in the name of the concept of the 'whole person'. Fear of the overweening power this implies has generated the first legislative responses to information technology: rights of privacy, data laws licensing keepers of files and limiting the scope for linking them. One of the most important rights is that of inspecting one's own record on files, a crucial constraint on sloppy and inaccurate techniques. Fifty-five per cent of federal files in the US were found to be incorrect. In this way the state's control over information is offset by the citizen's guarantee of transparent access. Transparency, rather than a right of privacy, restores the balance of control between citizen and state.

Most of the early modern control technologies, the files, tabulators, calculators and early mainframes stood alone. Information was brought to them, often physically, fed in by humans and processed, stored and produced on the spot. Only in the last quarter-century has processing become inextricably bound up with the transmission of information. John Von Neumann, one of the pioneers of computing, argued that a very small number of enormous computers would be able to serve the world's needs. These would exploit the economies of scale inherent in processing and would operate as utilities, providing a time-sharing access to companies, governments and institutions. Networks would be shaped like stars linking dumb terminals to the central computers. Instead of central utilities, intelligence is widely dispersed in cheap personal computers, as predicted by Vannevar Bush.[56] For some this is a countervailing force to any oppressive state: multiple sources of information and multiple routes for dissemination make it impossible for a government to maintain a monopoly of truth. There is some justification for this view. Its major flaw is that it ignores the fact that parellel technologies are simultaneously strengthening the potential for surveillance and control.

In considering the surveillance power of centralized bureaucracies it is worth recalling that the most oppressive forms of state control are not always the most centralized. Totalitarian systems, which could be managed with paper and pen, have often, paradoxically, used a very decentralized form of control, dependent on informers, party members and block leaders. They have often been militantly hostile to central bureaucracies. This degree of ubiquitous presence made totalitarianism possible without the help of extensive networks. Some would argue that the same is true in other modern institutions, whether corporations or religions. The most pernicious and oppressive forms of control come not from sophisticated computer systems but from the mobilization of loyalty, psychic bonds and peer discipline.

Control and Communications in Warfare

While government technologies remain constrained by arguments for civil liberty and privacy, military technology is in the midst of an apparently unbounded revolution in the application of control technologies. The extreme conditions of war provide an ultimate test for control techniques, and continue to lead the forced march to new forms of artificial intelligence, remote control, surveillance and counterstrategy.

In warfare there is little scope for weak power structures although guerrilla armies have sometimes begun with structures of this kind. Centralized intelligence, command and control have usually been critical to military effectiveness. Wars brought new uses of network technologies such as the undersea network built by Japan during its war with China in the 1890s, the telephone wires strung behind lines in the 1905 Russo-Japanese war, and the use of radio signals for coordinating ships, tanks or submarines. The value of control technologies derives from the fact that in the past, and even within its own terms, war has been enormously inefficient: according to one estimate during the US Civil War, only one bullet in 100,000 hit its target. Weapons such as tactical nuclear devices are also remarkably blunt instruments. Communications technologies, allied to robotics and artificial intelligence, promise a massive leap forward in the 'productivity' of military machines.

Transparency is essential to this leap. Describing the future, Frank Barnaby quotes General Westmoreland, then the US Army Chief of Staff, in a speech made in 1969: 'I see battlefields that are under 24 hour real or near real time surveillance of all types. I see battlefields on which we can destroy anything we locate through instant communications and almost instantaneous application of highly lethal firepower.'[57] This vision has yet to become a reality but many of its elements are in place: autonomous and intelligent missiles able to search, recognize, and attack their targets independently; optical, infrared, seismic and sound sensors capable of detecting the movement of people and creating electronic borders such as that between Israel and Lebanon; remotely piloted vehicles, and unmanned aircraft for surveillance or attack; functionoids, military robots which are being developed into the foot-soldiers of the future. The aim is instant and ubiquitous control, a transparency revolution whose aim is to detect and target enemy forces while hiding and communicating with one's own. Each machine and each combatant must be linked into networks which are mobile and secure. According to one expert, future wars will not involve conflict between offensive and defensive capabilities but 'between the visible and the hidden, between transparency and stealth'.[58] Forty per cent of all military satellites are used for photographic reconnaissance, continually enhanced by higher resolution and the digital processing of images. The electromagnetic spectrum is systematically 'vacuumed' for enemy signals. Fifth generation computers and artificial intelligence (AI) are being applied to robot vision and pattern recognition, speech recognition and language understanding to make it easier for pilots or tank commanders to control their machines. AI is also being applied to the enormous software problems of defensive systems such as the Strategic Defense Initiative (SDI), with programs such as the STARS (Software Technology for Adaptable Reliable Systems) seeking dramatically to reduce the costs and defects endemic to military software. Each new advance in turn creates a new set of counterstrategies. The science of 'C3I' (command, control, communication and intelligence) is now joined by 'C3CM': command, control and communication countermeasures: the production of misleading signals, jamming techniques, decoys and ever more complex cryptographic techniques.

As the SDI program began to take form, President Reagan's science adviser gave a glowing account to the US Senate of the importance of the computer to modern nuclear warfare:

It was data processing which overcame John Von Neumann's scepticism of ever making the ICBM work in the first place. It was data processing at the heart of the move to MIRVing. It was data processing which tied ICBM fleets together for coordinated execution. It was data processing which has provided the ICBM accuracy necessary for preemptive strikes. And it is data processing which will be at the heart of any defense against ballistic missiles.[59]

The ability instantly to see, decide and direct, means that in warfare at least the centre will know more than the periphery: distributed control of the kind finding favour in other spheres is more likely to be associated with the guerrilla movement than the modern army which uses technology to shore up the centralized command and control structure. The informatization of war has travelled fast: its limits are those of all military technologies and of all technologies deployed in competitive contexts. Each measure spawns its counter-measure, and each attempt to bring order and predictability to the chaotic carnage of war only brings a new form of uncontrollability. This is the essence of control in competitive situations: the attempt to achieve new orders of purposive or positional control introduces new kinds of volatility and danger.

4

Control Economies

One of the characteristic features of modern capitalist and socialist economies is the scale and scope of their methods of control: the various techniques of personnel management, inventory management and financial planning, of organizing management information or interorganizational systems. All are systematic disciplines practised by corps of professionals. In parallel their technological counterparts, the ordering systems, funds transfer and value added networks have evolved into complex systems that are the core of the information economy. All have become the object of enormous investment.

Their imperative, to improve and accelerate the circulation of materials, ideas and money, to eliminate waste and enhance systematic control, has been present throughout the industrial era. But its fullest realization has depended on new technologies of control and communication. These various techniques and technologies together form what can be called an economy of control, a set of practices, ideas and institutions that play an increasingly decisive role in modern societies.

Control in economic life works on two very different dimensions. It involves coordination of flows in space and time, and a whole set of problems concerning where information is to be produced, sent and processed, and how the problems of control can be minimized. Within these contexts information technologies are used to facilitate computations of one kind or another. The second type of control involves the authority and powers that operate through hierarchies and within the marketplace, and the use of technologies to enhance surveillance and to restructure work so as to tighten discipline. The everyday use of communications technologies to enhance control in both of these senses highlights its double nature. In parallel, and often in the same organizations, ways of working have been restructured both to enhance hierarchic control within a tightly controlled system and to encourage new forms of soft control, based on mutual coordination, cooperation and devolved responsibility. The two forms of control, the soft and the hard, have evolved both in tandem and in tension. Both have become ever more sophisticated. Where one brings greater predictability and order, the other brings that degree of risk, creativity and individual responsibility without which adaptation and change are impossible.

This chapter shows that the ambivalent evolution of the control economy has taken ideas about organization far beyond the philosophies of control of Frederick Taylor and earlier theorists of management and accountancy. Far from solving the problems of production, distribution and consumption, the various applications of apparently hard control technologies have simply emphasized the importance of those soft structures that govern the real working of an office, a factory or a market. A fully automated, programmed and predictable world remains a dream.

Control in the Past

Just as an awareness of information makes it possible to reassess the past in terms of its modes of making, storing and disseminating information, so the role of control in the modern economy allows for a different perspective on the history of economic life. In hunting and gathering societies the problems of control can be seen to have centred on the need to restrain population growth so as to maintain the ecological balance of the food supply. In what have been described as hydraulic societies control issues concerned the organization of water, and the use of control over water to extract a surplus for a ruling class. In subsistence agriculture, by contrast, harmony with nature rather than mastery over it is the task of control, a problem of correctly gauging how much grain to preserve for another year and of how to maximize the use and yield of animals. The aim is to control against unforeseeable threats such as flood, drought and pillage.

What distinguishes industrial societies is the restructuring of control around timescales different from those of nature: principally those of capital markets, of accumulated labour and discounted futures. A second distinguishing feature is the complexity of the chains that grow up between production and consumption. As these grow longer problems of control become much more complicated: the integrity of the good or service must be preserved against decay, theft and redundance in an environment of rapidly changing values. With complexity come new orders of uncertainty. Sudden shifts in market conditions must be hedged against or bypassed. Factors and agents must be used and monitored in distant markets. Credit must be kept in line with debt, as must present investment and future demands. Labour must be disciplined, and provided with incentives of fear and reward. As with the subsistence farmer, the unexpected must be planned against. Strategies to maximize advantage from the present go alongside strategies of position and security. Every move from money into commodities runs the risk of not being able to move back into money. Money, too, is always an unstable holder of value, requiring its own hedges and diversifications, and holdings of precious metals or property to minimize risk.

Historically, organizational structures have tended to evolve both in relation to their purposes and to the technologies with which these can be achieved. Decisive innovations in organization have often come from those sectors which first faced problems of dealing with complex flows on a large scale. In the nineteenth century, many of the key innovations in corporate forms came from sectors dealing with large inputs of energy and large throughputs of materials (primarily the railways and metal industries), just as in the second half of the twentieth century many of the key innovations have come from sectors like aerospace and computing that depend on complex flows of information and knowledge. Communications technologies were instrumental in permitting organizational innovation. The telegraph and railway were particularly important. The telegraph allowed long-distance control, in the first place through control of the switching of railway rolling stock. By permitting a division between transport and communication, and between control and direct management, the telegraph set in motion a long revolution in organizational techniques. In John Carey's words 'signalling was separated from muculature',[1] and weak power control became feasible. More recently the telephone has permitted the emergence of 'kanban' or just-in-time structures, the local area network that of fully integrated production systems.

The relationship between technology and organizational form was apparent in the nineteenth century armaments factories of Springfield and Colt, which did much to prefigure later mass production systems by embedding authority and control into the very layout of machines and production lines. Eli Whitney began the movement from skilled craft labour to semi-skilled labour when he introduced jigs to guide workers' movements. Control was achieved through disaggregation. By breaking the work process down into its constituent parts, introducing complex mechanisms for accounting of time, materials and money, management enhanced its ability to control value, time and quality. The informational problems of control were limited by modularization, which depended on the creation of a discourse or calculus with which to see what was happening in the workplace.

Management and cost accounting provided this discourse. Internal management accounting (as distinct from external accounting for bankers, tax inspectors or creditors) has its roots early in the nineteenth century, in the workshops and small factories of the period. As larger capital investments came to be made in textiles, railways and later steel, managers found that they needed measures of internal productivity and profitability. The more innovative of them invented new accounting techniques to allocate costs and to encourage cost-cutting. Ways of seeing and abstracting were the precondition for effective control. In textiles the primary concern was with the outlay of internally controlled resources per unit of intermediate output. The most important of these was labour. Control and monitoring of costs carried with it a parallel purpose of ensuring labour discipline. The railways, which were at the time amongst the largest and most dispersed organizations, needed systems for managing their huge cash receipts and disbursements, which came to depend on concepts such as the cost per ton-mile, and the operating ratio, the ratio of revenue to operating costs. In the chemical industry Du Pont developed the concept of the return on investment, used to gauge the viability of internal investments. As Du Pont and General Motors developed multi-divisional structures to exploit economies of scope and shared organizational functions, new concepts were developed to permit managers at the centre to 'run the organization by numbers'. Abstraction and preprocessing were mobilized for central control.

The sources of innovation tended to be those firms on the leading edge of their era. In the 1950s and 1960s new concepts such as 'project accounting', 'program budgeting', 'zero base budgeting' and accounting for matrix organizations arose from firms engaged in large-scale, long-term projects in aerospace and defense. Internal accounting measures evolved in parallel with older traditions of external accounting, using more conservative, verifiable techniques to audit in the name of outside investors.[2] Both continue to be revolutionized. Network technologies can be used to formalize these approaches and embed them in everyday processes. In the era of LANs the costs of monitoring costs and outputs are far lower than in the past: automatic recognition and tracking systems have created an environment in which much of a company's activity can be monitored continuously in real time, providing a direct link between physical movements and financial accounts.

According to Alfred Chandler, the pre-eminent historian of American business, control problems, particularly those of the new national railroads, were the crucial impetus towards the emergence of the modern corporation, and later the multi-divisional corporation of the 1920s.[3] In each case a balance had to be set between insufficient control and excessive control. With insufficient control the centre is unaware of errors or unable to correct them until it is too late. Excessive control means that peripheral units lose their incentive to act dynamically by using independent judgement and the centre is overburdened with the information needed to exercise control. At a macro level, in Chandler's accounts, control in the sense of coordination and the stabilization of markets passed from the external, dispersed control of the market to the internal bureaucracies of the corporation: the invisible hand was replaced by the visible hand. Control in the sense of discipline was also concentrated and restructured in the visible hands of the organization and the factory, the manager and the overseer. Loose networks of craftspeople and small traders, regulated by combinations of market forces and cooperation, were replaced by centralized, authoritarian corporations.

When markets spread and production chains lengthened exchange came to be carried out with strangers coordinated through the national market and the corporation, the telegraph and the railway. With complexity firms had to predict the behaviour of more different actors, gauging more variables and monitoring more exchanges within their own operations. As in biology or physics a change in scale will tend to demand a change in the forms of organisms and organizations. Just as a human-sized insect's leg would collapse under its weight, the changing scales of economic activity cannot simply be met by multiplying the size of pre-existing forms. Instead new specializations had to be organized, new motivational bonds forged, new disciplines and lines of accountability and command created.[4] Changes in quantity call forth changes in quality and form.[5] Growing complexity and scale demand a permanent restructuring in the forms of organizations: from the family firm to the joint stock company, the multi-divisional firm and the transnational.

Early managers were responsible for a wide range of tasks, for finance, planning, design and direct supervision. Their knowhow was wrung from trial and error experience; planning was, in Chandler's words 'highly personal' and communication was largely oral. The development of modern management techniques transformed these practices. Middle management in companies like General Motors pioneered new and systematic functions in financial control, inventory control and personnel management. Communication became more formal, less dependent on bodily presence. The tasks of coordination which could previously be carried out by skilled craft workers now had to be systematized, control tasks abstracted from other tasks. In general, the problems of complexity were solved with ever more complex pyramidal structures, evolving specialized roles and vertical lines of accountability, and following the underlying principles of the Weberian bureaucracy, the separation between person and position, the detailed specification of tasks, a complex division of labour and formal lines of authority.

The weaknesses of bureaucratic control are now well understood. They are seen in their purest form in the socialist countries and those making a painful transition to market economies. Previously they had made the most far-reaching claims for their ability to plan complex economies. In a planned economy, as complexity increases, millions of new products, skills and relationships must be planned, priced and quantified through the mechanisms of the five-year plan, the hierarchies of firm, sector, ministry, and planning ministry. In order to cope with vast inputs of information all bureaucracies 'preprocess' information, converting the heterogeneity of the real world into the homogeneity of the form or the statistic. Preprocessing always comes at a cost. In the planned economies it usually means dealing with goods in terms of a few quantitative dimensions rather than qualities. Preprocessing is essential if their already inefficient processing of information, most of which is directed to reproduction, is not to get completely out of hand. It is, however, inherently inefficient, as it must systematically ignore whatever is peculiar or individual. Humans must be treated as things, things as computable numbers. Markets also preprocess: prices, decisions to buy or not to buy convert the many dimensions of want or need into single quantitative dimensions. Only slowly have the various sciences of market research come to augment the market's information with more subtle and multi-dimensional analyses of needs, lifestyles and identities.

As control techniques and technologies have evolved to manipulate preprocessed information some of the limits of control have made themselves manifest. Within the socialist countries the machinery of planning proved unable to generate accurate information about what was taking place in the economy; lack of information in turn undermined the value and credibility of the commands passed down.[6] A study in 1964 revealed that a typical machine-producing enterprise employing 6,000 people generated 275 million characters each year, equivalent to about 450 standard-length books: each year the equivalent of 73 were sent to higher echelons.[7] In practice the information was used more for control and accountability than for planning. In the economy as a whole the quantities of information become phenomenal: 120–170 billion piece of information circulated (for a planning system with the capacity to process 2.7–3.6 million), while the plan itself ran to 12,000 pages.[8]

For a time it was believed that information technology could solve these problems, providing on-line up to date information about enterprises and the processing capacity to deal with hundreds of millions of variables. Oskar Lange, the Polish economist, claimed that computers could solve the problems of socialist planning.[9] This view ignored two critical issues. One was the organization of information. The most successful enterprises cope with massive information production by controlling and limiting its flow: multi-divisional structures and conglomerate forms can both be understood in these terms. As we shall see the most advanced forms rationalize information further, with vertical surveillance (primarily through financial indicators) combined with an emphasis on horizontal flows.

The second problem was the structural context within which information was produced. This is less a problem of communcations flows than of the lack of incentives for middle and junior managers to report accurately up the line. Optimistic reports sent up the hierachy would come back in the form of burdensome quotas. Pessimistic reports might threaten career chances. In such a context any rational manager seeks to construct a viable and appropriate picture of reality, rather than a true one. Precisely the same structural disincentives to truth exist in all bureaucracies, structures once described by the economist Kenneth Boulding as ideally suited to inhibiting the flow of information from bottom to top. Each distortion of information is a negotiation about control; it is a means of keeping control at a lower level of decision making, even though the formal hierarchy demands that control be kept at the top.

Similar problems constrain initiative and creativity within bureaucracies and planned systems. Any creative act at a low level of the hierarchy implicitly undermines the authority of those higher up. Bureaucracies are always averse to risk. Whereas a failed initiative will permanently harm an individual's career, a successful one will be unlikely substantially to advance it. These problems have existed for as long as tight hierarchies. One early solution was that of the Empress Maria Theresa who introduced a medal for officers who successfully turned the tide in battle by ignoring orders. This recognized that local knowledge and understanding would often be superior to knowledge at the centre. Similar arguments have been made by neoclassical economics emphasizing the costs of centralized coordination.[10] No amount of technological capacity alters the fact that at some point judgement must be used based on information of prevailing conditions.

What communications networks can do is to shift the locus of decision making. Budgets, always used as a control tool, can be regularly reviewed and revised at the centre. In modern warfare, even tactical battle decisions can be made at the very summit of political power. The existence of private corporate networks offers senior executives the means to review the operations of remote plants and initiate new strategies. All such extensions of centralized control run the same risk: greater control is achieved at the price of ignoring local specificities and undermining the initiative, identity and sense of worth of those whose autonomy is breached. In the words of the cliché, if people are treated like machines, they will behave like machines. This is one reason why strong power systems have nearly always in practice depended on parallel weak power systems of trust, ethos, authority and respect.

Control, Speed and Time

The modern obsession with speed, and with control as a means to eliminate time, is relatively recent. As long as the processing of materials and energy was carried out at the pace of rivers, winds and animals, speed was not an important variable in economic life. Rothschild's famous use of carrier pigeons to enable him to deceive London's financial markets in the wake of the battle of Waterloo, and the military use of speed as theorized by Clausewitz and others are exceptions to a general rule.[11] Even Clausewitz was oblivious to the possible significance of technologies for speed, although the Stockton to Darlington railway was in operation seven years before *On War* was first published in 1832. Steam power was to act as an accelerator for the embryonic world economy: more goods could be produced, processed and distributed at higher speeds. Alongside it there evolved a set of tools for controlling speed. Regulators, valves, Watt's governor, Andrew Ure's thermostat, and De Forest's audion, were all crucial to the development of manufacturing, though it was not until the twentieth century that what today might be considered the most basic of control technologies, the vacuum tube permitting electrical, weak power control of strong power systems, came into use.

The evolution of social equivalents of the governor and the vacuum tube also took a long time. As Beniger points out, the Bank of the United States of the 1830s, America's most complex institution with twenty-two branch offices and profits fifty times those of the largest mercantile house, was managed by just three people.[12] The methods of the East India Company, which as early as 1708 transformed its accounting system with monthly cash inflow and outflow controls and proper capital and current accounts that enabled it to assess the profitability of each branch of trade, were not widely replicated. This underdevelopment of control limited the scope of economic life. Alfred Chandler, writing about the American economy of the 1840s, points out that the 'merchants who carried out the commercial transactions and made the arrangements to move the crops out and finished goods in did so in order to make a profit on each transaction or sale'.[13] Any more complex, lagged movement out of money and into commodities remained too risky, too uncontrollable. What turned into extensive systems for financing trade, managing retailing and wholesale systems, chambers of commerce, trade journals, jobbing, auctions, laws, and insurance, spread only fitfully, repeatedly retreating under the impact of recessions and wars before advancing again.

As steam power became ubiquitous in the second half of the nineteenth century, it brought greater predictability and dependability and an enormous increase in volume and speed of material circulation. James Beniger argues that the disjunction between capacities to process and distribute materials and energy, and the capacity to control and coordinate them, forced a profound crisis of control towards the end of the century. There was no guarantee that the control economy would grow in step with its material counterpart. The crisis first took a very visible shape in the form of crashes on single-line railway tracks in the 1840s. Later it manifested itself in the problems of controlling the large dispersed corporations which ran the railways. Both were partially mitigated by the use of the telegraph network as a control infrastructure overlying the railways, but both demanded changes in structure as well as technology.

The same was true of production innovations such as continuous processing which required means of coordinating the large volumes of goods being produced. Standardization of production, parts and measurements, which had already been developed earlier in the 'American System' in gun factories and textiles, became the norm. Processing of flows in manufacturing of steel, motors and firearms created particular problems of coordination arising from the energy-intensive nature of metalworking and making. In other sectors continuous process machinery could itself act as a control technology. Ultimately, machines could themselves become communications devices. By integrating mechanical, electric and later electronic control capacities, machine technologies could save capital as well as labour.[14]

Numerous control solutions were adopted so that the economies implicit in mass production could be exploited: specialization in management; cost control systems such as those developed and obsessively implemented by Carnegie in the steel industry; shop floor accounting and order controls; Sloan's linking of production to market feedback at General Motors, standardization and interchangeability of parts, the redesign of plants to facilitate throughputs, and statistical quality control to ensure that consistency of quality is appropriate to what consumers will pay were all brought into use to bring predictability and order. Similar crises and solutions arose in distribution. In wholesaling, hierarchies of salaried managers were developed to permit centralized monitoring of mass distribution. New concepts such as stock turn, gross margin by department, standardized packaging and sorting developed to cope with higher speeds of movement of goods, prefiguring their modern counterparts, such as the direct product-profitability programmes which allow a retailer precisely to monitor the profitability of each good through an analysis of self-space, turnover and margin. From distribution, the same essential problem appeared in consumption, which had to be controlled, ordered and regulated if producers and distributors were not to amass vast stocks of unwanted goods.

Full-page advertising began in 1878, trade journals for the advertising industry in 1888, mass-circulation newspapers under Northcliffe in Britain and Pulitzer in New York in the 1880s and 1890s. Taylorism spread into advertising. Herbert Casson wrote that 'what has worked so well in the acquisition of knowledge and in the production of commodities may work just as well in the distribution of those commodities'. A. C. Nielson cast his company 'in the role of the Frederick Winslow Taylor of retailing and communications. Time and motion study was applied to the movement of products across grocers' shelves, and to the movement of viewers across broadcast advertisers' programs.'[15] In Britain, Northcliffe introduced the concept of audited circulations to provide an objective calculus for advertisers and soon forced auditing onto his competitors. In television Nielson's Audimeters (directly attached to the radio and television set) and the various other 'Peoplemeter' and diary systems of AGB (Audits of Great Britain), Dentsu and others have gradually been advanced precisely to measure the extent to which people really watch individual programmes, which ones they videotape and whether they skip advertisements.

If the first wave of innovations in marketing were designed for the systematic control of mass markets, more recent generations have been orientated to ever more precise targeting of individual consumers and groups. Communications technologies have been essential to this process, as the emphasis on 'cost per thousand' and 'cost per prospect' have been displaced by an emphasis on 'cost per sale' that more precisely monitor effectiveness. As Kevin Wilson has argued, this depends on 'response mechanisms that quickly determine success or failure'.[16] Videotex networks in particular promise that every transaction leaves a record which can itself become a commodity: the network produces information about consumer behaviour that in turn aids producer control.

Taylorism and its Apotheoses

The application of the philosophy of control, abstraction, dissection and reconstruction, to the whole of economic life is part of a much broader adoption of scientific and bureaucratic methods. Taylorist notions of breaking problems down into their smallest constituent parts, of intensive monitoring and study, and of step-by-step reconstruction originate more in the military sphere than in the economy. Anthony Giddens, for example, refers to the work of Maurice of Orange at the end of the sixteenth century in breaking down the 'handling of the musket into a series of fortythree separate movements, that of the pike into twenty-three, coordinated within a formation of soldiers in a battle unit . . .

precise timing is essential ... since weaponry and machinery have increasingly become designed to operate in a sequential way, each step in its operation being a prerequisite to what is done next'.[17] Michel Foucault's account in *Discipline and Punish* of the Oberkampf manufactory at Jouay in the late eighteenth century is another vivid example of the antecedents of Taylorism.

For Taylor, control was to be removed from the individual to be dissected and reconstructed by the manager or commander according to scientific principles. 'Joint obedience to fact and laws' would come to replace 'obedience to personal authority'. In Taylor's words this involved 'the deliberate gathering in on the part of those on management's side of all the great mass of traditional knowledge, which in the past has been in the heads of the workers, and in the physical skill and knack of the workman which he has acquired through years of experience'.[18] All manual work was reduced to simple labour, with intelligence, judgement and creativity specialized as a function of management. The organization would be based on a vertical pyramid of command, written communication and standard procedures. The benefits would be reaped by both labour and capital; scientific management offered true democracy. This division of labour, justifiable in terms of efficiency, concentrated control and information processing.[19] At the time this was widely seen as an inevitable effect of machine production. Marx, for example, wrote of a trend towards machines that cause 'the separation of the intellectual faculties of the production process from manual labour, and the transformation of those faculties into powers exercised by capital over labour'.[20] Gastev, Taylor's leading Soviet follower, sought to implement his principles and the 'total mathematicisation of psychophysiology and economics' under socialism.[21]

Frederick Taylor's was just one response to a profound crisis of control in the rapidly industrializing countries of the Western world. As we have seen, James Beniger argues that it was the concurrence of rapid advances in processing of materials and energies that produced an intensive control crisis at the end of the nineteenth century, a crisis that subsequently elicited a new set of techniques and technologies.[22] The familiar technologies of control in the office and shop, the typewriters, cash registers, shorthand, telegraph-tickers, carbon paper, filing cabinets, dictating machines and punch card tabulators, were all developed between 1840 and 1890, in parallel to the transformation of the techniques of control, the organization of management, accounting, advertising and commercial information. Between 1880 and 1890 the number of female clerical workers in the USA grew nearly fourfold. The major corporations of the information economy also date from this period: AT&T was founded in 1876 and General Electric in 1892, while Hollerith's companies were beginning the evolution that would lead to the founding of IBM in 1911 (though it only took on the name in 1923). Marconi's various companies were formed at the very beginning of the twentieth century and ultimately spawned such offshoots as RCA and Thorn-EMI.

Despite the remarkably rapid growth of economic sectors based on communication and control during this period it is probably misleading to see the control crisis as peculiar to the end of the nineteenth century. A more plausible view would see it as endemic to all modern industrial societies: rather than simply being an effect of a disjunction between material processing powers and informational processing powers, control crises can result from almost any kind of crisis, whether a crisis of demand, of disaffected labour, of finance or of foreign competition. Growth in the scale and complexity of systems automatically causes crises of control. They can also arise out of control technologies themselves, as these spawn new orders of complexity and uncertainty. Control innovations have continued to offer competitive advantage throughout the twentieth century: more effective control of existing resources is an alternative to devising new products and production processes.

Control in the Flexible Workplace

Taylorism was always explicitly concerned not only with overt control but also with flows of information. Information and knowledge had to be concentrated in the hands of managers and designers, while manual tasks were broken down into their component parts. The subjects of scientific management received commands rather than engaging in communication. One implication of this approach was that Taylorism was never successfully extended from the shop floor to the boardroom. Where managerial tasks were subjected to the techniques of scientific management they ceased to be considered as managerial. When Chester Barnard wrote of the 'art' of management that 'transcends the capacity of merely intellectual methods' he was not simply mystifying the manager's tasks.[23] Like craft work, management work depends on communication and communality. All detailed studies of the practice of management have stressed the importance of weak power structures and techniques, of bodily presence and of the short cuts to communication achieved by trust and shared intuition.

Shoshanna Zuboff has analysed this phenomenon in terms of the distinction between acting on and acting with. Much of the work of a shop floor or office involves acting on a machine (a lathe, typewriter or Visual Display Unit), usually in isolation; other forms of work involve acting with other people. White-collar work could only be analysed and controlled when it involved acting on pre-given tasks: a social and communicative environment by contrast proved almost impossible to model and systematize. This has had perverse effects. The automation of offices and factories has often involved separating acting-on tasks from acting-with tasks; jobs are separated and physically isolated, rationalized, automatically paced and monitored. Rather than amplifying human intelligence and creativity the machine is used to stunt and constrain it. Communications technologies are used to shut off communication.

The key terrain for the struggle between Taylorist ideas of control and alternative weak power approaches has been automation. Automation can be understood as the latest in a line of solutions to the three aspects of machine activity: power, action and control. Mechanical devices replace human energy with power and action from other sources. Power is provided by steam, coal or electricity, action by gearing devices, jigs and lathes. Automation replaces human control with control embedded in systems (such as the production line), programmability (through the software defining how a machine tool operates) and feedback such that the tool can respond to the properties of the material being processed.[24] Although the word automation was first used by executives at Ford in the 1930s, fully fledged automation depended on the existence of programmable computers, systemic automation on the ability to network computers together. Like management itself automation is in large part about communication, the ability to command, to monitor and to share information.

Automation has its roots in the eighteenth-century use of water power, gradually evolving from the transformation and movement of things, to the control process itself.[25] The automated factories promised by companies like General Electric, Fanuc and Kawasaki appear to offer the elimination of problematic human labour and the complete predictability and controllability of production. Time and motion can be literally programmed into the system's software and automatically monitored as robots and programmable logic controllers spread from very simple operations like injection moulding, spot and arc welding to more complicated assembly tasks. As sensors and pattern-recognizing vision advanced, quality control could be automated: control could be passed up the hierarchy and formalized in sets of decision rules. Automation or computer integrated manufacturing offer quality, consistency and twenty-four hour days. Computer Aided Engineering, manufacturing and design can in principle be integrated with each other as stand-alone machines are linked into networks, just as electronic cash registers can be tied together to form EFTPOS (Electronic Funds Transfer at Point of Sale) networks. Control can be centralized.[26] In pursuing integration the aim is to integrate the software guiding complex processes to allow machines to communicate with each other, for example about changing speeds or qualities, with maximum transparency, and to diagnose and correct their own defects.

The machinery of automation is clearly different from its predecessors. The successors to the typewriters, tabulating machines, machine tools and cash registers of the late nineteenth century have become communications devices that both use information and programs and produce it. The machinery of automation, the flexible manufacturing systems and computer-aided design, manufacturing and engineering (CAD/CAM/CAE) systems are generally organized as networks. The word processor can produce information about the number of keystrokes or errors made by its operator, the modern cash register information about which goods are being sold. A deeper transparency and flexibility becomes possible with 'reflexive' machines of this kind. Once linked to retailer and distribution networks, they offer a comprehensive solution to the control problems that have been faced since the last century: the whole chain from production to consumption can be knowable, transparent, predictable and controllable in real time. Production can be to order. A customer's demand in the shop can be instantaneously transmitted to the automated factory and subcontracting networks. In the case of a car, for example, the customer can specify colour, modifications, a choice of interior materials and accessories (as in General Motors' famous Saturn Project). These are in turn communicated via a VANS network to suppliers which produce the relevant parts with numerically controlled, flexible machinery and deliver it almost immediately. The manufacturer assembles the car which is then delivered to the retailer. For other kinds of goods sophisticated EFTPOS systems continually monitor sales and order replacements, simultaneously eliminating the problem of inventories in both finance and retailing.

The programmability and reflexivity of automated machinery also makes it suitable for producing diverse products, emphasizing economies of scope rather than scale. Within the production process itself cybernetic feedback means that unpredictable changes in the environment or in the quality of inputs can be immediately adjusted for. Numerically controlled machines can move from batch to batch of different products in response to changes in demand fed back from distribution and retailer networks. Systems can be designed to program themselves, to learn by their experience in diagnosis or pattern recognition functions. In general, the emphasis on communication becomes pervasive. The emergent 'best practice forms of industrial organization . . . [involve] a transition to close proximity, and the development of closer design and planning links. The important resource in these relationships is the ability to process and communicate information.'[27]

In reality automation has not been an easy concept to put into practice.

Incompatible communications standards (see chapters 9 and 11), and technical problems of integration, have meant that the great majority of automation at the end of the 1980s was 'no more than a few machine tools linked together by automated loading to form a production cell'.[28] But there are also deeper reasons why automation has failed to live up to its promise, for the appearance of total control is deceptive. Machines, like humans, require negotiation. According to Larry Hirschhorn, 'the cybernetic image of the perfect machine is utopian'.[29] The more complex a machine is, the more it is likely to break down. This is notoriously true of computer software when there are simply too many interacting variables to be preplanned. Autodiagnostic systems can work up to a point, but ultimately someone must control the controls. To do so, in the words of Hirschhorn, 'they cannot merely become competent at a fixed and predictable set of tasks'. Instead, post-industrial work requires that it is developmental, interacting and skill-building; in other words that people interact with machines to guide them, overcome faults and reshape them for new tasks. Such a perspective recognizes that machines are never perfect entities which can be set into perpetual motion.

Hirschhorn writes that 'in a polypropylene chemical plant, the computer was not designed to control all the feedback loops of the production system. Chemical engineers could not fully represent the dynamics of the chemical process in mathematical terms, and previous attempts at computer control in other plants had resulted in significant underproduction.' Instead, the computer system was designed to facilitate worker learning, continually interacting with operating staff who are responsible for decisions. Job classification is organized on the principle of pay-for-learning. In post-industrial settings, Hirschhorn argues, failures must be seen as a valuable part of the process of learning and creatively solving problems. The attempts to eliminate failure (bolstered in part by highly sensitive financial control through equity markets) can constrict growth and change. As in the over-rigid bureaucracy, excessive control, and its concomitant of excessive risk aversion, can by dysfunctional.

The limits of software are repeatedly found in the practice of automation: appropriate systems design requires a mix of skills from software, through engineering, to practical experience with machines. Much if not most of the software produced for numerically controlled machines is literally unworkable without adaptation by those involved in working with the machines. In Germany shopfloor programming has become widespread, and is especially suitable for rapidly changing batch production of specialized products.

Many of these communicational challenges of automation, were predicted. In *The Advent of the Automatic Factory* (published in 1952), John Diebold pointed to the need to link automation to new organizational forms, stressing the importance of 'multi-skilling, of the devolution of responsibility, and of integration of product and process development and design with production engineering and marketing'.[30] The greatest successes with automation have come where innovations with organizational form have matched innovations with machinery. The Japanese success with just-in-time (JIT) techniques is a classic example, dependent as much on social as technological innovation. JIT depends on retraining workforces and giving greater responsibility to shopfloor workers, reducing the numbers of middle managers and encouraging horizontal flows of information. These methods emerged as the successful alternative to material requirements planning, the attempt to computerize the systematic backscheduling of all components needs. Another Japanese technique is the horizontal integration of production engineering, design and research, in which the factory is treated almost as a laboratory. Rather than being concentrated and rationalized, the tasks of management and decision making are spread among the workforce. The ability of intelligent machines to produce information about themselves is exploited most fully by dispersing access and control.

Similar experiences have occurred in the service sector, particularly in financial companies which were among the first users of computers and complex networks. During the 1950s insurance companies used them for payrolls, accounting, actuarial and statistical jobs. More recently banks and financial institutions have retained their lead, applying sophisticated communications technologies to cheque-handling, bookkeeping, electronic funds transfer, the operation of automatic teller machines and credit analysis. In the automated office pace and sequencing could be controlled by computer. Training times could be cut when computers monitored workers; different tasks could be integrated into a single job, so that deskilling and reskilling evolved in parallel. More work could become temporary or part-time, shifting health and pension costs onto the public sector. But despite these apparent benefits for profitability, according to one commentator, 'the adoption of computer technologies initially led to decreased capital productivity and profitability' in the banks.[31] The remarkable failure of technology to enhance productivity can be accounted for in many ways: as a problem of learning times,[32] as a general problem of industrial revolutions (during the first it took decades for the productivity benefits of mechanization to show through) or as a problem of incompatible equipment. But the most convincing explanations are those that emphasize organization: the failure to adapt, a consequence of the attempt to use technologies to overcentralize and overcontrol processes.

Some of the more successful uses of technology have involved a range and subtlety of uses not present before: in some cases the need to be close to the market has favoured the use of distributed systems for which companies have had to retrain their largely female clerical staff. In other cases communications technologies are used to enforce standardization and conformity. According to a study in the US, 'the first stage of automation in the insurance industry tended to increase job fragmentation, centralize production by narrow function, heighten occupational sex segregation and make many routine keyboarding functions spatially "footloose". More recently, however, the greater sophistication of the technologies and transformed market conditions are dictating a new organizational logic which promises to reverse many of these trends.'[33]

This new logic, which has been described as replacing a functional with a systems approach, brings changes in the very nature of labour. The distinctions between professional and clerical work easily blur, and roles which previously enjoyed discretion and status, such as those of buyers or stock controllers in retailing, are swept away by automation, EFTPOS and other systems which automatically perform tasks according to set algorithms in place of the judgement of a person. The junior manager or overseer, if he or she survives, becomes a supervisor of machines rather than people. At the same time other tasks gain in breadth and depth. The great advantage of computer-based technologies is their adaptability and flexibility, which means that they are often best used in a spirit of experiment and reappraisal of old ways of doing things. Such a spirit is usually at odds with the structure of the workplace, and with its traditions of disciplinary power, of surveillance and control over the body and its labour. One report argued that 'the control oriented planning procedures typical of the early 1970s . . . and the strategic focus of later years [were] too detailed, bureaucratic and traditional for the exploitation of IT for competitive advantage'.[34] A typical view was expressed by Juan Rado, who wrote that 'there is a growing consensus that, for enterprises, the real benefit of office automation lies in the optimisation of the general control and managerial system rather than in specific increases in productivity at the work station or computer terminal level . . . it is the communication dimension or the interaction of equipment that makes the real difference in the rationalisation of office work'.[35]

As a result the focus is again put on 'soft systems', motivations and responsibility, the scope for creativity and problem solving, rather than on hard quantities. The same considerations apply in analysing many of the economic structures which are forming around communications networks: federations, cooperatives of small firms, long-term joint ventures, collaborative research and development. In each case trust and reciprocity turn out to be major factors explaining economic behaviour and the ways in which resources are allocated, functioning in a space between cooperation and competition. Softening structures reflect an economy in which material quantities are diminishing in significance. Effective control in human organizations depends on being able to combine the 'hard' analysis of quantities with the softer analysis of systems, motivations and meanings. No real institution can be 'run by numbers'.

All systems of control are bounded by their ability to gather and process information, in economic life to know about what is happening in the production or distribution process, about prices and demands. Within organizations the creation of hierarchies, of formal rules and procedures is one way of coping with increased complexity. But with complexity comes uncertainty, and classic Weberian bureaucracies are not well designed for unforeseen challenges, tending to force ever more information upwards where it overloads the decision makers. To solve this problem the structures of information and control have to change.[36] One option is to reduce the need for information processing: for example, by devolving authority to more autonomous units, by reducing the uncertainty present in the working environment (perhaps through a reduction in the numbers of parts involved in a production process), or by creating more areas of slackness. The second set of solutions improve the organization's ability to process information, by increasing vertical or horizontal communication and increasing processing capacities either with computers or with better qualified staff.

Within industries and bureaucracies both types of solution are being experimented with in a myriad of forms. The lack of obvious, mechanistic answers has brought a new order of fluidity and change in the forms of economic life. Moreover both sets of solution reflect an understanding of organizations as informational institutions, strongly shaped by the soft variables of knowledge, responsibility and interaction. The new emphasis reflects a concern with innovation and creativity as sources of value, and a recognition that they require a loosening of discipline and order. The changing structure of control at the micro level has effects at the macro level. Because a control innovation designed to perform an existing task more efficiently usually has the side-effect of making it possible to do a new task, there is no obvious limit to investment in control. This is the heart of the revolution in control, and why it has largely escaped economic study. For as control becomes more important to economic life, an object of bigger investments and more systematic analyses, it too becomes subject to a potentially permanent revolution, a permanent redrawing of boundaries.

5

Network Technologies

Technological change always takes place under the dead weight of habits and traditions, prevailing cultures and prevailing powers. But technologies are never simply moulded to given ends. They also bring their own generic properties, their own lines of least resistance and potential unforeseen by their promoters and inventors. This is particularly true of the intelligent and reflexive technologies used in advanced communications networks, technologies that are programmable, adaptable and open in nature. As networks have evolved into extensive computers, their flows of signals controlled by sophisticated electronic switches, their terminals either computers or telephones and televisions that have acquired some of the properties of computers, they too have taken on something of the character of the universal machine. Where the constrained and dedicated networks of telegraphy, voice telephony and broadcasting were relatively stable and predictable, more recent technologies have brought a new order of fluidity to technological change. The means now often precede the ends, and technologies emerge as solutions in search of problems.

The evolution of communications technologies is a remarkable story of massive misjudgements and surprising foresight. The recent past is littered with failed communications technologies such as the eight-track tape, the videophone or the waveguide and with technologies whose actual uses proved opposite to those initially intended. The telephone was initially conceived as a one-way communications system, an aid for the deaf or a means for multiplexing telegraphy. The radio was conceived as a medium for point-to-point communication. The gramophone was designed as a tool for storing telephone conversations. Radio was widely expected to render cables redundant. In the words of one reporter in 1902, 'Cables might now be coiled up and sold for junk.'[1] Until the invention of the Pupin coil, the huge costs of thick cables gave a particular urgency to experiments with radio. Similar comments are made today about satellites and coaxial cables. In the early 1970s a global copper shortage was predicted as the result of the growing use of electronics. In the event there was a glut. The misreadings of the future have been on a grand scale. Most strikingly perhaps, the computer was at first expected to fill a very narrow role, solving esoteric problems in physics. Howard Aiken, builder of the Mark I, one of the first computers, reflected the conventional wisdom when he forecast that four or five would meet all the United States' computing needs.

Technological change rarely follows a straight path. As in such fields as mathematics, old ideas are often more useful than those of the recent past: the optical fibre was first conceived in the 1870s but only became viable once glass of sufficient purity was developed in the 1960s and 1970s. The first fax networks were built in France in the 1860s but soon discarded.[2] Computers and digital communications systems use principles that owe their origins to Boole's binary mathematics, a set of ideas that were strictly speaking useless when first developed in the nineteenth century. Many 'mature' or discarded technologies have been given a new lease of life: superconducting switches using Josephson junctions, for example, were widely seen as failures in the early 1980s, yet suddenly took on a new significance when materials which could superconduct at higher temperatures were discovered.

Despite this chequered history, there are some consistent themes in the history of communications technology. There is a strong sense in which, in Raymond Williams's words, most of the key technologies 'were foreseen – not in utopian but in technical ways – before the crucial components of the developed systems had been discovered and refined'.[3] Alexander Graham Bell accurately described the future of the telephone in a well-known letter to a group of British engineers in 1877. Baird patented not only the television but the colour television and the three-dimensional television. Each inventor soon came to see the range of possible applications of his invention across several media. A famous 1879 *Punch* cartoon portayed a televised tennis match in which the viewers could talk to the players. In the early 1880s Albert Robida, a French artist, showed families watching distant wars, being taught by a distant teacher or examining goods for sale on a screen in the living-room. The impact of fiction on the development of communications technologies has been well documented, offering inspiration to the inventor of the robot, the television and the computer. As Williams points out, inventions such as the television depended on a complex cluster of technical and social innovations before they could become a reality and find a viable purpose. They were born neither of a purely technological logic nor of purely social function: rather the same transformations had created both the new needs and the new possibilities. Out of a range of possibilities economic realities and strategic perceptions determined outcomes. Television evolved as a domestic medium, rather than the communal one conceived in Germany and the Soviet Union, and planned for rural France after

World War II. Telephone networks were built without the bandwidth to carry moving pictures, and with a central organization of signalling which made it impossible for the receiver to screen calls, although very different choices were technically feasible.

Although the work of prediction and imagination has been remarkable, a whole raft of technologies have emerged without any clear understanding of where their practical, and economically viable, uses would be. Recent technologies have emerged not as pre-given wholes but rather as sites of contest for different uses, interests and visions. The personal computer has been torn between quite contradictory ideas, that of the game machine, the educational machine and the machine for home control or for ordered work in the office. Videotex has been caught between its conception as a vehicle for public information, its role as a medium for commercial transaction and its adoption as a public message board. Technologies have rarely rained down on passive user populations. Their history is better understood as one of absorption and redefinition by their users, whether they be armies, large corporations or households. David Noble has written that 'close inspection of technological development reveals that technology leads a double life, one which conforms to the intentions of designers and interests of power and another which contradicts them – proceeding behind the backs of architects to yield unintended consequences and unanticipated possibilities'.[4] This relatively open character is particularly apparent in the case of the basic communications technologies, the telephone (whose designers were initially resistant to the idea that it could be a tool of sociability),[5] the computer and the electronic messaging network, which offer a means of control or communication, while leaving the end for the user to define.

Digital Languages

Beneath the fluidity of technological change, and the broad scope for political and strategic choice, a number of generic trends are reshaping the nature of all communications technologies. However strong the social and economic forces shaping technologies it is not possible to understand the grain of change in the communications economies without a grasp of these trends. Four stand out: the move from analogue to digital forms of transmission and storage; the convergence of different forms of communication around the same processing and transmission technologies; the shift from electronic to optical systems; and the long-term increase in flexibility, programmability and adaptability. None is irreversible, and telecommunications engineers are experimenting with new forms of analogue transmission which could ultimately replace digital systems, just as ultra-fast valves are beginning to threaten the dominance of semiconductors. But all are having an impact on the whole range of communications technologies.

Before the invention of the computer, most communications technologies were analogue, that is recordings stored the sound waves of speech, film the colours and shades passed through a lens. In both cases, commodities were distributed physically rather than along a network. In radio and television, carrier frequencies are overlaid with the actual wave patterns of speech and image. Telephone cables carried electric analogues of speech. Morse code telegraphy was a rare exception. The digital technologies which are now becoming dominant in communications networks are best conceived not as a progression of machines but as variations on a single principle. Amidst the alphabet soup of new machines and applications digitization is the core innovation which allows networks to be extended and integrated. The basic principle of all digital systems is the use of the on–off binary language of zeros and ones used by computers, and pioneered by Claud Shannon's work linking binary Boolean algebra to on and off switches in electric circuits. Digitization provides a common language, a common code of immense simplicity and flexibility for all forms of communication, sounds, images and data. In principle any message or signal, even a taste or smell, can be captured and then replicated through a digital medium.

Originated in computing, the universal machine's universal language was soon seen to have much wider applications. By the late 1950s it was widely recognized that in the long term computing and voice telephony would become integrated. By the 1960s telephone networks were beginning to resemble distributed computers, using stored program controls. Pulse Code Modulation (PCM), the technique for translating analogue voice signals into digital signals in a 64 kbs channel which was first patented in 1938 and later developed by Alan Turing, the inventor of the computer, emerged as the building block for integrated networks capable of carrying any form of electronic information. Using somewhat different principles, and much greater channel capacity, video signals can also be turned into digital form, transmitted along the same networks and, in principle, through the same switches. To translate sounds or images into digital form the computer records samples thousands of times each second which are transmitted and reconstructed for the loudspeaker or TV screen. In the case of music stored on a compact disc, for example, sounds are sampled 44,000 times each second, stored in digital form in the 'pits' of the disc and then reproduced into sound waves. Most of the new generations of cultural technologies are based on digital principles: the compact disc and the digital audio tape, the CCD camera and digital radio. Though television signals are broadcast in analogue form new television sets include digital techniques to freeze frames, divide screens or replay sequences. This active engagement in scanning, sampling and reconstructing is distinctive to digital technologies. As I shall explain in chapter 9, although digital signals appear to share a common language this is only half true. It is as if they used the same letters but different words and grammars. Different combinations of ones and zeros are used to give instructions, to correct errors or to check access rights. As a result most computers and machines cannot communicate with each other without costly conversion of protocols.

Digital technologies are both cheap and expensive. Digital switches are enormously expensive, costing as much as $2 bn to develop. By far the largest cost is software, often involving over a million lines of code. Replication costs are less than one-sixth of the total, suggesting that switches are quintessential products of the modern communications industry, very expensive to produce and relatively cheap to reproduce. More mundane digital technologies are also cheap, once sufficient economies of scale have been achieved. The raw material of chips and optical fibres is abundant silicon; miniaturization means that less is needed of it and that it uses less energy; integration means that many different services can use the same elements. Once a part is designed, the basic manufacturing process is a form of printing. Photolithography, the basic technique for making chips offers enormous returns to scale. Design engineers now treat computation as free. This leads to the familiar throwaway presence of digital technologies in daily life: calculators and watches given away with petrol, machines which are cheaper to replace than to repair.

Digitization makes it possible to exercise an unprecedented degree of control over communication. There is an important sense in which the digital medium, unlike an analogue one, knows what information it is transmitting. The message itself can be controlled through error correction techniques, which ensure that the original message is precisely reproduced at each node without noise and interference. Errors can be checked, and addressing and packaging material can be transmitted alongside the main message. Messages can be screened, stored or re-routed. The fidelity of digital communication has proved vital in extending communications media into financial transactions where errors can be enormously costly. The transmission medium need no longer be a simple pipeline shunting messages from one point to another, and reproducing the message only as received. Given the application of some processing intelligence, messages can be manipulated, stored, re-routed, monitored and re-formatted.

One of the effects of the move from various analogue techniques towards digital technologies is the promotion of a convergence of previously separate media, cultural forms and industries. Digital distribution media can carry any form of message, whether voices, data or images. Storage technologies like the CD can be used to store music, text as with the CD-ROM) or video (the CD-Video or Laservision). A similar convergence is apparent in production technologies. Where early generations of technology for publishing, music recording or video editing used customized machinery, more recent generations use generic technologies with specialized software. Advanced personal computers can be used to produce newspapers or to edit, synthesize and sample music or images. In each case an open technology is replacing a dedicated one.

Parallel to the trend from analogue to digital forms is a shift from electronic to optical forms of storage and transmission. The basic advantage of light is its very large bandwidth, that is to say its capacity to hold information. Optical technologies first came into widespread use with the replacement of coaxial copper cables by fibre-optic cables in trunk and some local telephone networks. In the home they are most familiar in the form of the compact disc technologies. Holography and laser printing are also becoming widespread. In the longer run optical computers and microprocessors have the potential to replace electronic counterparts.

Another general trend is towards greater flexibility and control. The trend to greater flexibility can also be read as part of a much longer-term evolution of control technologies such as the amplifier. It was this ability to control the microscopic behaviour of electrons which made possible the construction of truly global networks.[6] More recently, with the use of digital technologies, sophisticated control has been made available to the user, the producer, the editor and the network manager. Programmability means that computer-based machines, descendants of the idea of the universal machine, can be adapted to very different uses. The main barrier to realizing flexibility is the existence of incompatible standards: the various operating systems (such as Unix or OS/2), television standards (PAL, SECAM, NTSC and the various HDTV standards), interpretations of OSI, and the differing dialects of more specialized digital languages such as the MIDI music programming standard all impede flexibility of use and interconnection. The underlying trend towards more open technologies, which remove flexibility and control from the designer to the user, is unmistakable.

Technologies of the Network: Switching

Each of these trends is reflected in the changing nature of telecommunications networks. Like all networks electronic communications networks consist of two main elements: on the one hand nodes, the switches, terminals, telephone sets and TVs, and on the other links of cable and radio. Their two primary functions are the transmission of information and its manipulation, which may involve switching it between different paths or turning it into a more usable form. In the modern network, where switches resemble computers, the task of switching bits of information from one place to another is simply one of the more mundane functions that a computer can perform. As well as routeing information, nodes also contain secondary functions, such as the means of input and output (keyboards, telephones, printers, voice recognition devices) and memory (in discs, tape or chips), while the network as a whole has its own, systemic properties, increasingly contained in software.

Communications networks depend on switching mechanisms because not everyone wants to receive the same signals at the same time. In the earliest networks, using fires and smoke, semaphore and flags, transmission was simply an effect of switching. In the case of the telephone, switching is carried out in local and central switching centres, physically and logically distinct from transmission. In broadcasting, switching is a function of the receiver, who can choose between a fixed number of channels, while in postal services 'switching' is carried out in mail-sorting offices. In the first generations of communications networks processing and switching were much more laborious and expensive than the transmission of items of information over copper wire. This was particularly true when switching was organized manually by armies of female telephone operators, precisely drilled and trained as to the appropriate words to be used in any situation. In early telephone systems the costliness of switching was reflected in the characteristic topography of the telephone network: at the bottom millions of telephones were linked through a pyramid of increasingly complex switches to a handful of central controlling switches at the apex. Nearly all links were vertical rather than horizontal. This technical structure had a number of implications: the terminal or telephone used by the user was a dumb slave of higher-level switches. Both the service and the equipment used was highly standardized: any deviation from the standard or tampering with end equipment was strenuously opposed on the grounds that it involved a threat to the integrity of the network. The pyramid logic also favoured monopoly provision by an entity able to benefit from potential economies of scale and, by the same token, a regulatory regime to prevent abuse of the monopoly position.

Within any communications network there is a trade-off between processing and transmission. By manipulating information, particularly with digital techniques, less need be transmitted: redundant information such as silences, or images that do not move, can be discarded, errors can be controlled for, sampling can replace real-time analogue transmission, and transmission paths can be divided and re-divided using time or frequency multiplexing. Even voice and video, which appear to be continuous forms of communication are, in fact, 'bursty'. Capacity is only used 40 per cent of the time in most telephone conversations, while television programmes are broadcast in the form of fifty or sixty discrete frames each second. In telegraphy, Samuel Morse's achievement was to provide a viable solution to the problem of compressing information so as to reduce the use of bandwidth: cheap skilled labour at the switches minimized the amount of information that had to be transmitted by converting words into dots and dashes and paring language down to its barest essentials.

The trade-offs between processing and transmission depend on patterns of relative cost. Between the late 1950s and the mid-1980s the relative costs of copper wires and transistors or semiconductors have shifted dramatically. While the techniques available for manipulating information multiplied, their unit cost halved every one or two years. The family of technologies which emerged from the invention of the transistor in Bell Labs in 1947 and evolved into semiconductors and microprocessors, LSI and VLSI circuits, brought the economies of scale inherent in printing to the very heart of communications. The impact of these, the 'heartland technologies' of the information economy, has been a revolution in the design of networks. The transition from human switching (including the skills of the morse operator), through Strowger's electromechanical switches to cross bar and now stored program digital electronic systems, capable of handling as many as 50,000 simultaneous conversations, has involved a change in the basic resource used to switch signals. Early switches used space, inserting plugs and crossing wires to make connections. Modern electronic switches use time, divided into tightly controlled micro-, nano- and pecoseconds, as the main resource for switching and use no moving parts. Logical connections and channels replace physical ones. The first switch mixing electromechanical and electronic tehniques, the ECASS (Electronically Controlled Automatic Switching System) was built by Bell Labs in 1947, the first fully electronic switch, the ESSEX, at the end of the 1950s. These failed to displace electromechanical switches until integrated circuit technology had advanced sufficiently and declined in cost. The first industrially produced digital switch, in effect a sophisticated computer, was built in 1969 under the name ESS-1 (Electronic Switching System 1). It too was a product of Bell Labs, and the first in a series of switches, the most recent of which is the ESS-5, now adapted for ISDN. During the next decades many of these advanced electronic switches look set to be replaced by optical switches, able to connect with fibre-optic cables without having to convert from optical to electronic signals and back again. The first optical switches, used in the transatlantic fibre cable TAT-8, were optical–mechanical, moving fibres in and out of alignment very rapidly. More advanced techniques are solid-state, using electric currents or other light beams to switch photons.[7]

Within any network traffic is both random and statistically predictable as to its patterns over the course of a day or between different routes. Probability dictates that a switch serving twice as many people does not require twice as many connections. With new generations of digital switches these economies are gaining in significance: with each upgrading of the network fewer and larger switches are needed. These switches can carry out a much wider range of functions than their predecessors, multiplexing signals, storing messages, translating protocols, switching data and images as well as voices and performing more complex routeing procedures. As switches are controlled by software, the actual funcion of switching can be removed from the control functions which determine where messages are routed or what processes are applied to them. Each of these trends helps to foster economies of scale, to reward the operation of a smaller number of multi-function switches and to foster concentrated control over networks.

Miniaturization, PBXs, LANs and the Dispersal of Intelligence

Tendencies towards greater scale have been balanced by other trends which point to a decentralization of control. The rapid cheapening of switching and processing relative to transmission had a profound effect on the actual and potential structure of networks. Intelligent machines have become widely available, dispersed in homes, offices and factories. Often these are linked in private networks run by corporations or governments. In principle a network linking one million people can consist either of one wire with a million switches, or one switch with a million wires. If transmission costs are much higher than switching costs, the first model is logical. If the reverse is true, the second model makes more sense. According to some observers a move from the first to the second is under way in many networks: switches and terminals with some switching capability are proliferating and becoming more intelligent. In large part this is a reflection of the ability of the computer industry to drive the direction of technological change. Responding to the data-processing needs of government and private companies they partially wrested control of the technology away from telephone companies. As switching and processing became cheaper new topologies emerged, closer to the model of a single wire and a million switches. IBM's Local Area

Networks, for example, use token ring systems in which different terminals are linked on a single, ring-like link with high bandwidth: messages stop only at the terminals for which they were intended.

As switches proliferated, the logic which sustained the pyramid structure of the telephone network began to dissolve. In its place a much more complex picture emerged in which intelligence exists both inside and outside the network, where smaller networks link to larger ones, private ones to public ones. As large organizations mimic the workings of the network within themselves, with private networks and private switches, the lines separating the service provider and the user blur. An American communications theorist, Peter Huber, has described the emerging topology as that of Benoit Mandelbrot's fractal, where, like a tree or a snowflake, the whole consists of a multitude of parts based on similar topologies. Each has its own intelligence and network capabilities.[8] Huber described this network as geodesic, a reference to Buckminster Fuller's geodesic domes. The geodesic image suggests the possibility of a proliferation of small pyramids around a larger ring or, conversely, a proliferation of rings within the basic pyramid. It is a vision which is explicitly directed against the traditional centralized and regulated pyramid network.

Central to this process has been the advance of the terminal: from being the 'dumb' attachment to centralized mainframes, the computer has become an intelligent, controlling element in networks. The PCs, Apples and IBMs, with their user-friendly 'mouse', GEM and WINDOWs, and more recent generations like the Sun Microsystems Workstation and the Apple MacII, suggest that the terminal can become extremely powerful. By the end of the 1990s it is predicted that there will be desktop workstations with a computing power as high as fifty to one hundred megaflops, roughly that of the 1980s' supercomputers.

Other technologies also play key roles in the decentring of the network. One set are the local networks, the Local Area Network or LAN (such as Xerox's Ethernet or Wang's Wangnet) and the PBX, the private branch exchange or switchboard used to connect telephones in a building or site. Both are themselves mini-networks, which can operate within an office or factory; alternatively, they can be used to link a company's operations dispersed across a whole country. Both can be used to switch and transmit data, voice and images within the private network. PBXs, for example, routinely offer features such as store-and-forward or least-cost routeing. LANs reflect the evolution of computer networks, originally used for batch processing and later time-sharing, into vastly more complex mixes of mainframes and VDUs, front-end processors ·dealing with routeing and protocols, and cluster controllers joining groups of terminals. Both sets of technologies, the one originating in the circuit-switching of telephony, the other in the bursty flows of computing, offer control to the end user, and challenge the control of the network operator over flows of signals and over tariffs. The challenge is similar to that posed by the various bypass technologies that have evolved around satellite communications. Of particular interest now is the emergence of Very Small Aperture Terminals (VSATs) for one- or two-way communication, which replace the large receiver dishes owned by the PTTs with much smaller ones under the ownership and control of the user.

The dispersal of intelligence away from central switches owes much to the speed with which the raw materials of communications have become smaller. Like the advance of digitization and semiconductors, miniaturization reflects the peculiar demands of the US military and space programs for very lightweight and compact control devices in rockets, spacecraft and missiles. Between 1958 and 1974 the US military bought between 35 and 50 per cent of all integrated circuits made in the US. More recently the Pentagon has been at the forefront of moves towards the use of gallium arsenide in place of silicon. As costs fell by 28 per cent each time output doubled in microchips, a feat achieved almost every year during 1970s, the effect of miniaturization was to make processing capacity economically and physically viable in a bewildering variety of different contexts. The array of machines which can be linked by communications networks now stretches far beyond overt communications devices such as the telephone, radio, television set or computer to include central heating systems, washing machines, missiles, mobile devices, cars, pagers, alarms, sensors, meters, production and distribution systems. The apparently contradictory tendencies towards greater centralization and greater decentralization share the same origins: the rapid cheapening of control made possible by semiconductor and integrated circuit technologies and by the underlying logic of digitization.

The ISDN

The emergence of digital signals as a universal code for all communications brought with it an apparently inevitable technological logic that all communications would be integrated on the same networks. The first real integrated digital network was built by the US Department of Defense in 1956. Initially digitization could be justified solely in terms of cost savings for voice telephony. Smaller solid-state switches would make fewer errors, would minimize noise and reproduce signals more exactly than their analogue, electromechanical predecessors. But it was immediately clear that digital networks would have wider application. Although voice continues to account for over 90 per cent of traffic on telecommunications networks, the demand for data communications has been growing by over 30 per cent each year in many countries.

The ISDN first crystallized around a set of institutions and concepts in the late 1960s and was systematically defined by the CCITT (the Consultative Committee of the ITU) in 1972: it was a vision of a wholly standardized system, the world's largest and most complex machine.[9] To realize it the CCITT defined a set of standards which would provide a framework for PTTs to upgrade their networks. The name implied not only that networks would be integrated but also that intelligence and functionality would be largely located within the network rather than in terminals attached to it. The same switches that routed telephone conversations would also be able to transform digital signals, to store and forward messages or check rights of access. These functions could then be aggregated across the whole system, allowing the network to substitute resources and maximize efficiency. The ideal was described by AT&T's public relations department as 'the graceful evolution of today's telecommunications network towards a powerful, unified network fabric featuring universal ports, dynamic allocation of bandwidth and other resources and adaptive, logically provided services'.[10] Although often presented as a radical break, the ISDN is essentially an evolutionary model for reorganizing the logical structure of the network. Much of its physical form can remain unchanged. Existing electronic switches can be adjusted through their software. Existing twisted wires into the home can be left in place so long as ISDN equipment is placed at each end.

The scope for evolution appealed to many of the interests controlling telecommunications. The public service coalition of PTTs, their unions, consumer groups, regional and national governments was reflected in the early rhetoric of the ISDN as a universal service providing access to the information society for every home and office.[11] Technical work built on the traditionally close links between the major laboratories, equipment manufacturers and operators: Bell, Western Electric and AT&T in the US; Martlesham, GEC and Plessey in the UK; the DBP, Siemens and HHI in West Germany; CNET, CGE (now Alcatel) in France; NTT, ECL and the DenDen family in Japan. As telephone penetration neared saturation point, the ISDN offered a continuous path of new products and services and a means of defining the convergence of telecommunications and computing in ways that would benefit the equipment industry. As the vehicle for all forms of communications, the standards setting process sought to encompass and define the whole range of telecommunications: architectural models defining network structures, interface standards for linking networks and terminals, and standards for such services as electronic mail (×.400), and packet-switching (×.25).

The ISDN has often been criticized as a classic case of technology push, a neat technological solution that meets no apparent needs. More fundamentally its vision of development as a set of planned rational solutions implemented by engineers came up against a reality of spreading deregulation and liberalization and a very different vision of private ISDNs being built by the major multi-nationals, GM and IBM, EDS and Boeing. By the end of the 1980s the ISDN was a fractured concept. Competing networks have come into existence: cable television and satellite networks, dedicated LANs, competitive microwave and fibre-optic networks all undermine the scope for an integrated network. Far from becoming more integrated, networks have become differentiated: packet networks, directory enquiry networks, mobile networks and switched circuit networks have evolved separately. The reality of sunk investment in separate networks has eroded confidence in the idea of the ISDN as a universal, public service network. In response, some PTTs have redefined the ISDN as a specialized business service, while others have experimented with home and small business uses, notably in Western France, in Bell South and around Mannheim in West Germany. Numerous quasi-ISDN services have come into being, only partially compatible with the CCITT standards. There has also been criticism of the core ISDN standards. The standard adopted for home use, the 2B + D (two 'B' communications channels of 64 kbs and a 16 kbs, 'D', signalling or control channel) seemed to offer more bandwidth than most homes would use, yet not enough for carrying broadcasting signals, by far the most significant home demand for flows of information. The 64 kbs standard was originally chosen as the speed needed for voice telephony, yet the advance of compression techniques means that voice can be carried at 16 kbs or less. For businesses too the 'granularity' of ISDN standards, offering fixed packages of 64 and 16 kbs channels, seemed inappropriate. As LANs have developed there is an interest in very high bandwidth D-type channels, run on packet-switched principles.

Technically, too, the ISDN standards have come to seem obsolete even before they are put into practice. The advance of fibre-optic technologies has made feasible broadband networks based on much larger bandwidths than the ISDN. Integrated broadband networks (IBNs) able to carry high-definition television signals or complex images for computer-aided design have become feasible. The IBN would have a capacity an order of magnitude greater than the ISDN: 140 mbs compared to 64 kbs. In theory, a fibre-optic cable could carry a quadrillion bits, or 100,000,000,000,000 compared to the 144,000 bits carried by an ISDN on copper wire.[12] An IBN would have a very different logical structure to the ISDN, probably based on packet techniques. The drive beyond ISDN is being pushed by the emergence of new switching technologies, assisted in part by large funding from the Pentagon's DARPA (Defense Advanced

Research Projects Agency) for the SDI program. Anthony Rutkowski writes of an 'unbounded grid of transmission systems and nodes' emerging from these technologies in which each network node is a switching system under human or machine intelligence: 'Gallium Arsenide for electronic switching and lithium niobate, indium antinony and zinc selenium crystals for photonic switches could provide a substantial leap in switching capacities creating new possibilities for parallel processing, AI applications with their requirement for enormous bandwidth, in integrated systems using optical switching and transmission.'[13] ISDN, the classic case of technology push, was itself falling victim to the push of technology.

Packet-switching and Fast Packet Technologies

Most telephone networks use what is called 'circuit switching'. When a call is made a line is allocated to the user to sustain a permanent flow of information until the call comes to an end. Many of the networks being built today are taking a very different form. Packet-switching, fast packet and ATM (Asynchronous Transfer Mode) technologies use the control capacities of digital technologies to break messages down and use the network much more flexibly than was ever possible in the past. Packet-switching originally developed in response to the special needs of computer communications; these tend to come in rapid bursts, followed by periods of silence. It was also shaped by the design needs of the military, attracted by the idea of robust systems not dependent on fixed circuit links. The standard telephone circuit, kept open for the duration of a call and charged according to time rather than information throughput, was clearly inappropriate and inefficient for these uses. The principle of packet-switching takes advantage of the cheapness of digital switching capacity relative to transmission: messages are divided into packets, series of bits which are combined with addressing and error control information at each end. Rather than keeping a single circuit open, these are sent through the network according to the availability of capacity: one part of the message may travel a different route to the next. Time division multiplexing means that many different messages share the same channel. Using intelligent switching capacity, the various parts are reconstructed in the correct order before reaching their recipient. When they have entered the network, the network's intelligence determines how best to move the message.

This apparently cumbersome technique has profound implications for the structure of networks. Given powerful control tools at the heart of the network, messages can be routed in such a way that shortage of capacity need not operate as a constraint. The network can be organized dynamically rather than being constrained by a pyramidal structure of nodes and links. In circuit switched systems the network cannot be designed to handle all possible traffic; instead a certain probability of traffic from any one source is assumed and capacity is built to meet a given amount of traffic with predicted probabilities for blocking. In packet systems blocking can be largely avoided: if there is a block on one route the switch can either re-route part of the message or hold it until the route is unblocked. Such a structure involves massive economies of scale: within the US 70 per cent of public packet switched service is controlled by just two companies. Much the largest network in the world is Transpac, run as a monopoly by France Télécom, which was responsible for carrying 1,200 billion characters each month in 1988 (most of them in Minitel messages), more than the combined traffic of all other public packet networks. The efficiency of advanced packet networks depends on a centralization of management and control. Hitherto packet technologies have been almost exclusively used for computer data, particularly financial transactions which are bursty and demand the error-correcting capacities of packet systems. However, the same principles are now being used for voice and video signals offering the possibility of a fully 'packetized' integrated network, continually breaking down, checking and reconstructing messages.

In the debates about ISDN and IBN new technological principles such as ATM, which like packet systems are asynchronous and avoid fixed channels, are extending some of the flexibility of packetization to new areas. In most telecommunications networks, including the ISDN, notional channels consisting of time slots are allocated to particular uses: for example a voice channel will be given what is called a positioned channel of 64 kbs. This arrangement helps when different networks are being linked together or when signals are being multiplexed, because one positioned channel can be linked to another. However, a system of this kind becomes inefficient when unforeseen and unpredictable demands are likely to be made on an interface or transmission cable. With ATM technologies the bandwidth of an interface or transmission link adjusts dynamically to the demands being made on it. The mechanistic division of bandwidth into channels for predetermined uses is replaced by a much more fluid structure able to choose when, where and how to send signals. If, for example, there are no voice signals passing through an interface all the available bandwidth can be devoted to data transmissions on smaller channels.

Fast packet techniques use some of the same techniques but either on a fixed route or with entirely self-routeing packets of information. Whereas in existing packet networks each message must be reconstructed, and errors and addressing checked at each node (so as to compensate for unreliable analogue transmission), with fast packet techniques the control functions operate only at the edges of the network, enabling a much greater quantity of information to be relayed at high speed. These various techniques are beginning to make switches more flexible: at present it is hard to build switches adaptable to signals of different bandwidths. Most existing digital switches switch 64 kbs or 2 mbs channels even if, for example, only 9.6 kbs of data is being passed along the 64 kbs channel. This substantially limits the benefits of integrating different kinds of signal. Although these more advanced systems are some years away from implementation on a large scale, they have clear attractions for a set of industries uncertain about the nature of the demands that will be placed on them in 15 or 30 years' time. They also suggest a profoundly different evolution to that of the geodesic or fractal network: a fully packetized network would require considerable concentrations of network control if the whole network was to use its capacity dynamically in response to demand.

Control Channels in Networks

Packet systems involve an alternative model for organizing control in networks. In the traditional telephone system control messages about where a signal is going or how it is to be charged are passed along the same copper wires as the communication itself. The move from human switching to electromechanical switching was in some ways regressive. Messages could no longer be kept by the operator. Because control was mechanized (the actual act of dialling directly guided switches to set up a circuit) the system became less flexible. With automation the system has reverted. Control is again separated from the message itself and organized through the software of the switch. ISDN networks use out of channel signalling, where a separate channel is used to control what flows of data or voice travel along the main channels. In such a system it is possible for control data to take different routes to the messages being controlled. In other words the control network exists at one remove from the main network.

Network control technologies are advancing rapidly. In most networks control can be concentrated and removed from switching. A single control centre can simultaneously command a number of different switches. Common channel signalling methods enable a channel simultaneously to control large numbers of different kinds of signal. Access to this control network has become a source of conflict. Large corporate users and private network operators want free access to control channels to limit their dependence on existing carriers. According to some researchers, control will itself become a key commodity: 'when further evolution towards implementation of B-ISDN, variable rate, networks proceeds, network control may become the most important commodity being bought and sold in the telecommunications market'.[14]

Within corporate networks the ability to manage and control flows of signals is already critical. Control can guarantee security; it can cut costs as channels are broken up and restructured; and it allows the uses of the network to be monitored. As new standards are agreed for computer communications (the 'OSI' model) the interrelations between control and communication are becoming increasingly complex. In the OSI model, a communication at one level can be used to control the flow of signals at lower levels, a prospect with dramatic implications for operators of current public networks with a monopoly of control. In packet networks much of the control information is again integrated with the message itself. Information about where the message is going is put in the address at the head of the packet. In principle, the end user is again able to play a direct role in managing the network. This evolution has an important implication for strategies and techniques of regulation. It suggests that in the future competition will focus less on ownership or control of the physical facilities of a network, the traditional concern both of regulators and of bypassers, and more on control over software.[15]

The control capacities of digital networks are ambiguous. The same increases in control capacity which have encouraged a dispersal of intelligence from the centre of the pyramid network to smaller private networks, microcomputers, Local Area Networks and a host of other machines, have also created the conditions for massive consolidations of control whereby a central computer can track precisely which part of which message is at a particular place at a particular microsecond. The real benefits of common channel signalling techniques, packet-switching and ATM technologies come from their ability to integrate and exploit whole networks, dynamically responding to demands and using the network as a unified system. Their technological potential depends in other words on centralized coordination. This must inevitably conflict with the idea that control can simply be bought and sold like any other service. What is more likely is a hierarchy of controls in which network operators maintain the power to control the basic flow of bits through the network, able dynamically to adjust bandwidth and aggregate services, while users have restricted access to signalling channels with which to define the details of the services they will receive.

There is also another sense in which new control capacities are ambiguous. The designers of ISDN were fearful of allowing access to control channels because of the experience of push-button telephones which gave an enormously powerful subversive tool to hackers breaking into apparently secure systems or manipulating switches to avoid paying bills.

Intelligent Networks

Alongside the ISDN, the concept of the Intelligent Network rapidly gained acceptance in the telecommunications industry during the late 1980s. It represents an interesting 'control compromise' between centralized and decentralized control. Rather than the infrastructure being a system that supports other services, it becomes itself intelligent, an array of intelligences that can be distributed, managed and reconfigured by the user. The concept was developed by Bellcore, one half of the former Bell Labs, as part of the Bell companies' strategy to bring large corporate users back within their public networks.[16]

The Intelligent Network depends on two sets of technology: high-speed digital switching and fast common channel signalling. In the intelligent network, control functions are located in a small number of control centres (Service Control Points or SCPs), distinct from the network's switches. Software for a new service can be located at an SCP and immediately made available through the network, rather than having to be provided at each local exchange. This instant ubiquity is achieved because of the ability of the SCP to communicate with local exchanges with common channel signalling techniques such as CCS-7. AT&T's Software Defined Network, a form of virtual private network (a network which appears to the user to be private but which is actually offered over the public network) that is being offered to large corporations, is one step in this direction. The software defining the shape of the private network, of who has access to whom and when, is located in a single point.[17] This can be quickly reprogrammed, bringing new sites into the network or removing access rights instantaneously.

The vision of instant ubiquity over an intelligent network has prompted IBM and other computer firms to lend more attention to the public network. Such a network could seriously threaten the fully private, specialized network structures which IBM has traditionally favoured as a way of weakening PTTs. Unlike the private networks, which usually operate well below capacity, Intelligent Networks exploit the economies of scale inherent in integrated networks. Rather than fighting the trends towards ISDNs and Intelligent Networks, IBM and DEC have sought to play a leading role in the production and implementation of the software for SCPs in collaboration with network operators, a move that calls into question who will ultimately own and control the heart of the networks of the future and whether intelligence will be concentrated in the network or in terminals.

The long-run evolution of Intelligent Networks is unpredictable. Designed as a strategic tool for network operators, who expected to maintain control over central databases, the continued regulatory shift towards separating networks from services suggests that the Intelligent Network concept could instead challenge the operators' ability to control the organization of services over the network.[18]

Open Networks

Alongside the broadband network, the ISDN and the Intelligent Network, one further concept is essential to an understanding of how networks are developing. This is the open network, a concept that combines technical meanings with regulatory ones. Technically the open network evolved out of attempts to network computers. Flexibility in linking different kinds of machine and different patterns of use turned out to be one of the most costly and difficult tasks in computing. Attempted solutions included the evolution of IBM's SNA (Systems Network Architecture) towards more open, non-hierarchical structures and the parallel development of the OSI reference model, designed to create the conditions for transparent communication between different computers and machines (see chapter 9).

The pressure to promote transparent communications had an unavoidable impact on telecommunications, as it became clear that telecommunications networks could be organized on similar principles to those emerging in computing. Ultimately anyone using a terminal attached to the network would be able to access its transmission and processing power. The OSI reference model came to be adopted within ISDN fora, and within the other standards-setting bodies concerned with MAP (Manufacturing Automation Protocol) for manufacturing, TOP (Technical and Office Protocol) for offices and GOSIP for governments. A web of institutions ranging from COS (the Committee for Open Systems) in the US to SPAG in Europe and POSI in Japan, all became committed to advancing the theory and practice of open and transparent networks. Within the CCITT study groups, the US's influential TI Committees and the ISO, technologists and network planners avidly explored the growing complexity of possible network structures, of broadband networks, intelligent networks, and the various ways in which they can be used to disaggregate the services offered by a network. All represent possible solutions to open networking. All serve to transform the ways in which network control can be structured, making it technically possible to disaggregate the provision of network functions and to shape the extent of openness or closure of the network. Photonic transmission and switching, superconductivity, fast and burst switching, parallel processing, artificial intelligence and expert systems all increase the potential powers of switches, and of terminal equipment, by an order of magnitude further reinforcing these trends.

Transmission Media

The balance between switching and transmission capacities has been transformed by the advance of processing technologies, an advance with no real parallel in the history of technology. Transmission technologies tend to be rather older, at least in conception. Most transmission technologies were conceived or experimented with well before they became widespread. Antecedents of the telegraph go back to the sixteenth century. Ways of transmitting pictures by electric wires were first proposed in 1842, and achieved by Caselli in 1862. Optical transmission dates to the 1870s. A century of intensive research into electric and electronic communications has resulted in the existence of a confusing diversity of transmission media. Cable and radio transmission have continually threatened to displace each other. The one universal trend has been towards greater communications capacity. This has been possible because of the advances in cable technologies: from twisted pairs, through coaxial copper to multi-mode and mono-mode fibre optics, from electric signals through LEDs (Light Emitting Diodes) to lasers; and because ever higher frequencies in the electromagnetic spectrum have been brought into use. By the late 1980s single mode fibre-optic cables with data rates of several gigabits were in use. Since the 1920s the whole range of the spectrum between 1500 KHz and 50 GHz has been brought into regular commercial use, while the ITU allocates spectrum up to 400 GHz. Medium wave and high frequency point-to-point broadcasting has been joined by VHF, UHF, microwave, waveguide, DBS (Direct Broadcast Satellite), cellular and other forms of mobile radio. Where the first Intelsat Early Bird satellite could carry 240 telephone circuits, its successors in the late 1980s can carry over 35,000. Where the first transatlantic telgraph could carry only three words each minute the TAT-8 cable of the late 1980s can carry around 30,000 channels.

For all forms of communication the basic resource is bandwidth, the capacity to transmit information. The higher the frequency, the more bandwidth is available. 1 GHz has a thousand times the capacity of 1 MHz. The huge capacity of optical fibres is a function of the high frequency of light.

Different kinds of signal have very different requirements for bandwidth. Personal computers communicating through modems require only 1–2 KHz; the telephone, reflecting the range of the human voice, uses 3–4 KHz, while television signals require about 6–8 MHz. Each of these has a parallel requirement for digital capacity: television signals for example are sampled in 9 bit samples 10 million times each second, requiring 90 mbs to be transmitted. This compares with 1.2 kbs for low-grade modems, and the 64 kbs standard for voice telephony. In parallel with the extension of bandwidth, technologies have advanced for preserving the integrity of communications over long distances. Fewer repeaters are needed, and signals can be reconstituted to remove noise and error. In fibre-optic technologies, one of the most significant recent inventions is the soliton: a means of shaping pulses of light in such a way that there is almost no dispersal and distortion over very long distances. By 1988, the distance between repeaters on undersea cables had risen to 65 miles.[19]

In principle any message can be transmitted over any medium. In practice each transmission medium has its own peculiar characteristics: the quantities of information it can transmit each second; the quality of signals; reliability (for example whether or not it is vulnerable to the weather); security (whether, as with mobile radio, signals can be easily intercepted or whether, as with a fibre-optic network, a single act of sabotage can cause immense damage); and flexibility, how easily capacity can be increased.

The chapter began with a quote from the first decade of the century when cables were written off as obsolete. The end of the century is witnessing an equally intensive competition between technologies. Crucial choices have to be made as to the relative virtues of the broadband technologies of optical fibres, with their potential for integrating services, in particular for integrating television distribution, and an array of radio-based cellular and microwave technologies offering the personalization of communication (with numbers attached to individuals rather than places[20]) and a cheap route to multi-channel television. Making choices between the two has become a crucial policy issue for governments and operators,[21] fraught with complexity both because of the speed of change in functionality and costs and because of the scale of money involved in replacing copper cables with fibres.[22]

Strategic uncertainty about the future of everything from regulation to technology inevitably shapes choices. Long-term investment becomes less attractive. Technologies which meet immediate demands take precedence over more speculative investments. This is reflected in accounting practice. Where the traditional telephone network was depreciated over forty or fifty years, modern networks are influenced by the far shorter depreciation rates of the computer industries, anything from two to ten years. Uncertainty is also reflected in investment patterns. Instead of spreading as a universal replacement for copper, by 1990 it was clear that fibre links were tending to be restricted to large users, with other new services being provided either with radio technologies or copper cable.

Technologies and the Limits to Abundance

Abundance has become a common theme in discussions about communications technologies. Fibre-optic cables with the capacity to transmit tens of thousands of television channels and compact discs capable of storing numerous encyclopedias seem to have outstripped human capacities to use information. Information overload is already a common experience. The basic raw material of communication, silicon, is abundant. As the density of components placed on a chip doubles every eighteen months, the continued miniaturization of microchips is ultimately limited only by the size of molecules. All communications channels are limited by the laws of physics and the rules applying to communication over noisy channels that were first described by Shannon, but switches and links are limited ultimately only by the speed of light, which can be approached as conversions and processing of signals are minimized. Transmission media are limited by the availability of spectrum, although the frontiers of spectrum continue to be extended both extensively and intensively as spectrum is used more efficiently. Higher orders of magnitude in speed of switching are potentially available on space platforms operating close to absolute zero temperatures.

Some of the most important limits to abundance are simultaneously technological and human. The advance of input and output devices continues to be constrained by the size of the human body and the capacities of human senses. The development of usable speech recognition devices has disappointed some expectations, although increasingly sophisticated human–machine interfaces are being developed for aircraft pilots. These involve speech-activated commands and firing programs which follow the movement of the pilot's eyes to track a target. Much of the SDI research is being devoted to natural language comprehension and simulation. The second type of barrier is also human. Of all the different elements in communications networks, processing, transmission, memory, input–output and software, it is software which has proved most resistant to cost-reducing strategies. As switches and computers become more complex the complexity and vulnerability of software increases even more. A modern telephone switch requires over a million lines of programming code. The US military communications network required an estimated seventeen million lines of programming. Such an endeavour requires huge quantities of skilled human labour. The use of expert systems, of the standardization of subroutines and programs and software engineering to enable computers to write software all begin to address the problem, but none can achieve the flexibility needed to write and rewrite software for complex and specialized operations.

The next phases of network development look set to depend on precisely these kinds of complex softwares capable of controlling extremely fast transmission, customized services, and the dynamic organization of bandwidth and services over interlinking networks. The application of AI promises to make networks more robust and user-friendly: number-based systems could be replaced by voice-activated name-based systems; user faults could generate prompts; terminal equipment could adapt itself to an array of standards. AI is also being used to design networks and diagnose faults.[23]

As tasks become more complex the structure of the computer itself becomes a barrier. The serial organization first developed for computers by John Von Neumann is widely seen as a barrier to higher speeds and greater complexity. With serial methods one processor shuttles back and forth between data and memory without communication between processors. Like the bureaucracy the serial computer works one step at a time in a strict hierarchy of function. Parallel processing, an idea as old as the computer, instead uses numerous processors simultaneously accessing a memory and communicating with each other.

The essence of parallel processing is that processors communicate with each other and that each has a flexibility of function. Networks become neural in nature, modelled on the workings of the human brain. The brute application of computing power gives way to more heuristic approaches that are essential if machines, like humans, are not to be overwhelmed by information. Many of these advanced technologies originate in the demands of the military for such things as speech and image recognition systems, and for robots that can make complex decisions and learn from their mistakes. Other applications include graphics and image generation, signal engineering, fluid flow dynamics and the design of integrated circuits.

Parallel processing turns the computer into a much more complicated network than was needed for serial processing. The bus, a single channel linking the various parts of the computer, is replaced by complex architectures such as the hypercube, with multiple links between processors or the binary tree where each processor is linked to two offspring. Complex software is needed to control systems of this kind, assigning tasks to arrays of processors. Like the computer and digital networks, artificial intelligence, parallel processing and neural networks, are all fairly open sets of ideas and principles with an almost boundless array of possible applications. Although they have failed to live up to some of the more extravagant claims made for them, their potential to replace control and decision-making functions in machines and systems is enormous.

If they realize their potential the implications for communications networks will be radical. Both parallel processing and artificial intelligence techniques tend to demand very large bandwidths and extremely high speeds as signals are continually passed between different processors. Workstations like Apple's Multifinder using hypercube programs to allow simultaneous access to data, text and graphics depend on large bandwidths to exploit their use of visual rather than textual functions.[24] Even the high capacity digital networks now being planned could become severe constraints on the scope for devising more distributed architecures. What looks like abundant bandwidth could soon turn out to be inadequate. Moreover, as billions are invested in digital terminals and switches, engineers are already discussing analogue concepts based on pattern recognition, which could replace them in the next century.[25]

Lewis Mumford believed that the telephone (like the fountain pen) was a perfect machine, impossible to improve. But if there is one consistent theme in the history of the open and flexible technologies of digital communication it is that apparent summits soon turn out to be foothills in larger and stranger landscapes.

6

The Limits of Free Flow: Commodities, Computers and Censorship

In most modern Western societies the free flow of information is seen as an obvious good, the guarantee of truth and honesty, and the means of uncovering tyrannies, abuses and falsifications. Free flow preserves the autonomy of the individual against larger powers while in economic life, speed and ease of circulation of information are seen to allow greater efficiency and more truly competitive markets, giving power to the consumer.

Looked at closely free flow turns out to be an unusually problematic ideal. Its problems mirror those of information more generally, a set of problems that are best understood as ones of control: of who has direct control over the production, packaging and dissemination of information and, more generally, of who has control over the informational environment within which people live. Free flow threatens a series of legitimate interests in controlling and restricting information. The oldest interest is that of the state in preserving national security and in restricting pornography and subversion; the more recent interests are those of industry, upheld by governments and laws. Private firms depend on the containment of free flow to protect copyrights, patents and trade secrets. All industries which produce and sell symbols, stories, ideas, images and sounds ultimately depend on the powers of the state and the law to control the free flows of piracy and unauthorized copying which can rob them of economic remuneration. Without laws and enforcement agencies to protect exclusive rights of this kind markets in information could not function.

The third set of interests are those of the individual. The right to privacy, like the right to remain silent under interrogation, is a right to maintain personal control against the demands for free flow of information made by a powerful system or institution. In her book *Secrets*,[1] Sissela Bok wrote that the realization that one has 'the power to remain silent is linked to the understanding that one can exert some control over events – that one need not be entirely transparent, entirely predictable'. Claims to privacy 'are claims to control access to what one takes –

however grandiosely – to be one's personal domain'. These interests in restriction are present, albeit in very different forms, throughout modern human history.

Technologies continually throw abstract ideals into new relief, demanding new concepts, laws and institutions. The idea of copyright had little meaning prior to the invention of printing. The freedom to broadcast, or the freedom of a community to refuse to receive signals, had little meaning before the advent of the satellite, the television and the radio. Today the ISDN and other integrated networks pose the question of free flow in new ways, with their implicit technical ideal of transparency, the smooth, unimpeded flow of communications across borders and between people and machines, and their power to record every communication and transaction. Whether in economic life or in the media each step towards greater openness and transparency brings costs as well as benefits. Free flow can be the enemy of control, whether the control of an oppressive or paternalistic state, the control of private corporations or the control of the individual. Free flow is in practice ambiguous, equally able to liberate or to destabilize the structures that sustain autonomy and freedom, to spread misinformation, propaganda and deceit, or the flow of legitimately private information.

This chapter analyses some of the problems endemic to the control of information, suggesting why there can be no hard and fast rules, no timeless rights and principles. Even as governments are coming to understand that the rules of control, copyright, patents and trade secrets are vital to the prosperity of large sectors of their economy, so is it becoming apparent that all solutions are conditional, temporary and unstable.

Information as a Commodity

The book was one of the very first commodities. As early as the fifth century BC active markets existed in Greece and Rome for papyrus books that were the products of slaves working in large *scriptoria*. In the absence of cheap copying technologies copyright was not a problem. It was only with the invention of printing, the first large-scale machine production producing the first repeatable commodity, that the commercial control of a text became an issue for governments and lawyers. Legally the commodity being sold ceased to be the physical form of paper, ink and binding but was rather the abstract information it contained.

Information and communication are resistant to any simple, structural controls. To be a tradeable good, which adds value and offers a return on investment, information must behave like a commodity: there must be viable, enforcible rights of property. Information must be given boundaries, within which use is legitimate, outside of which use constitutes theft. Without exclusivity, information may have a value but it cannot command a price: newspapers can be bought and sold but radio signals can command a price only if special measures are taken to make signals hard to receive. To this extent information is like all other goods: things which are abundant cannot be packaged and sold. But information has none of the familiar properties of scarcity of more material goods. Certain kinds of information gain in value the more widely they are distributed while others depend on narrow exclusivity. Information can be easily stolen or otherwise used without payment, and without the original owner losing anything tangible. In a famous 1970s court case in Britain, a student was acquitted of stealing the contents of an exam paper on the grounds that the university had not been deprived of a possession. The peculiar problem for information is its natural fluidity that carries it across organizational hierarchies, breaching secrets, spreading through gossip, ease of memory, and now through new copying technologies of tape, photocopier and computer disc.

The fundamental property which distinguishes communications networks from networks of transportation or energy is captured in the etymology of the word communication, derived from the Latin *communico* meaning 'to share'. Information can be shared, reproduced and transmitted without limit. It carries an opposite resonance to the word 'private', derived from *privare* meaning 'to deny', a sense retained in the modern 'deprive'. Its ease of sharing does not depend on technologies but only on common language. The problem for those engaged in turning information into an industry is that in order to exploit information, to turn it into a commodity for sale and profit, it is necessary first to publish, to go public and make the commodity manifest. By this very process its vulnerability to theft or misuse is emphasized.

Intellectual Property, Piracy and Control

There is little agreement as to the origins of the idea of an intellectual property right. There is certainly little evidence of it in the ancient world, which viewed ideas as the common property of the community and had only a weak notion of the author as an identifiable individual. The first evidence of artists signing works or of poets claiming authorship (and contesting plagiarism) comes from Greece in the sixth century BC. This is not to say that ancient societies were not concerned with controlling the flow of information: many religious movements believed in secret knowledge, and in the idea that different levels of understanding are appropriate to different audiences. Examples of banning and burning abound.

But the abstract idea of intellectual ownership and control was almost unknown. One exception is the Talmudic tradition, which stresses the importance of crediting principles derived from past authors. Other scattered exceptions include the Irish King Dermott's famed ruling on Columba's copying of Abbott Finian's Psalter: 'To every cow her calf, and consequently to every book its copy.'[2] Over time systems for controlling property rights in information have largely grown in response to particular technologies. With the invention of printing in the fifteenth century, the familiar principle of 'privilege', a limited monopoly granted by the sovereign, became the favoured means of exercising control. The first of these is reputed to have been granted in Venice, the early capital of book publishing, to Johann of Speyer, giving him a monopoly of book production. In 1486, the historian Antonio Sabellico was granted the first copyright for one of his books. This system of privileges gradually spread throughout Europe. Rather like the licensing of broadcasting in the twentieth century, systems of this kind were an effective means of indirect censorship. Government control evolved as the price for protection against privacy. In this period it was generally the publisher rather than the author who held the relevant rights and obligations. Despite the later rise of authors' rights, this remains true in many cases: rights of reproduction remain with the owner of the copyright rather than the creator, leading to many famous cases where authors have lost the right to write about fictional characters they had themselves created.

Printing was soon seen as a threat to established authority; its ease of use threatened social control. It threatened too the dominant integrated communications network based in Rome, which maintained outposts in every village, and the subnetworks controlling education and study in the great monastic orders. This monopoly was an explicit object of attack in Milton's *Areopagitica*, which also argued that 'every author should have the property of his work'. The long history of repression began soon after the first presses were brought into operation. In England, the Stationers' Company and the Star Chamber were the favoured instruments. In Europe the Church and the Inquisition were the organs of control.

From an early date it was clear that restrictions on information flow carried a high economic cost. In 1579 the introduction of imperial censorship in Frankfurt forced the book trade to move to Leipzig; similar English restrictions on typefounding in 1637 made English printers dependent on Holland. Throughout this period too governments used generous patent laws to compete for the best of the many itinerant craftsmen and inventors. Elizabeth Eisenstein writes that many of the most interesting developments in early printing occurred

under the aegis of merchant publishers who took advantage of late medieval political fragmentation to extend far flung trade networks from the shelter supplied by numerous petty principalities, relatively autonomous city states, republics, bishoprics, and walled towns. It is not in the major political centres such as Paris, Madrid, Vienna, Berlin, Rome and London but rather in commercial centres and quasi-autonomous 'free cities' like Venice, Lyon, Strasbourg, Basel, Antwerp and Frankfurt that one will find early print culture flourishing, so to speak, in its native habitat.[3]

The prosperity of a cultural industry seemed to depend on its distance from strong political control. Similar costs of control have become apparent in the late twentieth century. When the same networks carry both fiction and news and financial, research or trading information, restrictive controls can become massive fetters on economic development. In China in 1989, for example, economic imperatives made it impossible to close international lines; instead the state could only exert control through placing an armed guard on every fax machine.

It is sometimes argued that the problems of controlling commodity forms hampered the development of publishing as an industry. From the very origins of printing, piracy has been rampant; its earliest recorded example was in 1466. In part this reflected a culture which had little respect for the idea that stories or ideas could be owned and sold by an individual. By the mid-nineteenth century piracy had become an international phenomenon and a source of conflict between states. Publishers in the USA systematically pirated European authors. Within Europe, Belgium and Holland were viewed, particularly by the French, as pirate nations. But despite piracy and state repression, the publishing industry grew. Although individual authors and publishers may have suffered from piracy, the overall increase in circulation and availability probably served the industry well in the long run, creating new interests and new demands. The absence of strict copyright rules fostered cultural diffusion and almost never discouraged people from publishing. What economics describes as the positive externalities of publishing, the promotion of literacy and the vitality and relevance of print, helped the industry to grow. Flagrant disregard for property helped to make the printed word a common property.

Concepts of Intellectual Property

The idea of intellectual property, embodied in copyright law, grew in parallel with patent laws to protect the rights of inventors. Like copyright the patent is a means of controlling information. The idea of owning an invention has its origins in the prizes given for useful inventions in ancient Persia, China and in Greece from the fourth century BC onwards. These gradually became regularized in the form of monopoly grants to supply governments. In the modern era, patent law took shape at the same time as copyright, a similar response to technology. The first known example was designed to protect the Venetian silk industry. Weaving machines such as water-powered twisting mills required heavy investment in lay-outs, schedules and looms. The famous 1474 statute granted a ten-year monopoly to owners of inventions. As in printing, ownership was considered more important than the act of creation itself. The word 'inventor' carried both its modern meaning and a more general sense of practitioner. Inventors were usually employees. By the eighteenth century, however, the idea that the inventor or creater has rights of control over creations was becoming commonplace, associated in particular with John Locke's argument in his *Two Treatises on Government*, that rights to the products of one's labour have an origin in natural law.[4]

Copyright and Technology

Competing legal traditions offer alternative approaches. French and German traditions stress the concept of *droit d'auteur* and *Urheberrecht*, the idea that a creation is in some way an extension of the very personality of the author who must therefore be able to control its uses. In English and American law, by contrast, a parallel tradition stresses 'copy rights' and the economic need to reward the creator of information, the taker of risks. American law has traditionally taken a pragmatic view of copyright. Rights to reward are seen not as natural rights but as statutory ones, legitimate because of the benefit the public receives from creative work rather than because of a moral obligation to the author. This tradition attempts to balance fair reward with two economic interests: that of the widest possible dispersal of useful knowledge or information and that of encouraging the maximum innovation.

Copyright offers a temporary monopoly, either to reflect the author's moral rights of control or as the means of encouraging the economic output of information and ideas.[5] This monopoly clearly conflicts with two ideas at the core of Western ideas of freedom, the commitment to the free market,[6] and the commitment to the free flow of political and cultural ideas. In practice it has been the pragmatic need to encourage the production of ideas rather than a philosophical commitment to rights of control that has shaped laws of information.

In an earlier period the tensions between freedom and the need for control were far less apparent. Copyright was one of the means of removing control away from the dead hand of State and Church to the more decentralized control of the market. Freedom of speech and information was by and large incorporated in constitutions. Censorship was abolished in Britain in 1694, in Sweden in 1766, in the US First Amendment of 1791 and in Germany as a result of the 1848 revolution.

With exceptions in war and under dictatorships, the constraints on the dissemination of information since then have been largely economic: those of meeting the new economic logic of advertising-financed media, of capitalist industry, profit and takeover which displaced the idea of publishing as an activity undertaken to propagate opinions.

Within the European tradition this economic logic is overlaid with a set of ideas about authorial rights. Within it there is a highly individualistic view of art, creativity and the generation of ideas which bears only a loose relationship to the social realities of intellectual labour. Crystallized in the theory and practice of copyright, it protects the written form, rather than reading. Anything that can be recorded in physical form – tunes, characters and names – can be deemed to be copright protected. But the tradition excludes ideas, with no legal equivalent to Talmudic tradition: each creative work is treated as entirely new and entirely the product of the individual or individuals directly involved. Sociologically, it can be linked to the rise of a class of cultural producers competing for audiences in a market. It is an economic and legal solution to the problem of organizing a 'sphere of public discourse' beyond the control of Church and State. From it arose a powerful and persistent ideology of authorial control and sovereignty. This respect for *droit d'auteur*, however, usually combines with economic weakness relative to the institutions which package and distribute.

The author's weakness reflects the economic structure of publishing and indeed of all the cultural industries. All creative workers are dependent on those who control access to audiences, the distributors whose task it is to build audiences and service public demands.[8] Traditionally, and more than ever today, distribution has been far more concentrated than production; this is one reason why distribution, whether in the form of newspaper distribution, cinemas or broadcasting networks, has also been much more heavily regulated. Costs of production tend to be high, while costs of distribution and reproduction are low. The disparity has been growing rather than diminishing. First copy costs for films or records or software have tended to rise as costs of replication and distribution have been lowered by new technologies. Substantial economies of scale can be realized by a publisher, a record or television company because of the relative cheapness of replication. Yet because of the unpredictability of demand, and the uncontrollability of production, producers and distributors tend to spread risk, using a minority of successful works to subsidize a majority of loss-makers. The successful reap disproportionate rewards while the majority, of necessity, reap little reward and have little leverage with respect to their publisher. The freedom of the marketplace is also, for most, dependence on those with access to the market. The star system which ultimately confers great leverage on the most successful actors, musicians, writers and directors is inseparable from the pool system, the reserve army of unpaid, potential labour.

Similar structures have emerged in the computer programming industries. Moving away from their origins as craft industries, the software industries soon became dominated by a few international corporations such as Computer Associates, Microsoft, EDS and Cap-Gemini-Sogeti able to exploit economies in marketing and distribution. In the world of small computers there are similarities to the music and publishing industries: a small number of hits (such as the Lotus 1–2–3 which earned $270 m. in 1987 alone) subsidize a much larger number of failures. Operating systems such as DOS sell in vast quantities (10 m. for DOS), and create new markets for applications programs and networking software. Moreover, as in music or book publishing, the most able creative workers gain considerable economic power.

However, in computing as elsewhere the underlying weaknesses of the creative worker have been exacerbated by the changing nature of the cultural commodity. In computing there is endless scope for adapting, stealing and restructuring programs. Flow forms of provision in television and, to a lesser extent, the press, demand continual renewal and obsolescence at odds with the idea of the timeless value of a book. The editorial function in the production of both discrete commodities and flows has become much more important. The editor constructs repertoires, commissions specified works from authors and technicians and constructs the second skin of the commodity, its advertising, design and packaging, all of which are integral to the value sold to the consumer. The new significance of post-production in audiovisual and musical work further removes the product from original authorship. Editing and manipulation become central creative tasks. 'Scratch' forms emerge to feed off mainstream images and sounds, reconstructing them into different forms that subvert their original meanings. New creative practices call into question the line between theft and creative adaptation: they are a reminder that nearly all creative activity involves adaptations within a tradition, the reworking of older grammars and motifs. What these shifts symbolize is a change in the nature of control. The tradition of authorial moral right and control is superseded by a web of systems in which control resides with owners on the one hand and with editors and manipulators on the other.

Underlying the relations between the creators of vulnerable information and their publishers and distributors is a deep tension. Creativity and inventiveness are scarce but ubiquitous. The creator is generally weak (until turned into a star or bestseller), yet real creativity or creativity suitable for a dominant medium has immense value. Creative work has always proved resistant to rationalization and the techniques of Frederick Taylor and Henry Ford, resistant to the systematization of something that is inherently risky, inherently full of error. The industrialization of culture was a prime concern of the Frankfurt School, whose members coined the term 'cultural industry': as culture became mass-produced in industrial corporations they argued that the symbolic sphere would lose its ability to question existing forms of power. The autonomy of symbols and meanings would be constrained by the demands of profit and accumulation. One reason why these fears turned out to be exaggerated was suggested by Hans Magnus Enzensberger:

the mind industry ... does not, strictly speaking, produce anything. It is an intermediary, engaged only in production's secondary and tertiary derivatives, in transmission and infiltration, in the fungible aspect of what it multiplies and delivers to the consumer. The mind industry can take on anything, digest it, reproduce it, and pour it out ... this is its overwhelming power; yet it is also its most vulnerable spot; it thrives on a stuff it cannot manufacture itself.[9]

There is also a deeper reason why the 'mind industry' cannot control its own fate, the contradiction between the needs of commodity production and exchange for exclusivity and privatization and the needs of intellectual and creative work for social and convivial environments that foster the flow of ideas and arguments: universities and artistic milieus maintain a careful distance from commerce because they would be less efficient at meeting their goals if they did not.

Control in the Market

New communications technologies have consistently challenged the older structures of publishing. The music industry, to take just one example, took many years to adapt to the new realities of recording and mechanical copyright, creating a system of ownership over recorded sounds to parallel ownership of the abstract form of a song. In the case of records and films it was still possible to control the link between the copyright owner and the user; with broadcasting the relatively small numbers of broadcasters made it possible to impose compulsory systems of remuneration. But with the emergence of other technologies, the tape recorder and cassette, the video and the photocopier, these links between production and use were dissolved. Part of the problem arises from the nature of the monopoly being given, which applies not to the idea or information, but rather to its expression. The space between idea and expression is always hard to define, and when ideas can be expressed in multiple forms, in software, CD-ROMs or digital communications, and when they can be reworked, the very distinction breaks down. The repetitive power of technology undermines ownership, rendering impossible 'any coherent doctrine of private property in intellectual production'.[10] Moreover, where competing technologies can copy and distribute the same product – CDs, DAT (Digital Audio Tape), cassettes and records for music, books, CD-ROMs and photocopies for words – control becomes progressively harder to achieve. As a result the challenges of technology have tended to make copyright controls more draconian, increasing the scope and the bluntness of state powers over information. The spread of compulsory licensing schemes, of unified collection agencies sharing earnings in a pool, of government tribunals, and of special taxes on hardware, have emerged as solutions to the protection of copyright.[11] All go against the spirit of a free market and free exchange.

Each new generation of technology has made copying both cheaper and easier at a smaller scale. If production of printing plates, a film or record master is expensive and often highly labour-intensive, while reproduction is cheap, the openings for piracy are clear. When costs of copying were higher, centralized control, either to protect copyright or as overt censorship, was relatively easy. Printing presses could be licensed and pamphlets required to reveal the name of the printer. Transgressors could be found and punished. Advertising-financed media could be relatively simply controlled by penalizing advertisers, as was the case with pirate radio in the 1960s. With widespread access to cheap copying devices control became extremely difficult. These technologies reflect the value of free flow of information, of treating information as a public good. In many fields it has become hard to conceive of life without them: information is more useful the more it flows. This is one reason why the paperless office has yet to arrive, and why automation of offices has tended to increase the amount of paper used as more temporary paper hard copies are made to facilitate the use of information.

The hardware industries have exploited the utility of flow by moving from non-copying records to more versatile cassettes, and from film to video. Attempts to reverse the trend, with non-copying technologies such as the videodisc and the compact disc, may in the long run prove futile. Although it is generally accepted that copying for personal use is, if not acceptable than at least manageable, large-scale copying threatens all the software industries. Pirate markets now exist for all forms of software, with a heavy involvement of organized crime. Estimates for the extent of piracy are inevitably sketchy. Nevertheless it is clear that piracy is a far from marginal phenomenon. Industry estimates for losses from piracy were £1 bn for the book industry in 1986 (compared to only £1 m. in 1967), $1.5 bn for the music industry and around $1 bn for film.[12]

In 1986, *Variety* magazine estimated that 46 per cent of all video transactions involved illegal tapes. Computer software piracy is assumed to involve as much as 70 per cent of the market, while the spread of IBM PC clones, with almost identical operating systems, and forged ROM (Read Only Memory) chips, has revealed the blurred dividing line between hardware and software.

There are few means of protection open to the software industries. One is to make the product so cheap that copying is not worthwhile. This is the case with paperback books, which show little sign of being illegally copied (although textbooks are subject to rampant piracy). Attempts to create 'paperback' films using CD technology could provide a solution in the future. Alternatively, software producers can use technical ingenuity to make it either impossible or very costly to make unauthorized copies. The third option is the mobilization of the state and law to do the job of protection, a strategy which has become one dimension of the multi-faceted economic struggle between the USA (representing software interests) and Japan (representing hardware interests). An early sally was the failed attempt of the American film industry to prevent videocassette copying; despite the appeals of Jack Valenti of the Motion Picture Association of America who spoke of the 'savage rape and ravages of this machine', the Supreme Court accepted the reality of copying on millions of domestic videocassette recorders (VCRs).[13]

Having failed to mobilize copyright law, the audiovisual industries chose the second option, using technology to retain control over video property. Signals on rented tapes were manipulated to make them send confusing synchronization signals to VCR recording heads until it became clear that anyone with even a modest technical knowledge could circumvent the control. Digital television sets posed a threat since they contain algorithms which ignore irrelevant scanning signals of the kind used to prevent copying. Technologists have also developed 'open architecture' television receivers, with sufficient computing power to receive signals transmitted using any standard. Receivers of this kind could easily overcome the cruder encryption techniques.

There was a similar pattern of control and bypass in satellite broadcasting. By the mid-1980s around one million US households with satellite receivers were able to receive signals targeted at cable headends without paying for them. As in the case of video, the courts refused to uphold the broadcasters' property rights, forcing them instead to adopt technological solutions. Apparently sophisticated encryption systems, known as Video Cypher II (VC II), appeared to confer tight control over broadcasts: signals could be encrypted and, through the use of 'addressable converters', each viewer's ability to view could be directly controlled. When their credit ran out, the pictures would become unwatchable. Dish owners were offered the option of renting the means to descramble signals, a classic example of restricting the flow of information in order to make it function as a commodity. By 1988, however, it was estimated that around half of all receiver dish owners were using VC II decrypters without authorization. Electrical engineers were manipulating the descrambler to free it from remote control. Anyone wanting to preserve the exclusivity of their signals had to go one step further. Broadcasts of major boxing fights began to use the more advanced D-MAC standard, knowing that only the wealthier cable systems and cinemas would be able to afford to rent a D-MAC descrambler. In France in late 1988 films were broadcast to small cinemas in a scrambled HDTV signal. Rupert Murdoch's Sky channel has used smart card technologies (cards with optical storage or an implanted chip) instead of VC II to control flows of channels to viewers. Others concluded that the battle to control broadcast signals was ultimately unwinnable.

In the face of continuing technological change that undermines any strategy of technological control, the software industries have used political channels to force manufacturers, through the threat of legislative trade restrictions, to cooperate in joint hardware–software solutions, such as implanting chips in VCRs to make it impossible for them to record suitably coded signals. The containment of copying and signal theft came to a head with the emergence of digital copying technologies such as Sony's Digital Audio Tape (DAT). DAT offered perfect digital copying: in effect an endless stream of master copies made in the home. These could be recorded off the radio with the launch of digital radio in Japan in the early 1990s. In the medium term recordable compact discs are also likely. By forcing a modification of the DAT sampling method ('Copycode') the software industries prevented direct, on-line copying of CDs both in the USA and Europe. Their next step was to seek legislative controls on DAT's copying capacity. Again, technological battles were bound up with economic ones, in this case between the Japanese hardware industry and Europe and the US which, through Philips and RCA, had invested heavily in compact disc technology.

These battles took a new turn when Sony purchased CBS, the leader of the campaign against DAT. The manoeuvre suggested both the strengths and weaknesses of copyright control. In the 1970s and 1980s many observers had predicted that the last decades of the century would bring a restructuring of the cultural industries as the production of software, the publishing task of developing artists and exploiting material across different media and markets, disengaged from manufacturing. According to this view, as technologies changed with increasing rapidity, software production and control would emerge as the commanding heights of all industries concerned with symbols. An alternative view saw new technologies such as the video or the DAT as potential saviours, high-value added goods which would create new markets and inject dynamism. Neither model seems set to realize itself in a pure form since neither can alone control the system of communication, of software and hardware, that allows a new device to establish itself. What has become clear instead is the interdependence of software and hardware industries: new forms of hardware create demands from the software industries while new items of hardware depend on the availability of a wide range of software.

Computers and Software

The computer is the single most important villain wreaking havoc with the neat lines of intellectual property and control. Turing's original conception of the computer was as a universal machine, capable of copying any other. Such a copying capability is fundamental to the computer's operation. Whenever it uses a piece of software or receives a message it automatically copies it, storing it in some kind of buffer. Its Central Processing Unit depends on 'store and delay' for its serial processing to function. Similar principles apply to computer-like digital telecommunications switches: all routeing decisions and messages are stored, if only instantaneously. A related problem is that a computer must write, or at least copy, before it can either read a piece of incoming information or be read by a user. The basic principle of copyright, that reading is permitted and copying prohibited, is turned on its head. The fundamental weakness of copyright controls, namely that they protect representations from copying rather than protecting contents, is also highlighted in the world of computers. All these problems are exacerbated by more open networks linking terminals and databases over ever greater distances. An originator of information has no way of controlling the uses to which that information is put or the ways in which it is read. Computers linked to the network can easily copy a message or file and re-transmit it to any number of destinations. The problem becomes one of scale and speed.[14]

Copyright problems have become particularly acute in the computer software industry. Just what is genuinely original and what is in the public domain is open to interpretation. Legal authorities in different countries rarely come to the same conclusions. Codes are generally built up from previous ones and ultimately all are based on common mathematical algorithms. All software writers use the work of others. As software engineering techniques become more widespread and artificial intelligence programs themselves write software, the question of what is genuinely original becomes even more intractable. A deeper problem is that in order to be useful software must often be adapted to special uses. Large proportions of information technology budgets in institutions and organizations are spent on software maintenance and adaptation. In many institutions annual costs of software maintenance amount to between 10 and 15 per cent of the original costs of production.

Adaptation of software by individuals or institutions depends on access to the source code which is generally kept secret to prevent the user making multiple copies. Although control over the software is useful to the user, it clearly breaches the property rights of the author. Equally problematic is the definition of exactly what constitutes software. In computing the distinctions between hardware and software are very blurred. Any software can, in principle and at a cost, be frozen into hardware. Microchips rather than traditional software can control processes. These pieces of hardware, which may form a diagnostic medical system or the control system for a missile, may in turn be endlessly reproduced. None fits easily into traditional ideas of a text that can be protected by copyright.

In principle software is covered by a panoply of legal controls ranging from copyright and patent law to the law of trade secrets. In practice, copyright has been favoured as the means of control: bizarrely, computer programs are treated as literary works. There is, however, no clear distinction between what should be treated as copyrighted literature and what should be treated as patented machinery. Timescales of copyright are also controversial: what is appropriate for the author of an essentially timeless work of literature is quite inappropriate for a piece of computer software that may be obsolete within five years.

As the legal issues surrounding copyright have become more controversial, unusual alliances have formed between those opposed to over-rigid copyright restrictions, for example between business users wanting the flexibility to adjust software, and less developed countries wanting cheap access to First World technologies. A simple solution favoured by some neoclassical economists is to remove software from copyright protection altogether. This 'market' solution would force producers to use encryption and other techniques to block copiers, just as encryption techniques have been used in video and broadcasting. Perhaps the biggest single problem with this approach is that it goes against the powerful economic logic pushing towards greater compatibility of operating systems and programmes.

The problems of control have made it essential for software firms always to remain one step ahead of the shadow industry, continually offering enhancements. Any product has a short half-life before copying cuts its value. One response has been to make a virtue of the vulnerability of software as property. Formed into cooperatives in the US and Britain, software writers offer unprotected 'shareware' for anyone to use. They then persuade users to subscribe to user clubs which provide periodic enhancements. The software is recognized as a common property while the clubs provide a structure for rewarding the software writers. Another approach uses a form of copyright, 'copyleft', to provide programs with their source codes in such a way that users could not then sell programs without making the source code available. The laws of private control are thus used to ensure that information remains fully within the public domain.

Cooperative approaches to software are in many ways the most efficient, enabling the maximum exchange of ideas and criticism, and ease of adaptation. As programs become more complex and labyrinthine, software production becomes dependent on communities of producers and users continually interacting. A soft structure replaces the hard structure of property rights.

The trend towards seeking software by subscription is in line with other software industries. In broadcasting pay-per-view channels have generally been replaced by pay channels paid for by a monthly subscription. Other software companies have simply given up the struggle, dropping copyright protection for their products. WordStar and Microsoft are notable examples. Just as academic publishers can price books on the assumption that they will be bought by libraries and subsequently photocopied, so the software house can price on the implicit assumption that multiple copies will be made.

Stemming Flow in Networks

In practice, it is hard to keep signals private against determined efforts to intercept. The very structure of the network, interconnecting numerous nodes, makes it vulnerable to abuse. All mobile communications can be intercepted and, in principle, all encryption methods broken. Radio Frequency Interference is leaked by most electronic equipment including visual display units, so that signals can be intercepted and reconstructed by a nearby receiver. The popular vision of hackers breaking into military or educational records to launch missiles may be exaggerated but, in practice, most of the passwords used to restrict access to networks and computers can be easily worked out using powerful computers going through huge numbers of permutations. Defence networks tend to be relatively secure because they are not linked to public telephone networks, but this is not true of most corporate and government networks. For each new security technique designed to uncover illegal access a counter-technique can be devised. In this, the electronic spy is assisted by the fact that evidence of breaches of security can be erased. As electronic surveillance techniques proliferate so do the counter-measures: the transmission of disinformation, padding of communications with meaningless bits so as to disguise sudden bursts of real communication, and ever more complex encryption techniques.

Cryptology, the art of secret communications, has been transformed into a fully fledged science based on advanced mathematics. Sophisticated coding devices are now produced on an industrial scale. Digital transmission makes encryption much cheaper, while future transmission technologies such as Code Division Multiplex encode automatically. The American National Security Agency (NSA), widely seen as a world leader in communications technology, was responsible for overseeing IBM's development of what emerged as the dominant commercial encryption technique, the Digital Encryption System (DES). DES, like most sophisticated modern techniques, relies on a 'public key' system that makes it almost impossible to discover the decoding function from the encoding function. The basic algorithmic principles used to transform data or voices are made public. This economizes on the number of different algorithms needed to communicate to different groups of recipients. In traditional encryption the same code can be used to encode and decode messages. When secret messages are being sent to many different destinations, the numbers of codes needed can escalate out of control. With public key systems the user need only know its own secret key and the common public key. DES was approved by the US Federal Government in 1977 and by the American standards body in 1981.[15] Although NSA has ended its endorsement, DES is widely used throughout the world and is mandatory for electronic banking in the US (despite the assumption that NSA is able to decrypt any DES signals through 'trapdoors').

A major industry has emerged to cope with the security problems of open networks, with fraud, embezzlement and industrial espionage. DES and other means of encrypting messages, token and public key systems to authenticate authorized access to services on a network are all directed both to security and, equally important, to the need to ensure that those receiving services cannot avoid paying for them. Without this ability to control flows of payments (dependent on common standards and perhaps common gateways) the whole economy of symbolic production and indeed of material production could face destructive crises.

As OSI standards are developed to permit transparent connection of computers over networks, security has emerged as one of the biggest stumbling-blocks. New security methods for checking authorized access to files account for as much as 20 per cent of all data flows on secure networks, inevitably slowing down their basic operation. New threats from interconnection have also appeared. Best publicized are the computer viruses, simple codes and instructions which can rapidly multiply throughout networks, destroying information and disrupting processes.

If there is one indisputable fact about the crisis of network security it is that there are no foolproof barriers. There will almost always be mistakes in millions of lines of operating system code offering openings to hackers. New and more effective viruses are limited only by the ingenuity of their devisers: there is simply no way of screening against all possible forms of attack. 'Trojan Horse' instructions that erase all trace of their actions, and destructive 'logic bombs' that destroy programs are among the unavoidable strange new phenomena of a networked society.

The Limits of Control

Governments have always tried in different ways to limit information flows, using overt and indirect censorship, the control of writers' and artists' bodies, secrets laws and a panoply of official and quasi-official levers. Most of the leading companies involved in producing software, whether it be in the form of texts, records, videos or films, have tried to devise methods of maintaining control over their property. In response, in almost every society, ingenuity and technology have been used to circumvent controls. Famous examples include the use of cassette tapes in Iran, of samizdat cassettes and X-ray plates in USSR, of illegal satellite receivers in the USA, bootleg record and tapes. Informal video networks now exist throughout the world, sometimes linked to transmission media, as in the Australian aboriginal 'Imparja' television project. Video-recorders are used in large numbers throughout the world, from Poland to Chile to New Guinea. One video is a viewing medium; two videos can reproduce indefinitely.

Radio signals are also particularly hard to control. Short-wave broadcasts, which travel great distances, are expensive to jam. Pirate radio transmitters can be quickly assembled and moved. Television signals, because of the properties of VHF and UHF, tend to remain within national boundaries, but satellite broadcasting signals can be received anywhere within a hemisphere. The sheer scale and number of communicating technologies makes centralized control hard to achieve beyond a few mass-media channels.

It is easy to conclude that a simple expansion of freedom, led by technology, is imminent, a final challenge to the rights of governments to contrain the thoughts and expressions of their citizens. The erosion of power and hierarchy that this implies would create an abundance of knowledge, a library of Alexandria in every home. In a world of fibre-optic cables, vast optical storage systems and extremely fast integrated circuits, older scarcities, and the inequalities they caused, would lose their significance.

Unfortunately, this attractive vision of technologically based abundance in the supply of information conflicts with basic economics. Unless information can be kept scarce it cannot command a price. Without a price, private capital has no incentive to provide it. If production industries are unable to control the commodity form of what they produce the end result will be massive underproduction. After all patents and copyright systems have evolved because, in the words of one American legal theorist, 'the very fact that ideas are free creates a disincentive to the development of ideas'.[16]

In the past, control was structured into the technologies used to make and reproduce information. According to Ithiel de Sola Pool, 'what protects the author or publisher is physical control of the text for there is no control of reproduction once it is out of his hands'.[17] As control in this sense dissolves, new solutions are needed. Some have already been mentioned: the production of immediate information which loses its value very quickly, such as news or financial information, and real-time transactional information; the use of encryption to create an artificial scarcity; the locking of software and hardware, such that what is sold is a system of information or processing power; subscription models, where the consumer purchases a flow of magazines, software or television programmes on the basis of past performance; the regulated transfer of resources from hardware to software as with television licence fees or levies on blank audio of videotapes. None is a total solution, and none a permanent one either.

For the individual, too, the open networks of the twenty-first century will demand very different approaches to privacy and ownership. Greater network flexibility brings with it new problems: the called-line-identification, call-forwarding and itemized billing debates of the late 1980s are harbingers of the future, suggesting just how hard it is to balance the rights of senders and receivers, operators and users.

The Dutch Commission on Computer Crime suggested one way in which our understanding of ownership of information may change as networks become more pervasive. Rather than seeing information as something that can be owned, the Commission sought to define controls in terms of flows. Control is defined in terms of the intentions of the transmitter or producer. If, for example, a piece of information is addressed or encrypted for a particular transmission, then unauthorized use constitutes theft. Otherwise, use is permitted. The law begins to recognize that communication is concerned with channels rather than with things. Similar principles can apply to rights of access to flows of information that concern one's life, to psychiatric patients, to school students, to prisoners or to employees. Transparency can become a tool for democracy and self-control rather than coercion.

Copyright was designed to bear on physical forms. Today the emphasis has moved to control over flows and to sophisticated technologies to determine who has legitimate access to flows: PINs (Personal Identification Numbers), signature and retinal identifications, and DES-type codes all serve these purposes. As they evolve, the one thing that is certain is that shifting technologies will continually undermine any systems of control. In a networked, interconnected world all control over information is at best conditional, temporary and unstable.

7

The Limits of State Control and Deregulation

All communications networks are operated within tight institutional and legal frameworks, organized at the level of the nation state. Governments, laws and regulatory bodies have traditionally set stringent rules determining what equipment can be connected to networks, what lines can be used for, what prices can be charged and what kinds of service can be provided. The 1980s brought profound changes to these structures and to the traditionally close relationship between governments and their communications industries. In Britain, the US and Japan, and to a lesser extent Germany and France, a varying menu of privatizations, liberalizations, new laws and regulatory bodies was put into practice. Lumped together under the term 'deregulation', these changes disrupted the stable regimes within which broadcasting and telecommunications had operated for many decades.

In the past, the control of communications networks was primarily determined by considerations of security, nation-building or social equity. By the late 1980s and early 1990s the needs of the economy for productivity growth and competitiveness far outweighed other considerations. Paradoxically deregulations coincided with an ever more active role for governments and state agencies in creating what they believed to be the best climate for the communications economy. What was happening was not the end of state control (although there was a clear erosion of the powers of the national state) but rather a change in its forms, a change that can best be understood as one from control within a closed system to control within an open one.

This chapter offers an analytic framework for understanding the nature of recent changes, outlining the history of the various forms of sponsoring, restricting and arbitrating control. Running through the argument is the idea that new forms of 'arbitrating' regulation are replacing and redefining older models. These suggest, in embryonic form, how public institutions will be able to exercise control in the open and intelligent infrastructures of the twenty-first century and why regulation will become more rather than less important in a world of increasingly sophisticated and complex communications.

The Origins of the Regulatory Crisis

Regulators' often chaotic adaptation to the changing environment of the 1970s and 1980s can be traced to three sets of causes. One set is ideological and political, part of the long-term shift of the world's ideological tectonic plates away from state and public controls and towards the market. This seismic shift is bound up with a sense that in situations of uncertainty and flux governments are ill equipped to make far-reaching decisions on future technologies and needs. There is also a more narrowly political origin to the deregulatory movement, well described in an influential recent book by two American writers, Martha Derthick and Paul Quirk, who argued that political advocacy had played the decisive role in the deregulatory movement in telecommunications, trucking and airlines in the USA.[1] Others have highlighted the coalition between radical consumer groups and business that set off the deregulation of industry-specific regulatory bodies like the Federal Communications Commission (FCC), while leaving intact the more general regulatory bodies, the agencies of social regulation which above all others were anathema to business.[2]

A second set of causes are technological. Convergent technologies have brought together at least three different regulatory traditions: of common carriage telephony, of content-regulated broadcasting and of the free market press and computing. On an ISDN or broadband network a continuum stretches between point-to-point private communications and mass broadcasting, disrupting the neat demarcations between different models of regulation. The digital network and the computer transmit and manipulate information regardless of its meanings, and origins. Controls placed on one distribution medium can be circumvented through another, while controls on the contents of communication seem to demand a level of monitoring and policing that would be wholly impractical even if it was desirable. Technological change has also called into question the idea of a natural monopoly in either broadcasting or telecommunications, an idea which had provided a theoretical base for provision through regulated monopolies. When networks can be easily interconnected, and when radio- and cable-based networks can offer the same services, competition comes to seem more natural.

Technological convergence has been accompanied by a new interest in the idea of the open network. The idea of openness in networks first developed among technicians working on distributed processing and distributed architectures in computing. At the core is the idea that the infrastructure, rather than being a closed system controlled by a single entity, becomes an open resource which gives access to users, to service providers and to different types of communication.

Political and technological pressures towards more open and liberalized networks have been magnified by economic ones. The growing economic significance of communications meant that firms in other sectors looked for ways to enter formerly protected markets. Large firms also wanted greater control over their own communications. The two factors combined to encourage companies as diverse as General Motors and IBM, the Midland Bank, BP, Mitsubishi and General Electric to move into communications. At the same time broadcasting companies began to broadcast data to closed user groups, telecommunications operators to carry and invest in television channels, and cable companies (at least in the UK) to offer voice telephony. This interpenetration of different sectors has further strengthened the theoretical assault on the idea of natural monopoly. How competitive an industry is deemed to be depends on where the boundaries are drawn. Telephone companies can now be seen as minor participants in a vast, open and sprawling communications industry rather than as dominant players in a more narrowly defined and largely closed telephone industry.

There is also a more fundamental economic cause for the loosening of controls. A flexible and advanced telecommunications infrastructure supporting value added services has become the *sine qua non* for economic growth. Advanced capitalist economies have become dependent on specialized services, such as consultancy, advertising and market research, accountancy and on electronic flows of codified information, in the form of electronic funds transfer, data interchange (EFT and EDI) and innumerable other services of varying degrees of standardization. These various VANS are seen as the nervous systems of the more interconnected and flexible economies of the future. In Europe the VANS sector is predicted to grow to $4 bn by 1992, while in Japan by 1989 there were over 600 'Type II' carriers, using computers to offer services over the public infrastructures.[3]

It has been estimated that each 1 per cent growth in GNP in OECD countries produces a 1.5 per cent increase in demand for telecommunications services.[4] The converse of this relationship is that any constraints on new services act as a constraint on economic growth. In the words of the European Commission's 1987 Green Paper, 'telecommunications is the most critical arena for influencing the "nervous system" of modern society. To flourish, it has to have optimum environmental conditions'.[5]

This relationship between the changing nature of economic activity and deregulation explains why countries have deregulated at different speeds. It is no coincidence that the leading deregulators, the UK, US and Japan, are also the leading competitors in financial services. Their survival as trading centres depended on their ability to offer flexible services. Within

Europe, Britain's role as the first deregulator reflects more than ideology. It also reflects the UK economy's position as the leading user of data communications in Europe, accounting for nearly 25 per cent of Western Europe's total transborder data flows largely because of the concentration of banks and financial services in the City of London, and the unusually large size of its businesses which consequently have a greater need for data communications.

The need for resources to build networks to carry advanced digital services has also been a pressure towards liberalization. Network investment in the OECD countries will need to rise by 5 per cent each year in real terms to achieve current modernization goals, a figure which could be much higher in countries like the US and UK where competition is favouring the spread of duplicate networks.[6] Traditionally these funds would have come from within the public sector. By the late 1980s this was precluded by fiscal problems and by aversion to large public investments. The alternative was to make private investment attractive. By the mid-1980s the public contribution to investment in the network had fallen below 50 per cent for the very first time. The national strategic imperative of building new networks appeared impossible to achieve unless the sector was opened up to new private investors. Similar considerations applied in the Third World. In Latin America, the combined pressure of massive debts and consumer complaints about the quality of service forced governments to relinquish control to foreign capital. Indonesia considered a solution whereby foreign suppliers and operators would build and run a network, passing it back to state control once they had recouped their investment. Similar pressures appeared in Eastern Europe, forcing governments to consider privatizations and deregulation as a means of attracting foreign capital.

All three sets of causes, the political, the technological and the economic, can be summed up in a single word: complexity. The complex world of competing technologies and firms, of the blurring of geographical and sectoral boundaries that has occurred as telecommunications finds itself integrated with broadcasting and finance, computing and office equipment, has come to replace the bounded world of the national telephone company which once offered a simple set of services. Complexity has replaced the previously closed world of national networks with a more difficult world of cross-frontier flows, transnational organizations and intensified international competition. With complexity has also come uncertainty about which are the technologies and services of the future. Within this fluid and complex environment top–down control has become an ineffective, costly and blunt instrument.

The Nature of Regulation

In its narrow sense regulation refers to controls that function through rules: laws, decrees, administrative orders and judicial rulings. Its reality is rarely simple. The judiciary, governments and quasi-independent regulators continually jostle, each bringing different languages and traditions to the problems of control. Public interests, consumer interests, the interests of the market and the corporation all compete within the artificial terrain of regulation. The history of deregulations and liberalizations is also far from simple. Policies of privatization (BT, NTT) have conflicted with policies to introduce competition, since capital markets always prefer to invest in a monopoly.[7] In the US former advocates of deregulation like the company MCI have become the most fervent supporters of regulation in order to protect themselves from AT&T, while AT&T has become a leading supporter of deregulation. Strictly speaking deregulation means the removal of rules. Implicitly it also carries the suggestion that communications can be removed from the realm of politics. In practice, the opposite has been the case: regulations have had to become more detailed and more legalistic; AT&T, a private company, was always more tightly regulated than its public, European counterparts, and Britain's independent television companies were always more strictly and formally regulated than the BBC. Inevitably deregulation has been accompanied by the formalization of regulatory theories, structures and rules.

The Three Types of Control

Although the practice of deregulation has been confused and contradictory, there are a number of consistent themes. The history of regulation and deregulation can be understood as a succession and accumulation of three different types of control. One is a sponsoring type of control. The government uses its powers in the manner of a plan towards given ends, such as the creation of new infrastructures, the enhancement of national defence and social or regional equality. Direct or indirect sponsorship was crucial first to the success of the European PTTs, then to the dominance of AT&T and IBM, funded through the US 'military–industrial complex' and, finally, to the emerging dominance of Japanese companies like Fujitsu, NEC, Hitachi and Toshiba, founded on VLSI and related technologies sponsored by MITI. Government sponsorship in many countries went far beyond support for research, involving the government as the main provider of communications, operating telephony and telegraphy directly through a government department.[8]

The second type of control is restrictive: the problems of communication come to be seen either as those of overpowerful institutions needing restraint, or as those of public services needing protection from the danger of disruptive competition. Associated with this approach are anti-trust laws, rules on rates of return and pricing policies, and rules preventing companies from entering new markets. Through the FCC's controls on AT&T, the US provided the classic case of restrictive regulation.

The third type of control is a logical development of restrictive regulation. Instead of constraining a handful of dominant companies, regulation takes the form of arbitration, in which the government oversees such things as access to the electromagnetic spectrum, open standards or the terms on which networks are interconnected. This type of control can be every bit as interventionist as the two others. What distinguishes it is the idea that the state's role is to manage the parameters of an open ecology of communication, rather than directly to plan it.

These three types of control, the sponsoring, the restrictive and the arbitrating, often overlap. To take just one example, the creation and allocation of a property or monopoly right (over spectrum, a network or a copyright) involves both arbitration between claimants and restrictive control to sustain it. The distinction is useful, however, as a means of understanding the shifting role of governments over the last 100 years, the history of which can be read as a move through each of these forms of control, with each new one complementing rather than displacing its predecessors. This historic shift reflects both the weaknesses and the strengths of governments in an increasingly internationalized communications industry. Governments can no longer treat their communications networks as closed systems. Instead their policies have become increasingly orientated to the global economy, to attracting investment, to creating the conditions for competitiveness in domestic firms and towards meeting the needs of dominant firms.

Control through Sponsorship

In the nineteenth century, government intervention in networks largely took the form of subsidies and promotions. In varying forms this tradition remains intact to this day, now integrated with much larger programmes to accelerate the transition to information-based economies. Communications networks have always been seen as infrastructures, webs which support and are indispensable to the mass of other economic activities. They are the keys to political and military control (Michael Mann uses the term 'infrastructural control'[9]) and to economic circulation. As infrastructures they permit the coordination of flows of goods and services, a physical coordination of production and consumption that runs parallel to the control functions of the monetary system. Their nature as infrastructures affecting all other economic sectors was instrumental in persuading most of the world's governments to invest in and organize them. The intuitive understanding of their role was also theorized by economists: Adam Smith wrote that 'good roads, canals and navigable rivers, by diminishing the cost of carriage put the remote parts of the country more nearly upon the level with those in the neighbourhood of the town. They are upon that account the greatest of all improvements.'[10] Smith argued for public support on the grounds that infrastructures of this kind are 'of such a nature that the profit could never repay the expense to any individual or small number of individuals'. From a different perspective Schumpeter stressed the importance of the great infrastructural innovations of steam, rail and electric power in the process of economic change;[11] similarly one prominent justification for public investment in broadband is its potential to unleash a new wave of innovations around such things as videotelephony, teleshopping and parallel processing.[12] Achieving social innovation in the use of networks depends on the realization of critical masses of use (particularly for interactive services), which may in turn depend on initial subsidies.[13]

Though the links between infrastructures and growth appear intuitively obvious, they are difficult to pin down. Many economists have commented on the close correlation between GNP/capita and telephone density,[14] but it has proved much harder to determine which is cause and which is effect.[15] Similarly, economic historians such as Robert Fogel have offered convincing evidence that the impacts of infrastructures have been exaggerated.[16]

Support for infrastructures now forms part of much larger, highly publicized national plans of varying degrees of coherence and substance to guide the transition to the 'information society'. In most cases these have been closely aligned to monopoly national telecommunications providers, many of which long acted as driving forces in research and development. AT&T's Bell Labs (now split in two) was the largest private laboratory in the world and the originator of the transistor, the semiconductor and several of the earliest computers. Implicit in the preservation of AT&T's monopoly was an assumption that Bell Labs would license many of its inventions at little or not cost, acting almost as a public national institution. In other countries NTT played a crucial role in supporting the Japanese semiconductor industry, France's CNET in developing digital switches, British Telecom's laboratories in Martlesham in the development of videotex and optical fibres. In each case monopoly was used to finance research which in turn irrigated national industry with technologies and personnel.

During the late 1970s and 1980s these implicit roles began to become more explicit. In the USA the National Telecommunications and Information Administration (NTIA) was set up under President Carter to develop coherent policies ranging from regulation to trade and research issues. Because of the peculiarity of the American polity these policies largely took the form of an industrial policy at one remove, carried out through the Pentagon. In this they followed a long tradition dating back to the formation of RCA (Radio Corporation of America) at the behest of the US Navy in 1919, as a response to British dominance in cable and in radio technologies. After World War II close links were forged between industry and the military. Comsat was created in the early 1960s as the government's instrument for overcoming the USSR's lead in satellite applications. Computing, aircraft tracking, microwave and radar, rockets and space exploration have all passed from the military/space public sector into the private sector, establishing the pre-eminence of American electronics. Close personal links and intertwining career paths tie the various elements of the US communications elite in AT&T, NASA (the National Aeronautics and Space Administration), IBM, FCC, the Department of Defense, Comsat, and Bell Labs. Since the mid-1970s this elite has shared a belief in the need for a strategy of national renewal in communications, aimed in particular at regaining industrial leadership from the Japanese. The Air Force, for example, was behind one of the most concerted programmes for developing US CAD/CAM capability in ICAM (Integrated Computer Assisted Manufacturing), just as in earlier decades the Air Force promoted numerically controlled tools and paid contractors to learn how to use the technology.

A major factor behind the Justice Department's decision to drop the long-running IBM anti-trust suit in 1982 was the need to release an exemplary corporation from any constraints which might prevent it leading a national recovery in communications. DARPA, the creator of ARPAnet and much of the technology of new networks, recently claimed to Congress that 'the domestic commercial applications of this new technology will certainly complete the transformation of US society to the information age'.[17] DARPA has been heavily involved in developing artificial intelligence applications in pattern recognition and vision for robots, language-understanding and speech recognition, and in financing 'functionoids', robots used in reactor maintenance, mining or oil explorations. It has also committed substantial funds to high-definition television technologies, justifying them for simulation and training systems. The apotheosis of the US industrial policy at one remove is the Strategic Defense Initiative (SDI), both a defence initiative and an overt attempt to regain US industrial dominance through unprecedented public research and development spending. One Pentagon document argued that 'spin offs from a successful Stategic Computing Program will surge into our industrial community'.[18] Many of the problems of SDI are similar to those of ISDN and other advanced networks involving tracking large numbers of objects at extremely high speeds and operating enormously complicated programs with tens of millions of lines of software.

There are many doubts as to whether SDI-type initiatives have the effects they claim: some would argue that they erode competitiveness because of the lack of real market discipline in defence contracting, and that the concentration on the most advanced technologies ignores more commercially valuable products.[19] Videotex, a civil technology, remains remarkably underdeveloped in the USA. The important point, however, is that arguments for national plans and public spending continue to be politically effective even as an anti-statist deregulatory rhetoric appears dominant.

In other countries national mobilization has also taken forms appropriate to local political conditions and traditions. In Britain, the development of a coherent strategy was hampered by the absence of a tradition of industrial policy, despite the initiatives in the 1960s of the Industrial Reorganisation Corporation (IRC) (in particular regarding ICL and GEC) and of the National Enterprise Board (NEB) in the 1970s with its investment in the transputer company INMOS. In spite of the Conservative Government's stated antipathy to industrial policy in the early 1980s, Margaret Thatcher appointed the world's first Minister of Information Technology and launched a concerted intervention in the computing industry through the £350 m. Alvey programme (named after the British Telecom executive who chaired the committee) concentrating on developing VLSI technologies, expert systems and software engineering to help the British software industry move beyond its specialist niches. The Cabinet's Information Technology Advisory Panel (ITAP) committee produced a series of reports designed to engineer the way to the information society, recommending new policies for information production, training, copyright and cable. Information technology training centres (ITECs) were launched alongside an ambitious plan to educate a new generation in computer literacy. Ambition reached a peak in 1982 when it was announced that cable television would rapidly pave the way to a 'wired society' based on information services. Like the government's plans for Direct Broadcast Satellites the proposal to use entertainment-led cable as a short cut to high-capacity networks without government funding failed to take off. The perceived need for a national plan conflicted with free market ideology.[20] Intervention in shaping the infrastructure was explicitly ruled out.[21] Instead, private companies spearheaded national revival in communications, redefining it in terms of success in international markets. British Telecom rapidly made the transition from domestic utility to international communications company, heavily involved in overseas ventures (such as McCaw and Tymet in the US), and aggressively providing new services in the UK.[22] Cable and Wireless, also privatized in the early 1980s (continuing an earlier cycle of privatization in 1929 and renationalization in 1946), began building the most ambitious network in the world, a fibre-optic network linking Japan, South-East Asia, the US and Europe to its UK subsidiary, Mercury.

In West Germany the debate about communications networks has reflected local conditions, the peculiar, guaranteed position of the Deutsches Bundespost (DBP) in the Federal Constitution (the *Grundgesetz* or Basic Law) and the polity's commitment to more corporatist and consensual policy making. The Kommission für den Ausbau des technischen Kommunicationssystems (KtK) report in 1976 set off a series of detailed public inquiries and expert commissions, special party congresses and debates which have resulted in limited moves towards deregulation (promoted by the 1987 Witte report) alongside a continuing commitment to the social goals of regulation.[23] The expert commissions recommended a series of experiments in *Bildschirmtext* (videotext), cable television and fibre optics. Much of the debate in Germany has also focused on issues of privacy and the protection of the individual against the state. Resistance to deregulation has been led by the Bundespost, which remains the largest single employer in Europe. The DBP has successfully protected its role as the guardian of transition to the communications society, notably in high-profile experiments such as BIGFON (a large videoconferencing network), BERKOM (a broadband network in Berlin) and the promotion of ISDN. The need to protect the DBP's financial viability for investment in ISDN weighed heavily against any more radical liberalization.

France has been the classic example of 'dirigisme' in communications. The best-selling Nora–Minc report *The Computerization of Society*,[24] commissioned by Giscard d'Estaing and completed in 1976, was the first step in a series of bold moves to counter what its authors saw as the overwhelming threat to national sovereignty posed by IBM. Nora and Minc favoured a European PTT cartel to oppose IBM. Within France, the report set off a string of initiatives aimed at boosting the domestic communications industry and the *filière électronique*. Priority was also given to acquainting the population with information technologies. The report wrote that 'there is no spontaneity without regulation and no regulation without a hierarchical system', suggesting the need for a strong state to achieve its goals. In the *étatist* tradition this programme has already transformed France's telephone system from one of the most backward of the industrialized world into probably the most modern. The Direction Générale des Télécommunications (DGT) accumulated enormous debts in modernizing its network, in giving away five million Minitels terminals (at a cost of around $220 each),[25] in creating the Transpac packet switched network and more recently in offering ISDN services in conjunction with user groups.[26] In each case supply largely preceded demand: infrastructural provision was used as a catalyst to generate new uses and new services. The 1982 Plan Cable proposed to cable the whole country with fibre optics, though it fell far short of its objectives.[27] As in West Germany the PTT, now France Télécom, successfully positioned itself as the main medium for national plans, forged alliances with local powers and sponsored experimental schemes such as the fibre-optic cabling of Biarritz, and 'technopolises' such as Sophia Antipolis near Nice.

Of all the industrialized countries it is Japan which has probably had the most coherent and successful programme of all, aiming to achieve the *johoka shakai* or information society through a process embedded within its traditions of negotiation, planning and consensus in industrial policy. Their origins reach back to the state's role in introducing the telegraph soon after the Meiji restoration. Yoneji Masuda, among others, successfully argued for over twenty years that the creation of an information society should be a primary goal for government and industry. Much of the strategy was outlined in a 1971 report, the 'Plan for an Information Society', and in a series of articles and books dating back to the early 1960s. MITI's *johoka* or informationalization policies formed part of the 'dynamic comparative advantage' policy whereby Japanese industry has moved into knowledge-intensive sectors ahead of the rest of the world. *Johoka* was particularly attractive in the late 1960s as a way of avoiding the pollution endemic to Japanese industry while simultaneously escaping new competitors like Taiwan and South Korea. Alongside consensus, institutional conflict has also been pervasive: the *johoka* programme had to bridge the gap between telecommunications, a relatively inefficient domestic service industry, and the dynamic export industries, a gap that was reflected in government in the tensions between the MPT and MITI. Deregulation allowed companies, particularly the large trading companies like Mitsubishi and Mitsui, which had previously been excluded from NTT's purchasing, to enter the communications field, often in collaboration with overseas companies like IBM and AT&T.

Institutional tensions have not impeded the launch of ambitious experimental schemes such as MPT's Tama New Town project, the Higashi-Ikoma (Hi-Ovis) experiment and the Teletopia plan, each designed to pave the way for the wired city or *yusen toshi*.[28] In the early 1980s the Technopolis project was launched, with the goal of building dozens of knowledge industry cities around the country, cities which would bring together government, academia and private industry, to achieve a critical mass of innovation and creativity. Partly because of the size of the large electronics companies, MITI's role is not as central as it was in the past; nevertheless, following its tradition of targeting key sectors and technologies, eight companies were brought together to collaborate in the fifth-generation computing project managed by ICOT (Institute for New Generation Computer Technology) to develop parallel processing, artificial intelligence and non-numeric logic programming into a major industry for the next century. Sometimes in parallel and sometimes in competition with MITI, NTT has pursued its own plans to build the Information Network System, to provide a high-capacity digital infrastructure for voice, data, video and other services, on which it plans to spend up to $200 bn during the 1990s. As in every country, narrow political considerations also play a part. The ruling Liberal Democratic Party's commitment to large-scale infrastructural spending is in part a reflection of its financial dependence on the big contractors responsible for digging up roads and building microwave towers.

A very different approach has been taken in Sweden, a country notable for having one of the highest telephone penetration rates in the world and one of the communications industry's most successful companies, Ericcson. Sweden is also notable in that its PTT, Televerket, does not have a legal monopoly, and in that it combines high quality and low tariffs. Since 1980 Televerket has been subject to a law enforcing competitive international purchasing, forcing domestic manufacturers to compete.[29] The gradual introduction of competition into advanced services, mobile communications and terminal equipment, under the socialist government, offers a case-study in controlled liberalization, designed to foster more advanced services without jeopardizing the social commitments of Televerket.[30]

While national governments have taken the lead in developing industrial plans, transnational agencies are also beginning to play a role. Much the most important is the European Commission with its attempt to implement a coordinated European plan for communications. The plan links advanced collaborative research in the 1 bn ECU (European Currency Unit) RACE project on broadband communications networks, the STAR regional programme to enhance communications infrastructures in less developed regions around the Mediterranean, and moves towards the harmonization of regulation in such areas as VANS, common approvals procedures for equipment and common standards setting through ETSI, the European Telecommunication Standards Institute.[31] The European high technology research initiatives, ESPRIT and EUREKA, have also mobilized several billion ECUs for collaborative work on the leading edge of information technology. Each of these must be seen in the context of the EC's plan to create an open internal market by 1992, and its belief that the existence of an open and transparent communications infrastructure will be essential if European companies are to compete with the US and Japan. Collaborative work has also begun on key technologies including semiconductors, HDTV and advanced switches. Compared with Japan or France the EC lacks the density of institutions and links, and the history of common interests between PTTs, equipment manufacturers and key ministries which gives the more coherent national plans their power. Nevertheless the EC's work is another symptom of the perceived need for some overall planning functions to pave the way to new networks and to promote productivity growth. Only a body like the EC is in a position to engage in that 'organization of knowledge', the creation of networks linking technologists, manufacturers and users, out of which successful innovation flows. In their different ways each of the plans is evidence of the dynamism of political institutions, a reassertion of the historically close links between advanced industries and state patronage.

Beneath the appearance of bold plans, however, there remains considerable uncertainty as to whether plans retain any real meaning. Part of the problem lies in defining what constitutes a national economic entity. European governments, for example, have proved markedly incapable of reducing the power of IBM, the single dominant power in the world information industry. Within each country's borders national IBM subsidiaries employ large numbers of people (over 100,000 in the EC), contribute to balance of payments surpluses, and inevitably figure in any national plans for exploiting information technologies. For any government the cost of exerting control too forcibly is the permanent removal of investment. European telecommunications companies have also tended to follow the economic logic of forging links with US and Japanese counterparts rather than the political logic of pan-European stategies.[32] Similar boundary problems hampered the US government. Moves to protect the US semiconductor industry from Japanese encroachment, such as the block on Fujitsu's attempted purchase of Fairchild in 1987, were fatally compromised by the fact that large sections of the US industry had already made strategic alliances with Japan. Excessively rigid controls on trade hit US companies as hard as Japanese ones. NEC makes memory chips in California, Hitachi in Texas, while US companies make them in Japan. Globalization of finance too makes it hard to define what is an American or a British company: both exist within a network of matrix, displaced and therefore removed from control.

Similar problems face the governments of less developed countries seeking to maintain some control over national economies. The achievement of marginal successes in gaining control over the exploitation of natural resources merely emphasizes that the real terrain of struggle has moved on. The communication of data across national boundaries, much of it highly sensitive information about economic conditions and resources, has proved virtually uncontrollable. Once a country is integrated within the global communications network, whether through the private networks of transnationals or the public networks of the PTTs, the costs of monitoring and controlling communications become prohibitive. Only a handful of the larger countries, notably Brazil and India, have managed to maintain a degree of control over their own information economies through the resolute, and costly, pursuit of self-sufficiency. Brazil, for example, controls access to all foreign data bases and protects a domestic computer industry as well as running its own videotex system.[33] Like India it runs remote sensing satellites to compete with the American Landsat and the French SPOT. The weakness of the less developed countries becomes apparent in the fora of the ITU in which they have a nominal majority, but lack either the resources to exploit it or the incentive to concern themselves with technologies which they may not use for many decades. While the ITU devotes its resources to the ISDN, no Africa, Latin American or continental Asian countries (with the exception of South Korea) have announced any plans to implement it. The main role of the non-OECD countries has been in providing labour pools for manufacturing the equipment of communications networks (Brazil, Philippines and Korea), for keying data (Barbados, Philippines), and for editing and typesetting material produced in the First World (India and Pakistan).

Restrictive Regulation

The proliferation of national and regional plans represents a return to an earlier era before communications companies had come to be seen as dangerously powerful behemoths. By the turn of the century it had become clear that there was a need to defend the public interest against the possible abuse of power by monopolies and near-monopolies. In most countries the task of regulation was merged with executive functions within the government department responsible for the PTT. In the US, regulation as it is understood today grew up as an adjunct to anti-trust law. The struggle to constrain the abuse of power by monopolies and large corporations at times took on a high profile. It is worth recalling Roosevelt's words on accepting nomination in 1936: 'the age of machinery and of railroads, of steam and electricity, the telegraph and the radio; mass production, mass distribution – all of these combined to bring forward a new civilization and with it a new problem for those who remain free. For out of this new modern civilization economic royalists carved new dynasties . . . they created a new despotism and wrapped it in robes of legal sanction.'[34]

The ostensible role of regulation was to constrain this new despotism. Its methods were restrictive, setting limits on rates of return on capital, on prices that could be charged and on the markets that telephone companies could enter. Two types of restriction balanced each other: restrictions preventing the monopolists from abusing their power or entering other markets were balanced by restrictions preventing competitive entry by outsiders. It is this structure which is usually referred to as regulation and counterposed to the movement towards deregulation. Deregulation is generally held to involve the removal of both types of regulation. On the one hand monopoly network operators are given more freedom to move into neighbouring sectors such as broadcasting, computing and information services; on the other, competitive entry is permitted into some or all of their formerly protected markets. In practice, the process has been less simple than this. Since many PTTs were run as government departments some have needed to create formal structures of regulation, such as independent regulatory bodies, at the same time as they liberalize markets: deregulation has been better described as deregulation. This is why the US experience has been so important: it provides the clearest model of a division of roles between an independent regulator the (FCC) and the operators of the network (AT&T and the various independent telephone companies).

In the US as elsewhere, restrictive regulation came to be seen as a barrier to industrial development. Frequently invoked was the argument that the restrictive approach carries costs because of the growing disjunction between national governments and international industries. Regulation has had to become just one component of economic statecraft. As early as the sixteenth century the imposition of government controls in communications could be met by a movement of capital and labour to more congenial climates. In the 1980s multinational corporations have removed data processing and corporate headquarters from countries like West Germany which maintain strict regulatory controls over telecommunications. One-third of American transnationals now maintain their European data bases in the UK and 25 per cent of Western Europe's transborder data flows pass through the UK. The implications have not been lost on other governments. In the words of one study, 'administrations are aware that multinational enterprises seek to locate their network nodes to take advantage of the most flexible regulatory environments'.[35] In Europe, rules to guarantee that network operators bought domestically produced equipment and maintained domestic control over the leading edge of telecommunications equipment reputedly led to costs 40–60 per cent above these prevailing in the more open markets of the US. In general, so the argument goes, the internationalization of the communications industries has substantially increased the costs of restrictive national regulatory control.

The international dimension suggests why for countries like the US and UK deregulation came to be seen as necessary for national survival. The US's ratio of telecommunications exports to imports fell from 2.9 in 1965 to 0.5 in 1985, while Britain's fell from 3.6 to 1.0 during the same period.[36] Japan's overwhelming share of world electronic consumer goods export markets (85 per cent in 1985), is being matched in telecommunications, where its share rose from 8 per cent in 1965 to 34 per cent in 1985. Newly industrialized countries are also making rapid inroads into First World markets. Korea has targeted telecommunications equipment, and sectors such as PBXs, LANs and fibre optics, following the Japanese model of government-funded research centres, working in collaboration with major companies like Daewoo and Goldstar. In the USA and UK it was argued that unless domestic firms were exposed to the full blast of competition they would be unable to remain competitive in international markets.[37]

Similar arguments have been made in Europe, linking the need for deregulation to industrial policies for domestic computing and equipment manufacturers. Traditionally European PTTs maintained close links with domestic manufacturers. Although this made Europe no different from the US and Japan where equipment markets were dominated by three or four suppliers (or in Japan's case by the so-called DenDen family), because of the differences in scale it proved a much more serious fetter on their success in international markets. Companies like Siemens, Thomson, GEC, Plessey, AEG, CGE and ICL were all supported as favoured 'national champions' through government purchasing and investment policies. During the 1960s and 1970s these policies undoubtedly helped preserve domestic control and avoid dependence on the much larger foreign producers such as IT&T or Ericsson and now AT&T. By the 1980s the costs of autonomy were becoming prohibitive. Rising capital costs and shorter lead times for new generations of technology made it hard for relatively small European companies serving national markets to survive.[38] To learn how to operate on the world market they were seen to need the pressure of competition within their home market, pressure which could prove destructive. As the UK and USA had shown, this could be a difficult tightrope to walk. By 1986 the UK and USA had trade deficits in computing and communications of $2.2 bn and $3.4 bn respectively. The beneficial impact of competition proved inseparable from its costs: the tendency to manufacture more foreign products under licence, lower research and development spending and shorter time horizons.

From Restrictive to Arbitrating Regulation in the US

Deregulation of communications is widely and correctly seen as an American export. Through AT&T, the US had previously provided a model of the efficient, regulated monopoly telecommunications provider and it continues to account for 40 per cent of the global telecommunications market. Because of its size it exercises an enormous influence on policies and decision making throughout the world.

If there has been one consistent feature of deregulation both in the US and elsewhere, it has been the pivotal role of the large corporate users. Within any market large users prefer to have competing suppliers to guarantee competitive costs and responsive service. If large capitalism's defining characteristic is the ability to choose, its characteristic political struggles seek to win the right to choose. For the large corporate users the right to choose whether to use AT&T's service and equipment was inseparable from their material interest in avoiding what they saw as cross-subsidies to residential telephone users.[39] There is considerable doubt as to the true existence of cross-subsidies.[40] The important point is that new microwave, satellite and fibre-optic technologies made it possible to build cheap alternatives to the monopoly network. As costs fell newer networks could offer services more cheaply than old ones. At the same time the significance of communications costs raised its profile from that of a cost (like energy or water) to that of a strategic tool. Together these factors prompted large users to mobilize the power which accrues when 1 per cent of users can account for as much as 33 per cent of telephone company revenues. Their ability to exercise market power in a deregulated environment has also been proved in transport, where 50 per cent of rail traffic and 40–80 per cent of motor carrier traffic in the US is now carried under secret contract rates benefiting large users.[41]

Each of the key decisions in the deregulation of US networks gave large users more flexibility and control. The Carterphone decision, which in 1968 permitted an acoustical coupling device linking a private network to the AT&T system; the 'Above 890' authorization of independent transmission networks for specialized uses by car manufacturers, oil companies, retailers and others that was agreed in 1959; the 'Open Skies' satellite policy in 1972, which liberalized the satellite industry; and the three 'Computer Inquiries', all extended the sphere of competition first in customer premises equipment and private networks, and later in packet networks, private satellite services and long distance.[42] AT&T's divestiture of its local telephone companies, agreed in the Modified Final Judgement overseen by Judge Greene, freed it to devote its resources to providing integrated and specialized services to large business customers, a field which it believed would in the long run prove more profitable than the mundane operation of local networks.

The actual process of deregulation was both lengthy and stormy. What now looks like an inevitable process of liberalization often seemed chaotic at the time, shaped by the peculiarities of the division of powers in American politics and the whims of judges. Moreover, contrary to popular perceptions, the key deregulations in the US preceded the revival of right-wing economic theory and the political ascendancy of Reaganism. Complex political battles involving shifting coalitions shaped the actual course of deregulation: often the large users were not the decisive actors. General Electric and Control Data, for example, played major roles in representing small users as they themselves worked to fill the niche for specialized networks and data bases. Relatively small companies fought involved legal and political battles often as surrogates for much larger financial interests to carve an economic base out of deregulatory rulings.[43] MCI, originally intended by the FCC to provide private services to corporations, exploited the position to carve out a role as a competing public long distance carrier. The most visible battle, that between the Justice Department and AT&T, excluded the large users entirely.[44]

The large users' main goals of lower prices, better services and greater control could be met through two complementary routes: legal and political strategies to remove the structures supporting cross-subsidy on the one hand; corporate strategies to use the bypass of the network as an economic lever on AT&T on the other. Since IBM, oil companies and utilities pioneered the first private networks in the 1940s and 1950s bypass has taken many forms. Private networks for voice signals within a company and closed user systems, such as airlines reservation systems, generally used lines leased from AT&T (see chapter 11). More recently companies have built their own fully private systems using microwave, satellite links, fibre optics, PBXs, LANs and teleports. Private networks were able to take advantage of the price differentiation between leased lines and long-distance calls to abritrage and resell space to third parties. IBM's SBS (Satellite Business Systems) began by providing a specialized service to business users in 1980, but instead evolved as the first real competitor to AT&T's cable-based network. By the end of the 1980s bypass had become a major industry. One of the most prominent examples is the New York Teleport joint venture of Western Union and Merril Lynch, which provides fibre-optic links from Wall Street and lower Manhattan to satellite earth stations in Staten Island, completely bypassing the local public network.

Bypass is relatively insignificant in the context of the whole network. In the US in 1987, 99.9 per cent of all long distance traffic, generated by

99.9999 per cent of customers, continued to be carried entirely or in part by the public networks run by Regional Bell Operating Companies (RBOCs).[45] Physical bypass of the network accounted for only 250 million minutes of use each year compared to 170 billion carried by the RBOCs. The significance of bypass lies not in its relative weight but in its dynamic impact on the public network. Within the dominant operator bypass provides a rationale for reallocating resources to meet the needs of large corporate users. The network operators soon find they share the large users' interest in a 'rebalancing' of prices, so as to stop bypass reducing public carriers' revenues and their ability to exploit economies of scale in network design and operation. This now familiar pattern of liberalization of rules on bypass prompting a reorientation of the public network towards corporate users began in the US in the wake of the FCC 'Above 890' decision in 1959. In response AT&T offered discounts for bulk leasing of private lines and introduced the WATS tariff service for large users of long distance. In retrospect AT&T overreacted and underpriced its services for business. Nevertheless this pattern has been repeated ever since, in the US and elsewhere: the greatest impact of deregulation and competition is less the entry of new competitors than the transformation of the erstwhile monopoly. The unbalanced distribution of telecommunications usage has always created openings for market segmentation and price discrimination.[46] Deregulation has allowed much fuller exploitation of these differences: AT&T for example now offers varying packages of service, from those for occasional residential users to large users of special services such as the Software Defined Network, MegaCom and Tariff 12.

Although large users have been the primary beneficiaries of US regulation, they alone do not explain it. Deregulation also reflected a deep shift in the perspectives of government. Whereas in the past the FCC laid down standards for new technologies and had to be persuaded of their value for the public interest, the prevailing view now is that technologies are deemed 'innocent until proved guilty' and that governments are practically incapable of determining which will prove either viable or socially valuable. Instead, it is argued, the market should decide which succeed and which fail and should determine the standards under which they operate. A similar view was taken by the UK MacDonald Committee report on the future of the communications infrastructure.[47] In part this is an ideological shift: the deregulators see themselves as cutters of red tape and enemies of inert bureaucracy. But it can also be understood as an inevitable response to the complexities resulting from industry convergence. The simultaneous decisions to drop IBM's anti-trust suit and break up AT&T in 1983 signalled that thenceforth both would be operating in the same, much larger and more complex industry. Without deregulation, this new level of complexity, combined with the proliferation of new technologies, would have massively overburdened any regulatory system. Under the traditional procedures there would, quite simply, have been too many difficult decisions to be taken.

Complexity is hard to avoid. Although it was predicted that deregulation would allow companies to move resources away from the 'political marketplace' towards the economic marketplace, this has not in fact happened. Communication remains highly politicized, each decision to deregulate or reregulate actively contested by shifting coalitions seeking to exploit the various governmental agencies involved in setting the shape of the regulatory environment.

The massive economic pressures on the US and UK to stem eroding competitiveness have already been mentioned. They are complicated by the interpenetration of the national economy by overseas companies. These pressures have quickly had an impact on regulators, forcing them to reconceive the nature of their task: regulators like Oftel and the FCC, and others like Judge Greene, have increasingly had to justify their actions in terms of national competitiveness. As this has happened, a profound theoretical tension has arisen between economic theories and practices concerned with national competitiveness in an open market and the traditional models of regulation, concerned with such things as rates of return, economies of scale and monopoly, all of which conceive of the telecommunications network as a self-contained, closed system. All forms of regulation, whether of markets or of biological systems, involve both the management of internal relationships, and the terms on which exchanges are made with an external environment. The sponsoring types of regulation can be conceived as ways of injecting new resources into the system, chronic trade deficits as ways of taking them out. The evolving thinking on regulation has attempted to reconcile these two aspects of the system. Each move towards introducing greater competition into networks has been predicated on a belief that greater internal competitiveness, and a more effective structuring of competition, would lead to greater competitiveness for national companies operating in external markets.

Regulation and Structured Competition

Traditionally, the main tool for controlling AT&T was the use of rate of return regulation, which kept returns within a narrow band by adjusting tariffs. Similar controls were applied to nationalized companies like British Telecom which had to meet targets for returns on capital. This approach has been widely discredited for its bluntness, for its failure to reward efficiency and for the 'gold-plating' it fosters as companies over-invest as the only way of increasing profits. A similar pattern in railway regulation is reflected in the palatial late nineteenth-century railway stations of many American cities. Economic theorists argued that competition would prove a more effective tool for sustaining 'reasonable' tariffs and returns, while also freeing AT&T (and BT) to perform a global role. Competition would gradually replace restrictive controls, offering the discipline of the market in place of the discipline of the regulation, order and decree. Competition is seen as particularly important in a rapidly changing and expanding industry, which stands to benefit from what Hayek described as 'competition as a discovery procedure': the benefits of innovation and dynamism outweigh the costs of duplication and waste.

The introduction of competition in the network depended on a theoretical assault on the traditional view that the whole of the telecommunications network, like the railways and other networks, formed a natural monopoly.[48] This view had been one of the main arguments for regulation. Instead, it was argued, changing cost structures and technologies made competition viable in certain parts of the network, while ultimately only the free working of market forces could answer the empirical question of which parts of the network are naturally monopolistic. The question of natural monopoly hinges on the extent of economies of scale and scope. According to the influential contestability theory (largely developed by economists associated with AT&T), a monopoly is sustainable if there is a set of prices which can both repay the monopolist's costs and discourage competition. If there are low entry and exit costs the latent threat of competition could act as a surrogate regulatory pressure on the monopoly forcing it to behave as if in a competitive market.[49] Even if a competitor gained only a small share of the market the desired effects would still obtain.

There are few unambiguous answers as to the nature of economies in the network, or as to the contestability and sustainability of telecommunications monopolies.[50] According to some analysts, switching and transmission technologies are becoming increasingly modular, reducing the significance of economies. Others argue that digital integration and intelligent networking create a new impetus for scale economies which could be undermined by competition.[51] An equally confused picture exists in equipment markets. Although economies in fields such as switch manufacture have clearly risen, other data communications equipment sectors such as modems and multiplexers sustain small companies serving niches. Experience has clearly shown the scope for competition in customer equipment and value added services.

In long-distance services the viability of companies like MCI and US Sprint is less clear: each initially lost heavily in competition with AT&T's

more extensive network, which retains an overwhelming share of the market (by 1988 MCI had roughly 9 per cent of switched telephony and US Sprint, roughly 4 per cent). In Japan by 1990 there were three carriers providing network infrastructures in competition with NTT on the most lucrative intercity routes. Their true viability is hard to judge, since they were indirectly subsidized by the absence of access charges and by rules preventing NTT from lowering its prices. NTT still retained 98.9 per cent of the leased line market. Entry and exit costs in telecommunications networks remain high, as evidenced by the huge capital write-offs of United and GTE in the US, by AT&T's write-off of $20 bn of investment in analogue systems between 1984 and 1989 and by IBM's absorption of debt (estimated at several hundred million dollars) from the failed Satellite Business Systems venture.

These figures are reminders that telecommunications is a heavy industry, characterized by large investments and slow depreciations. For all the surface glamour of new technologies, change is slow. Long-term trends tend to outweigh the short-term effects of changing policies, as in the case of productivity where liberalizations and privatizations have had little discernible effect. The productivity records of both NTT and British Telecom have simply continued their long-term secular trend. In the US, too, through all the policy changes, telecommunications has continued to experience a steady, rapid growth in capital per person employed.[52]

In the US, UK and Japan competition has had to be encouraged. Excessive competition could undermine the accumulation of capital and investment in research; inadequate competition would inflate prices and remove the incentive to innovate. All newly deregulated markets include very large, experienced companies such as AT&T, BT, NTT and the divested Regional Bell Operating Companies. Dominant companies can exploit their economies of scale and scope and knowledge of customers, and can manipulate prices to squeeze out competitors. Even the most ardent free marketeers recognize the onus on the state to maintain the conditions for competition by supporting competitors against erstwhile monopolies.

There is a long history of state intervention to preserve 'fair' competition in communications. In Britain in the mid-nineteenth century it was widely believed that telegraph companies used their power manipulatively, for example in the maintenance of exclusive contracts with news agencies such as Reuters. This abuse of market power led to a vocal campaign by the press, especially the smaller newspapers, against the 'arbitrary and despotic' management of the telegraph and contributed to the telegraph being handed over to the Post Office in 1868 on condition that it took no further part in news gathering. Their inherent economies of scale have always made the communications industries conducive to monopoly. Many countries have 'fair competition' rules in the press, subsidies for start-ups or for the use of newsprint, and, as in France, common carriage distribution systems. In each case the aim is to lower barriers to entry as as to discourage monopoly. In the US, a string of anti-trust cases involving communications has dominated the history of communications networks. Examples include the separation of the ABC radio network from NBC, a succession of cases against AT&T which prevented the company from entering computing and eventually resulted in divestiture, and the failed anti-trust suit against IBM which ran from 1969 to 1982.

Regulation and Variety

Deregulation in no way ends the role of government. Instead government and its agencies become arbiters, continually redefining the parameters of competition and the distinctions between naturally competitive and monopolistic activities. W. Ross Ashby's famous principle that a controlling system must have as much variety as the system it seeks to control has been vindicated.[53] Attempts to simplify regulation through the use of price caps, for example, have simply resulted in other parameters, such as profitability or quality of service, moving out of line. The maintenance of multi-dimensional competition appears to depend on multi-dimensional controls on price, interconnection rules, technology standards and access to markets. However much they might wish to remove their own *raison d'être*, regulatory agencies continue to police boundaries and arbitrate. One inescapable reason is that the terms of interconnection are necessarily arbitrary: there is no objective measure for the true or fair cost of access to a network or the creation of a gateway between several networks. Instead, a desired end, such as the maintenance of competition, depends on the regulator's use of arbitrary tools in an arbitrary situation. An open and competitive communications environment appears to depend on the continued presence of a regulator to structure competition.

This role is inevitably bound up with the changing nature of technologies. One of the most persistent problems of regulation has been the definition of the boundaries between the basic transmission functions of the network and the enhanced or value added services that overlie it.[54] In the past transmission tended to be seen as a natural monopoly, while services were seen as more naturally competitive. After thirty years of attempts to define boundaries it has become clear that there can be no unequivocal technological answer to the problem. For example, when two incompatible computers communicate over a network, their protocols must be converted or translated in order to make communication possible. Although this is a basic requirement of transmission and can now be embedded within the network's switches, it involves the processing of information. A service such as this, once considered a rare premium service, can make a rapid transition to become basic. In different countries definitions tend to follow a mixture of historical precedent and political bargaining. Boundaries between the basic transmission of bits and their processing blur even more in advanced broadband networks, as routeing and other functions become embedded in the same complex software packages.

Common Carriage

One focus for the reconciliation of industrial and regulatory goals has been the concept of common carriage. In principle, common carriage can guarantee fair competition and the provision of infrastructure, while also freeing dominant operators to compete overseas. Within open network models common carriage can provide an organizing principle both for competition in services and for competitive, but integrated, provision of infrastructure.

The basic principle of common carriage has a long history, going back to fourteenth-century Milan and beyond, and the Italian Tassis or Taxis family. In an early example of economies of scope they soon branched out from mail transport into human transport. Prussia set up a state-run monopoly post office in 1614. Britain followed suit in 1656, having previously used private contractors, so establishing a long tradition of state monopoly in communications. In common carriage the carrier is required by law to provide a service to all at the same price. The same principle has been used for taxis, bridges and utilities. In communications common carriage implies that the carrier must exercise no control over the messages it carries.

Common carriers have generally been subject to restrictive regulations preventing them either from discriminating in favour of their own services, or from cross-subsidizing other operations from the common carriage monopoly. In telecommunications rules of fair competition ensure that the operator provides common carriage at common prices to all potential users. Rather than simply defining the terms whereby messages are carried, common carriage rules now shape the terms of access and interconnection to the network. The French Minitel network is an example of a new form of common carriage. The PTT acts as a common carrier, providing an infrastructure, electronic gateways, common billing, and menu functions (in particular the 'kiosk' system which saves users from having to subscribe for individual services).[55] At no point does the PTT intervene in the context of services.

Common carriage principles can also be used in the distribution of video signals. At present cable systems are not subject to common carriage rules, retaining instead the right to shape channels and services as they see fit. When broadcasting systems were first set up, common carriage was rejected in favour of the idea of broadcasters as regulated publishers, usually bound by some idea of public service. When spectrum and channel capacity become limitless, however, as might be the case with fibre-optic broadband networks, common carriage becomes a feasible way of organizing broadcasting, with the network carrying signals regardless of content for those able to pay the price.

In the UK this model was recommended by the 1986 Peacock Committee as a way of guaranteeing a free market in broadcasting.[56] Instead of financing television through licence fees and advertising, viewers would be able to pay directly for the programmes they wanted. Programme providers would simply use the network as they might the postal service. Although the recommendation was rejected, it remains a possible model for the future, combining the technical virtues of integrated networks with limits on the power of the network operator, diversity in programming with light regulation.[57]

Open Networks and the Future of Regulation

Redefined for a world of advanced networks, common carriage is providing a model for regulating networks that takes the arbitrating approach to its logical conclusions. These methods, based around the concept of the open network, are evolving into a set of general principles for regulation. In the USA the FCC is committed to the Open Network Architecture (ONA) model for regulating the boundaries between basic and enhanced services, while the EC is proposing Open Network Provision (ONP) as a foundation for a pan-European telecommunications market after 1992. Both are interesting as models, since they propose the very detailed regulation of highly fluid and competitive industries. Both are also significant as they suggest how regulation could adapt to 'denationalized' telecommunications networks run by transnational corporations.

The essence of open network models is the idea that the basic services offered by a network can and should be provided in a modular and open manner to anyone, whether an end user or a seller of advanced services. The network takes on the character of a common property, a collection of resources of intelligence and transmission. Open network models also make another promise, that different networks can be integrated without needing to be owned by a single monopolist.

Both ONA and ONP are designed to produce a multi-dimensional approach to guaranteeing the terms of common carriage: they involve rules relating to technical conditions, prices and conditions of use. They can also be understood as attempts to answer the challenge of two powerful trends in communications networks: the parallel push towards integration and common broadband or ISDN infrastructures and the trend towards specialized, decentralized networks under fragmented ownership and control. The two trends overlap around the terms on which networks and machines interlink, which involve issues of technical compatibility, pricing and knowledge about future developments.

Historically ONA arose out of the FCC's failed attempts to draw a line between basic and enhanced, monopoly and competitive services. Its third Computer Inquiry concluded that open network models would be able to achieve what the previous 'structural separations' could not: a competitive and 'level playing field' between the dominant companies and much smaller competitors. Competition could be achieved without telecommunications fragmenting into a myriad of incompatible networks.

The US Department of Justice defined ONA as permitting 'all would be providers of competitive service, including the company that presently holds the bottleneck monopoly to provide service on the basis of relatively equal costs of interconnection to the bottleneck'.[58] ONA, though not strictly speaking an architecture in the sense of IBM's Systems Network Architecture, promised ultimately to structure openness into the workings of the switch, rather as restructured long-distance switches in the USA gave users a choice between different carriers. A fair allocation of costs would be guaranteed by breaking the network's services down into their 'basic service elements' which would then be priced according to cost, alongside new cost accounting rules designed to prevent cross-subsidy.

As well as making sense within the regulatory history of the FCC, open network schemes were attractive to the deregulatory economists who had become influential within the FCC. ONA promised a totally free market in telecommunications: a perfect market in which every service is broken down into its constituent parts and priced according to marginal cost principles. Many economists and technologists were intuitively hostile to the idea of the ISDN, seen as a way for PTTs and AT&T to re-establish their monopoly and dominate the field of advanced services. ONA by contrast would overcome the last monopolistic 'bottleneck' of the local switch not only for enhanced services, but also for complex, enhanced voice services. Voice telephony is no longer a single, contained service; it includes a range of possible enhancements such as call storing and forwarding, personal numbers, freephone, advanced freephone, prompting and so forth, all of which are logically enhanced or value added services.[59]

In Europe, a somewhat different history has led to similar conclusions. Open networks are seen as essential for the creation of competitive markets for terminal equipment and telecommunication services right across Europe; these in turn are seen as essential elements in the economic survival of all sectors of the European economy after the creation of the internal market in 1992. Open network provision (ONP) was first announced in the 1987 EC Green Paper which set the framework for the creation of an integrated telecommunications market within the EC.[60] It argued that the EC would 'have to develop common principles regarding the general conditions for the provision of the network infrastructure by the Telecommunications Administrations to users and competitive service providers, in particular for transfrontier provision'. ONP would allow private companies to offer value added services on the same terms throughout the European Community, reconciling the maintenance of PTT monopoly over the physical infrastructure with a commitment to competition in services.[61] As in the US, open network rules could be seen as historic compromises, both between the regulator (or the European Commission) and PTTs, and between the latter and their larger private users.

Putting ONA and ONP into practice proved extremely complex, belying the idea that deregulation would bring a simplification of the state's role. Instead a series of heated debates arose over the exact terms of access to switches (for example, whether competitors would be able to load software into the PTT's switches), over the precise nature of the basic elements of the network, and over tariffing rules. It was initially thought that open networks would usher in the 'privatization of regulation', since the public sector was rapidly falling behind the private sector in its understanding of the complex technical and economic issues. According to the FCC, the ONA process 'most appropriately should occur in the private sector, where interested parties can participate in the development of ONAs that are suited to specific enhanced and basic service markets'. Regulation would be replaced by self-regulation even though in asymmetric industries, dominated by very large carriers, the idea of self-regulation is an odd one.

The long-term implications of open network models remain unclear. Theoretically they could give users access to network control channels, conferring enormous choice, power and control on organizations with sufficient computing resources. Making the network a common resource necessarily leaves the network operator with less control, not only over signals but also over such things as tariff structures. This is one of the deep political issues that lie one step beyond open network schemes, a question of which entities will ultimately control the switches, the flows of signals and thus the evolution of the network.

In the mean time open network models will emerge as just one more element in the economic competition between the world's leading powers, as they ensure that networks are exploited to the full in the evolution of new forms of economic life. State regulation and control will be primarily subordinated to this requirement, intensively regulating industries to construct the most appropriate competitive environment. It is this shift which ensures that the long tradition of state involvement in communications will survive even if its earlier supports, such as the various theories of public interest, fall into disrepair. It is this shift which continues to give momentum to the deregulatory process even if many of its promises (such as lower prices and better services for the comsumer) fail to be delivered.

8

Communicative Values

The Economics of Information

In the space of ten years after the end of World War II a dramatic cluster of breakthroughs transformed the ways in which information had been understood, revealing it to be as fundamental to the make-up of the universe as matter and energy. The Shannon–Weaver theory of information,[1] the advent of cybernetics and systems theory, the discovery of DNA, and the invention of the transistor and the computer focused attention on the manipulation of information, its characteristic modes of replication, selection and transformation. Information came to be seen as present in all organized structures. With this focus on information came a new interest in understanding processes of selection, adaptation and control.

Despite flirtations with systems theory, the study of economics resisted this intellectual revolution. Its concepts and structures remain essentially Newtonian, reflecting the eighteenth-century world of equilibria, of mechanically interlinked sectors, and of processes that are reversible in time.[2] While carrying the outmoded baggage of the physical sciences, economics also failed to reflect the insights of the social sciences. Unlike the other social sciences, economics still tends to seek ahistorical laws and universal regularities to map, model and manipulate with sophisticated mathematical tools.

These methodological deficiencies have impeded economics as it tentatively grapples with the evolution of an economy dependent on flows of information and knowledge. Economics has been much better at modelling information in the abstract than at understanding the structures within which it is used. Often it has simply seemed to wish to ignore the challenge posed by a world in which material and non-material values increasingly merge. Its approaches to consumption remain far cruder than those of anthropologists and cultural theorists who have been quicker to understand the role of identity and difference in consumption, the use of goods as bearers of messages. It has found it hard to model an economy in which the distinctions between supply and demand dissolve, as users gain control over the nature of services (as on advanced telecommunications networks) and as they participate in customizing products. More fundamentally, too, economics remains wedded to concepts such as relative scarcity and marginal cost which break down in the world of non-material production and exchange.

These deep theoretical problems have not impeded the emergence of a fully fledged discipline of information economics, with large numbers of publications, scholarly journals, conferences and research projects. Information economics is a prestigious and confident field. It has mapped out its own history, starting from the studies of information and uncertainty in markets carried out by Frank Knight and Friedrich Hayek. The general aim has been to modify the classic idea of equilibrium, perfect information and perfect competition, and to model the behaviour of the economy either as a system of computation, in which prices act as sophisticated message bearers between consumers and producers or as an imperfect informational machine, following Hayek's argument that only a few have correct information and gain a monopoly profit as their reward, and that it is precisely the absence of perfect information that gives the market its dynamism.

During the 1970s and 1980s the emphasis on the nature of information within markets moved to the centre of economic theory. Rational expectations theories profoundly changed conceptions of how markets work, and of the effectiveness of government policies.[3] Theorists became interested in the nature of behaviour in conditions of uncertainty, of 'noisy' information and strategic interaction. Ideas such as those of the Grossman–Stiglitz paradox moved to centre stage.[4] This argued that if people believed goods to be correctly priced (as is assumed by theories of perfect competition), there would be no incentive to search for information. In the absence of demand, no information would be supplied. Grossman and others answered paradoxes of this kind by focusing on the nature of noise and of the external shocks that affects markets. George Stigler's work on search costs, the costs of finding relevant information, was also highly influential.[5] This body of work suspended the assumption of perfect information demanded by Walrasian equilibrium and applied economic analysis to the task of finding and evaluating relevant information about such things as available jobs or prices of raw materials. Information could then be treated as a commodity like any other, subject to a calculus of costs and utilities.

The analysis of information searching falls within a broader research programme into patterns of behaviour under uncertainty and into what Herbert Simon described as the 'bounded rationality' within which people come to make decisions.[6] Rather than seeing the profound uncertainty of the world as a threat to the mechanics of neoclassical equilibrium, this approach attempts to incorporate defined uncertainties within the model. A similar theoretical goal informs theories of human capital that treat knowledge and skills as embedded within people and analogous to other forms of capital. Again, underlying theories are seen as sound: the task is to extend them to other spheres. Human capital is shown to bring returns and to depreciate. In the work of Gary Becker and others education is seen as an economic investment that will generate financial returns over time.[7]

The use of neoclassical theoretical tools comprehensively to incorporate the whole field of information and knowledge is particularly associated with the name of Fritz Machlup. Machlup carried out the first major employment analysis of the information sector as well as detailed studies of the peculiar features of knowledge, software and culture as commodities, the economics of patents and copyrights, research and development.[8] Again the interest is in information as a thing rather than as a relationship.

The same is true of the economic study of organization. As early as 1931, E. A. G. Robinson had written of the ways in which coordination costs might act as a limit to the scale of the enterprise even where there were increasing economies of scale in production.[9] The idea that an organization can be defined by its flows of information also dates from this period. The economic study of organization remains concerned with the costs of coordination. The theories of the firm of Coase, Penrose and Williamson all focus on the need to minimize costs of coordination and transaction and on the trade-offs between interfirm and intrafirm exchange.[10] Institutions are analysed, in an essentially static way, as to the efficiency of their channels of communication.

Despite the sophistication of their analyses of information, questions of control, of the contexts within which information and knowledge are actually used, remain a blind spot for neoclassical economics. The space between input and output is treated as an unproblematic black box, linking the equilibrated markets within which inputs and outputs perform. When neoclassical analysis does reach inside the organization, as with transactions theory, it brings with it all the flaws of a mechanistic, static analysis. Control is conceived simply as a short-term task of coordination, a problem of routine transactions and adjustments to bring marginal variables into equilibrium. Neoclassical economics sees the economy as constrained by limits to finding and processing resources, but not by limits of coordination and control. In equilibrium models, the workings of the price system solve all relevant problems in an optimal allocation.

The more sophisticated analyses of the information economy recognize the limits to coordination and control, and that these become major targets of investment in themselves bringing productivity in the control economy into line with productivity in the wider economy of material exchange. They also point to the relationships between complexity and greater demands for coordination: as markets grow and interconnect, search costs inevitably rise. But this conception of coordination is itself limited. It excludes conflicting interests on the one hand; on the other, the dynamic properties of control in situations of uncertainty, the role of positional control. In uncertain situations positional advantage and control, the chance to exercise choice in an unknown future will often outweigh considerations of profitability and short-term coordination.

There is a simple and a complicated reason for the gaps in orthodox economics. The simple reason is that equilibrium economics is blind to time: as in a mechanical system, all changes are theoretically reversible in time. In real life time moves in only one direction; futures are uncertain and threatening. The need to hedge, to predict, pre-empt and control against unforeseen dangers is intrinsic to all strategy and behaviour. This is why concepts such as 'sustainable competitive advantage' are common in business theory, reflecting a world of asymmetric time in which firms must protect against aggressive entry, against the bargaining powers of suppliers and buyers, and the threat of unforeseen substitutes. The deeper reason why neoclassical economics resists questions of control is that they reintroduce issues of politics and purpose. Where the analysis of marginal properties unites labour, capital and commodities on a single plane of appropriate reward, approaches orientated to institutional structures and control techniques tend to disentangle the conflicting purposes of economic life. To take just one example, albeit an important one, the idea that profit maximization is a universal and unproblematic goal is called into question, revealed as only one of a repertoire of goals. These may include the stabilization of prices, maximization of market share, the goal of positioning the firm on growth phases of product cycles, or the maintenance of labour discipline which may be achieved by means, such as the artificially created crisis, which hinder the achievement of other goals. Control over the labour process or markets, or control that is used to externalize costs, can be understood both as purposive (perhaps as a route to long-term profitability) and as a contribution to positional control. Neoclassical analysis recognizes no fundamental difference between the individual entrepreneur and the multinational firm: conflicts of interest within the firm, between workers and managers, middle and top management, centre and periphery, are simply ignored.[11]

The various approaches of orthodox economics all seek to bring the dimensions of information onto a homogeneous plane of economic analysis, of directly comparable prices and utilities. But information and communication are better understood as embedded within a world of competing purposes, of asymmetric time and profound uncertainty: a world of multiple economies. As a result, the variables which can be quantified are rarely the most relevant, just as in practice the tasks of management and control remain resistant to systematization. Instead we are inevitably faced with a set of soft variables that demand a qualitative rather than a quantitative analysis. The softness of information, and its resistence to innumerable attempts at classification,[12] explains why, in George Stigler's words (written at the beginning of the 1960s), it continues to occupy 'a slum dwelling in the town of economics'.[13]

Communicative Values

The heart of the problem is the uneasy relationship between information and value. All human societies produce and exchange both material goods and services and symbolic ones. Each economy, the material one producing bread and cars, and the symbolic one producing novels, scientific theories and weather forecasts, operates with a distinct system of rules, habits, structures and flows of value, and each economy has characteristic forms of work, status and reward, time horizons of creation and decay and rules of access and openness. The two economies are also woven into each other. Material economies depend on a symbolic economy of money, on the transfer of skills and knowledge through time and space, on motivations and disciplines, all of which are essentially symbolic, cultural and informational. Conversely symbolic economies have always been dependent on technologies of communication, on books and paper, radios, cables and computers. The personal computer or video-recorder would be inconceivable without the solid material base of industrial production systems, synthetic materials and cheap disciplined labour.

In the past very different rules and priorities governed the operation of these two economies. Where the material economy was governed by material needs, subsistence and the extraction of surplus, by the workings of markets and the demands of capital accumulation, the world of symbolic production and exchange traditionally maintained a degree of autonomy from a narrowly economic logic, ruled instead by the great institutions of Church and State, by religious and artistic codes. The material economy was much more closely bound up with the economy of money and exchange, while money was seen as a corrupting intrusion into the economies of symbolic production. During the course of the twentieth century the social organization of symbolic production has undergone a massive and possibly irreversible shift, part of that change that Enzensberger described as the industrialization of the mind.[14] The symbolic economy has become much more like its material counterpart.

Information and symbols are increasingly produced within industries, sold in markets and used as means to accumulate capital. Control over information has been wrested from Church and State to become embedded within the structures of economic exchange. Even where information remains the domain of state bureaucracies, its production and dissemination must be justified in utilitarian and instrumental terms.

Value Theories

This confluence of the two economies has called into question traditional ways of thinking about value, ways which have always been beset by semantic ambiguity because the word's meaning combines a sense of relativity, where value is defined by relative scarcity and the calculus of what something can be exchanged for, with the ethical sense of intrinsic worth. In the case of information, the concepts of relative scarcity and intrinsic worth lose much of their meaning. The problem is exacerbated because the traditional view of information and communication as separate from the world of commodity production retains some of its resonance. Claims are still made and upheld for the removal of certain spheres of activity from the realm of monetary exchange: certain goods, such as the right to an education, or rights of free speech, are deemed to have a different kind of value to other goods.

Value marks the point where economics meets, albeit reluctantly, with ethics, aesthetics, anthropology, cultural analysis and politics. It is from the start an overloaded word. It should not be surprising that its semantic ambiguities, above all that between scarcity and worth, have been at the root of the many conflicting discourses of value which have succeeded Aristotle's famous distinctions between exchange and use value, and his assertion that for a transaction to be just the ratio of rewards must be equal to the ratio of contributions (a view that is echoed in a very different form in modern marginalist theories).

Following Aristotle the medieval church counterposed the *justum pretium* to the *rerum pretium* or natural price that Roman law had derived from Stoic philosophy. Prices were seen as inherently ethical, the just price as a countervailing force to the coercion that is often implicit in economic exchange. The ethical economy was both a highly regulated economy and one that continually slipped out of control. Barbara Tuchman in *The Distant Mirror* writes that: 'to ensure that no-one gained an advantage over anyone else, commercial law prohibited innovation in tools or techniques ... selling below a fixed price ... and advertising ... merchants regularly paid fines for breaking every law that concerned their business and went on as before'.[15] Despite evasions, fixed prices and rigged markets were normal up to the time of the industrial revolution.

Some idea of the just price lingers in the pricing policies of many public services to this day. Prices of transport or health are designed not to reflect costs but rather to be fair or affordable. The same principle has often held in telephone services. The pricing of telephone rental and calls has often in practice reflected what was felt to be a fair price rather than an underlying cost. The practice of charging the same prices for access in cities and rural areas reflects this too, while in the US regulation explicitly called for residential telephone services to be provided at 'affordable' prices.[16]

Conflicting value theories have proliferated since the days of the *justum pretium*. Mercantilism located value not in ethics but in the act of exchange: value was produced in a profitable sale, and could subsequently be hoarded by successful nations. In the eighteenth century a string of contradictory theories sought to give value a more scientific interpretation. An English economist, Petty, is supposed to have originated the idea of labour as the source of all value, the Physiocrats the idea that it is located in agriculture. This implied that industry could not produce 'real' value, an idea that has its counterparts today in the view that the manufacturing sector is somehow more truly productive than the service or information sector.

Labour theories of value, and particularly Marxian ones, have been handicapped by their logical need to distinguish between the price of labour, and thus the prices of all commodities, and their value. Given this starting point it has proved impossible to quantify values and to track their movements between different sectors. These same problems have also weakened recent attempts to update labour theories to account for information and knowledge based economies.[17] Marx himself had written of the likelihood that the worker would 'step to the side of the production process instead of being its chief actor' as the source of profit became the private accumulation of 'accumulated social knowledge'. The largely socialized production of knowledge by educators, technicians, scientists and planners becomes the primary source of value which is subsequently appropriated privately. Rather than commodities being produced by means of other commodities, knowledge workers bring free knowledge and turn it into the artificially scarce forms of the copyrighted text and the patented product.

The purpose of labour theories is to explain the world, rather than to create a tool for controlling it. In this sense they suffer from being both accurate and analytically useless: clearly nothing of economic value can be produced without intellectual or manual labour. The problem is to create an analytically useful theory to track the web of connections which link past and present labour and the very different kinds of labour embodied in complex products. In the case of information, for example, products such as computer software can be almost infinitely reproduced at very little cost. The relationship between labour input and the value of the final product dissolves. Similarly in the case of creative work there can be no minimum socially necessary labour needed to invent a new superconducting material or to write a novel.

In each of the value theories mentioned so far, value is treated as a constitutive phenomenon in the Kantian sense, one that is distinguishable from the epiphenomena of price. Value is embedded in the workings of the real world rather than being an analytical construct that is projected onto the world. For classical economics it is the hidden reality which alone can explain the long-term behaviour of the surface phenomena of price and profit. Value has a single, identifiable source, whether in exchange, agriculture or labour. Following on from the theories of J. B. Say, modern neoclassical economics is based on a similar view, understanding value as a subjective and individual phenomenon of utilities and revealed preferences. Value derives from the individual's calculus of pleasure and pain, a subjective, cardinal and measurable calculus. As such, value ceases to be a question of ethics or justness; prices are by definition just since they reward marginal contributions.

Accounting for Information

According to Paul Lazarsfeld every society keeps the records most relevant for its major values. We could take this a step further. Every society keeps the records that it can use. In the various techniques used to understand investment, depreciation, the allocation and apportionment of costs and, above all, profit, what matters are usefulness and comparability. Hence the compromise of economic theory, tradition and ad hoc pragmatism in accounting's attempts to bring order to the fluid and unstable flow of money through processes of production and exchange. Order makes control possible. Weber justifiably claimed that double-entry book-keeping was one of the pre-eminent inventions of the Renaissance. National Income Accounting too was an essential tool for macroeconomic management while, more recently, input–output techniques have provided complex tools for the control of physical flows.

The analysis of informational and communicative values has proved much harder. They are harder to map over time because of the innumerable factors that devalue information, and harder to make commensurate across space. New technologies are inherently destabilizing, since they accelerate rates of devaluation of machines, buildings and skills. Informational technologies seem to do this with particular force.

Within a capitalist economy the prime role of accountancy is to find the true sources of profit and value. As such it develops in parallel with new systems of production. To take just one example, an accounting approach that stresses the need to use all resources as close to capacity as possible breaks down in just-in-time systems. Equally, accounting must reflect appropriate time scales: the time needed to develop, market and upgrade a new computer operating system requires project-based accounting systems that are often at odds with the demands of external accounting for regular profit and loss accounts, balance sheets and cash flows.

But although it faces pressures to evolve, accountancy is generally conservative and cautious, favouring quantities over qualities, real prices over estimated values. Accountancy's analysis of depreciation, for example, designed for investment in physical machines, simply avoids the problem of investment in abstract forms of knowledge. In current accounting practice, information, software and databases are treated as operational costs rather than as assets which show up on balance sheets. Human assets such as knowledge, ingenuity or loyalty are also seen as problematic and, therefore, strictly speaking valueless.

Accountancy shares the weakness of all discourses of value, whether theoretical or practical. All seek a single set of homogeneous quantifiers, a unified and simple realm into which can be compressed the heterogeneity of millions of different goods, services, monies and forms of labour. For the theorists the aim is to grasp the real dynamics of economic life, while for the accountant the aim is to create consistent tools for accountability both externally and within organizations. Preprocessing makes value manipulable. All homogeneous schemes which make everything commensurable are, however, vulnerable to the criticism that they mimic in theory the faults of an economic system that knows the price of everything and the value of nothing. 'True' value by contrast has many dimensions combining utility, aesthetics and ethics.

The homogeneous schemes are also flawed because they situate information at the wrong level. Information is, in an important sense, meta-economic and thus not reducible to it. Klaus Krippendorf has written that in input–output tables

information participates in the process by changing the table. It may change the transition function within one cell (e.g. when information is geared towards a more efficient organization of the process), it may change the interaction between cells otherwise considered independent (e.g. when industries etc become more informed about each other and coordinate their production and consumption) or it may add new cells, rows or columns (e.g. when information introduces new technologies). In such an analysis information is seen to be about or superordinate to the economy. It guides, controls and rearranges the economic activities and has, hence, the characteristic of a meta-economic quantity that cannot easily be built into a system of analysis that is essentially flat and provides no opportunity for self-reference.[18]

Information and Value: The Limits of Communication

Economics is founded on the concept of scarcity. Value relates relative scarcity to utilities. Yet information is almost never scarce in this sense. Useful or inspiring information may be hard to find, but the barriers are ones of organization and structure rather than of available quantities. Theoretical knowledge, long recognized as one of the driving forces behind economic change, is another example. There may be scarcities of people with Ph.D.s and artificial scarcities sustained by patents law, but there is no scarcity of plasma physics or biochemical knowledge.

Currently dominant economic theories were developed in a world of physical production. Inputs of labour, capital and raw materials produce physical outputs. Each can be subdivided into its constituent elements, and each can be mapped along continuous cost curves. In the case of information there are few stable production functions and no easy subdivisions. Marginal costs of reproduction tend to zero. Economies of scale are potentially enormous. The same product can take many different physical forms.

These problems are well known and limit the utility of economics. But it remains important not to lose sight of the basic use of economics as a means of using limited resources to meet ends. The world of communications is still bounded by limits. For people there are the limits of audibility and intelligibility. There are the physical limits of channel capacity, first theorized by Claude Shannon in his equations describing the limits to the communication of information over a noisy channel. The limits are a function both of the physical bandwidth of a medium and of how information is communicated. Shannon's theory emphasizes the importance of logical structures of intelligibility – the information content of a message is defined in terms of the improbability of a particular letter or word. Through this approach Shannon hinted at the social nature of communication; the transfer of information depends on shared languages, shared formats and shared ideas about what kinds of messages are likely. Value is seen to derive from the nature of the communicative circuit, a labour both of transmission and of reception. Value formation 'for information commodities is guided by conditions of scarcity related to the information transfer structure of communication channels'.[19] The approach is thus sensitive to the fact that a small amount of information can be rich in meaning.

A second set of limits concerns the usability of what is communicated, the structures within which communication takes place. Telephone networks only become useful when there are dispersed companies, bureaucracies, friendship and family networks, packet switched networks when there are dispersed computers which need to communicate. Information becomes meaningful when it is located in a specific place and time in relation to real needs and powers. This has become increasingly apparent as the volume of flows of information grows. Greater flows of information have brought diminishing returns. According to a study by the Japanese telephone company NTT the percentage of information disseminated that is actually useful has declined from 11 per cent in 1970 to around 5 per cent in the late 1980s. This universal experience has fostered attempts to discover how artificial intelligence in all its forms can be exploited to select and order information, to think heuristically rather than mechanically and thus turn quantity into quality. The faculty to select and ignore is also being developed within the human mind. It is estimated that the average US household watches seven hours of television each day and sees 1,600 advertising images of which only twelve are responded to: people in 'information-rich' environments develop a remarkable ability to filter.

The question of usability is relevant to control. Information is most easily used when it is consistently formatted and structured. Quantities are more easily used than more subjective or qualitative kinds of communication. Control requires less energy and expenditure when its parameters are predictable. This general rule helps to explain the huge and continuing investments in finding ways to make communications and decisions routine, whether through invoicing systems or programmed trading. The notion of usability also helps to explain why a company like Lexis, provider of videotex legal data, copyrights not the laws, which are in the public domain, but rather its page breaks. The value it offers is the ability to search and index, the structuring of information that makes it useful.

A third set of limits arises from the position of communicational activities within a larger economy of monies and commodities. The production of culture, knowledge and inventions has been threatened by continually rising costs as productivity rises more quickly in other sectors of the economy less dependent on labour. This 'cost-disease' was theorized by William Baumol, in an extension of his famous theory of the artistic deficit which argued that the theatre and other arts would face continually rising costs as productivity rose elsewhere. In the extended model Baumol showed that costs in sectors such as television production and computer software, both of which depend on a mix of advanced hardware and skilled labour, will tend to match those of the most labour-intensive sectors in which productivity is most stagnant.[20] As the application of software in factories and offices displaces labour and reduces costs, so it inevitably increases its own relative cost, creating a fetter to its own development. Networks and information technologies can be used to overcome these limits: Electronic News Gathering and automated cameras can increase productivity in broadcasting and expert systems can incorporate the knowledge and working procedures of experts in such fields as organic chemistry or medicine. Software engineering and the use of standardized subroutines can be used to industrialize what is currently a craft industry, and to replace intuitive work with mathematical rigour, while in the longer run more complex artificial intelligence applications have the potential to rationalize and restructure large sections of professional life. But dependence on creative human labour, a dependence that brings with it inevitable symptoms of cost disease, shows no signs of diminishing. Moreover, the more that complex networks interconnect, the greater is the dependence on problem-solving abilities in systems design and integration.

A fourth set of limits derives from other people's use of information. Much of the highly structured information bought and sold over networks is characterized by shrinking half-lives: the time it takes for a piece of information to halve in value.[21] This period is gradually falling as links become more instantaneous, rendering a piece of commodity or financial information that is a few hours old as valueless as a month-old newspaper.[22]

Value and Productivity

Unifying and preprocessing techniques exist because they simplify control. Investment decisions are easier to make if they can be based on apparently hard, quantifiable market research and cost predictions. An unpredictable and chaotic world can be made to appear controllable. The appearance of techniques and languages systematically to control flows of values and goods is characteristic of modern economies. Value comes to be conceived in terms of flows: as a product is developed, passing through different branches of the organization, value is progressively added. Models can be devised that map information flows as if they were analogous to physical ones.[23] Within the economic chain value can be seen to accrue through the successive links of information collection and creation, processing, storage and distribution.

The view of value as a product of processes that add value is distinctive of a society familiar with the idea of productivity, an idea that can be applied to everything from education to warfare. This is a relatively new perspective. From neolithic times to the industrial revolution economic value could be appropriated in one of only two ways: through the zero sum games of conquest and booty or through the struggle to achieve a surplus from nature by hunting, gathering and cultivating. In both cases value was associated with physical products and was extracted either from the soil or from enemies. Merchants might trade goods for profit and might invest surpluses in primitive industry such as mining but, because control could not be reliably exercised over time or space, the chains linking commodities and money inevitably remained short. The idea of processing a set of materials through a productive chain, of adding value at each stage, was not understood. This idea of productivity has its roots in the industrial revolution and in the mobilization of powers of discipline and control. At each stage of a productive chain criteria of productivity can be applied, tasks can be broken down and reconfigured, the flows of materials monitored, timed and speeded up. Much of the economic history of the last 150 years concerns the growing mastery over time through the discourses of accounting, production engineering, Taylorism and industrial management, ergonomics and market research. Today, in relation to information and communications technologies, questions of productivity focus on such things as the rationalization of existing processes (for example cutting the 70 per cent of computer output which is rekeyed into other computers), the elimination of waste (of time, materials, capital), and the elimination of error (such as those estimated to be contained in at least 50 per cent of complex documents such as bills of lading[24]).

The idea of productivity has two less obvious offspring. One is the possibility of abundance: the positive sum game of productivity has no intrinsic limit. Through the expansion of productive resources, the economy can render economics, the study of scarcity, redundant. This idea was common to Marx and to much nineteenth-century utopian thought. Both capitalism and socialism share a weakness for fecund, abundant utopias free from ecological or economic limits. In our own time these ideas have reappeared in visions of technological and informational abundance: automation plus scientific progress in conservation promises abundance in consumer goods, while the possibility of endless-ly, costlessly replicating information and knowledge promises an abundance of creativity and solutions, and the boundless amplification of human intelligence. Alongside faith in abundance stands the idea that natural cycles of birth and decay can be overcome; that control and productivity can be society's perpetual motion machines.

The second, latent implication of productivity, is the idea of a greatly expanded realm of choice and flexibility in production. The scope for experiment in extractive processes is very limited and very risky. Subsistence farming, like mining, was for long a gamble against nature. With industrialization and the emergence of what William Connolly has described as a culture of productivity,[25] change and innovation become central structuring principles of production. The notion of natural limits to the game, set either by nature or by the available stock of wealth to plunder, is replaced by an idea of infinitely flexible, extendable value. Just as a society experiencing abundance would have transcended the idea of price, so a malleable production system escapes the simple lines linking inputs of labour and materials to the value of output. Both effects of productivity can be linked to knowledge. The endless accumulation of knowledge offers the means for endless growth in productivity.

The Contradiction between Commodities and Knowledge

Knowledge and creativity are hard to control. Their sources of value are as indeterminate as the values they produce. The principles of control learned in industry have little to offer in the domain of intellectual work. Taylorism involves, almost by definition, the separation of intellectual labour from all other tasks, though there are in practice many routine tasks in the laboratory or the production studio which can be Taylorized and automated. The classic examples include Carl Duisberg at Bayer and Hollywood just before World War I. In general, effective control of the creation of knowledge or creative values requires quite different modes of organization. Creativity depends on experiment and error, on the irrational and the unthought, and on the ability to combine apparently incongruous elements into a new whole. It depends also on social structure, both at a macro level and at a micro level in the ways that people work together, 'acting-with' in Shoshanna Zuboff's phrase. The systematic production of codified knowledge, which Daniel Bell has described as the key resource of post-industrial societies, also depends on an environment able to absorb, adapt and use it. It rests on a communicative structure, usually combining the university, the academic discipline, the trade journal, producers and users.[26] The history of invention and innovation certainly indicates that usage structures have been as important as the availability of resources or the ingenuity of inventors. The Egyptian aeolipile and the Greek computer (the Antikythera device) are just two famous examples of inventions that found no resonance within their environment.

The communications industry played a pivotal role in the emergence of structures of systematic research and diffusion. According to J. D. Bernal, the 'telegraph companies and later cable and telephone companies were the first purely scientific commercial enterprises'.[27] Value was seen to reside not only in control of labour and of the physical world but also in control of knowledge. Vail's AT&T used its patents to establish a monopoly in telephony, fighting over 600 suits against infringement. When the patents ran out in the 1890s it sought instead to 'occupy the field' through the systematic production of inventions. When it failed to produce the key breakthroughs it simply bought them.[28] Large-scale scientific production became the source of industrial dominance, as evidenced by the statistics which show the percentage of patents held by individuals in the USA to have fallen from 81.7 per cent in 1900 to 23 per cent in the early 1970s. For the modern corporation 'scientific knowledge has become a strategic tool for company planners, a way of guiding them towards future products and markets, if possible ahead of rival companies and countries'.[29] Direct investment in research laboratories parallels systematic sponsorship of academic institutions.

The exploitation of knowledge as a source of value depends on careful engineering, a mix of a loose creative environment and tight appropriation of what is produced. The knowledge that is shared goes far beyond that which can be defined by patents. Indeed an 'almost universal error of high technology policy is the assumption that it is scientific and technical information which is most highly valued ... of much more value, and much harder to procure, is the stuff of which learning curves are made, knowledge gained through practical experience of rendering the technical commercial'.[30] The need to create structures within which knowledge of this kind can flow explains why the construction of networks and investment in new technologies has been paralleled by an intensive competition between states seeking to create an appropriate environment for knowledge creation, whether through technopolises (as in Japan's plans for 55 information cities and 128 teletopias[31]), science parks, or long-term finance of a scientific community (as in the US). This public spending is justified by orthodox economic theory. According to Kenneth Arrow:

we expect a free enterprise economy to underinvest in invention and research (as compared with an ideal) because it is risky, because the product can be appropriated only to a limited extent and because of increasing returns in use. This underinvestment will be greater for more basic research ... for optimal allocation to invention it would be necessary for the Government or some other agency not governed by profit and loss criteria to finance research and invention.[32]

Arrow's comment highlights the importance of being able to control and appropriate knowledge. Without control there is no incentive for investment. In theory patents offer control, as do the laws surrounding trade secrets. In practice, many patents can be 'invented' around, and the legal costs of protection can be substantial (in MacDonald and Kimbel's words both society and inventor cheat, 'society providing protection that is rarely effective, and the inventor revealing as little information as possible about his invention'[33]). As with all knowledge there is a tendency to slip from the private to the public domain. All trade secrets are vulnerable once a product is sold on the market, rather as the act of publishing renders the cultural product vulnerable to illicit use. These problems are effects of the shift in the nature of knowledge away from its origins in experience and teaching, towards its modern status as something that is codified and separate from the person. It is a shift that makes knowledge more like other informational commodities, more footloose and harder to control. The implicit knowledge of a craft worker or an individual scientist is, by contrast, less fluid and less easy to steal. For similar reasons, in trade it is better to sell goods than the knowledge to make goods.

The problems of appropriation and control lead to many of the characteristic strategies of the late twentieth century. The many forms of corporate alliance, of 'user lock-in' and continual adaptation, are all partial solutions. At the level of a society the solutions are harder to find: any resolution of the contradiction between viewing knowledge in terms of economic values and the traditional view of knowledge as having a different type of value to other goods must be moral and political as well as practical. Leon Wofsey of Berkeley has articulated the conflicts: 'the business of business is to make money ... and the mode is secrecy, a proprietary control of information and the fruits of research. The motive force of the university is the pursuit of knowledge, and the mode is open exchange of ideas and the unrestricted publication of results and research.'[34] The greater emphasis on limiting and controlling knowledge goes against the grain of the creative and open environment. According to the computer scientist Michael Dertouzos, 'the [US] Government has become increasingly preoccupied with possible leaks of research to military adversaries and commercial competitors ... However because of the freedom that much research requires, this trend towards increased management could do far more to damage innovation than to accomplish the intended goals.'[35] A similar problem often afflicts governments. Mary Cheh writes that 'some government administrators and policy makers believe that knowledge should be hoarded and traded like any other commodity'.[36] Instead efficient innovation depends on extensive flows and exchange of information, as is recognized by the many firms which deliberately circumvent the rigidities of patents systems.[37]

A fertile knowledge economy rests on communities of knowledge in which cooperation, argument, the sharing and stealing of ideas can all take place. Innovation tends to arise out of networks, from marketing and production as much as basic research. It is no coincidence that the two most famous centres of high technology production in the US, Silicon Valley and Route 128, grew around universities and not around the huge concentrations of knowledge workers who worked for the rigid hierarchies of AT&T and Bell Labs in New Jersey and IBM in New York State.

The knowledge economy is an open system: neither its inputs nor its outputs can be entirely commodified and controlled. This may also help to explain the USSR's relative failure, despite having over a third more people working in research and development in the 1980s than the US, a failure that is more often explained in terms of the separation of research and production.

Culture, Identity and Value

Culture brings another dimension to the question of value. Cultural consumption is itself communicative; it is good to think with and good to communicate with. The values of commodities exist within a space of interconnected social difference and distinction, where individual utility and identity are inseparable from those of other individuals. This economy of difference and distinction is inherently social; pleasures and meanings are bound up with those of other people.[38]

Economic activity has always been concerned as much with meaning as with matter and quantity. Polanyi wrote that the 'monks traded for religious reasons and monasteries became the largest trading establishments in Europe . . . The Kula trade of the Trobriand Islanders, one of the most intricate barter arrangements known to man, is primarily an aesthetic pursuit . . . with the Kwakiutl, the chief aim of industry seems to be to satisfy a point of honour.'[39] Today, the characteristic modern commodity is surrounded by a 'second shell', its packaging in meanings, associations and identities that is now as important a value added as its traditional utility.[40] Goods and services can be creatively bundled into packages that are more than the sum of their parts; they can be 'editorialized' like a pure cultural commodity or redefined so that what is sold is a relationship rather than a utility. Product designers and market researchers are trained to conceive of commodities not as a single dimension of utility and price but rather as elements within clusters of consumption, lifestyles within which goods become meaningful. Rather than simply pursuing the maximization of a narrowly conceived value so as to widen the gap between revenues and costs, the principle is rather to pursue the fecund heterogeneity of values.

If it is hard to model the value of the information being used or consumed it is also hard to model how it should be priced. This has long been understood in the electronic media, and in the record and book industries where pricing is generally strategic rather than based on underlying costs. In broadcasting the traditional economic structure reflected the absence of any link between use and payment, value and prices. The rationale for financing broadcasting through licence fees, advertising or taxes was its public-good nature: signals could not be made exclusive, and additional users could be reached at zero marginal cost. As a result, broadcasting was sold at zero price and financed through systems which took no account of use.[41]

Fluid Values in Telecommunications

Telecommunications has also been continually buffeted by the problem of accurately describing costs and providing an objective basis for pricing decisions.[42] Even with dedicated networks like the telegraph there was little objective guide for pricing, other than the limit of needing to cover short-run variable costs. With integrated networks like the ISDN, merging different kinds of signal onto the same networks, objective criteria disappear almost entirely. Costs are largely fixed, and once capacity is installed the costs of using the network are relatively low: the marginal cost of carrying signals tends to zero. Even in older networks the idea of a marginal cost is very imperfect: marginal costs are usually almost zero, but when demand is at a peak they become very high, perhaps as much as $100 for a single telephone call since this is, strictly speaking, the cost of additional capacity.

With supercomputers and optical technologies scarcity becomes largely irrelevant. There may be scarcities of software writers or superfast chips but the capacity to communicate is abundant. Within the new networks based on advanced packet-switching techniques, the idea of the margin disappears altogether as capacity is almost limitless and switches are designed not to block. Proposals for mesh topologies, for flattened pyramids of switching and control, are only possible because the scarcity constraints that previously required concentration of traffic and switching no longer hold. As in culture and the production of knowledge, there is no clear relationship between the value of the network to the user and the costs of providing it. Moreover setting prices for interconnection of more than one network becomes almost entirely arbitrary.[43] This absence of any clear relationship between costs and values has been reflected in the common carriage rules governing telegraph and telephone networks. Unlike common carriers in transport, both recognize only the value of the physical message rather than the value of the information that is contained in them.

It should be clear by now that in the world of information and communication values, prices and costs bear only a loose relationship to each other. The costs of producing a song or a piece of computer software bear little or no relation to the extent and nature of use. In some cases value is maximized by diffusion, in others by scarcity: use of knowledge may destroy its value but does not destroy the knowledge itself. What is valuable to one person will be valueless to another. Moreover information's value merges imperceptibly with that of material objects. In Porat's famous study of the information economy, for example, it was estimated that nearly 50 per cent of the value of a typical pharmaceutical product was accounted for by its informational content.[44]

This discussion of the problems endemic to communication and value has a common theme. It is that value is becoming more rather than less fluid as new technologies are used to reshape the forms of economic life. The widespread view that communications technologies are bringing everything within a single sphere of exchange and replacing qualities with quantities, turns out to be misleading.

The political philosopher Michael Walzer has written that 'every social good or set of goods constitutes, as it were, a distributive sphere within which only certain criteria and arrangements are appropriated'.[45] At different times scarcities of physical strength, of family reputation, of money, of land or of knowledge have been the key social scarcities, the one social good that is privileged over all others. Today it is capital, in both its financial and cultural forms that plays this role. Yet even its values are by no means fixed.[46] One of the interesting social struggles likely to be endemic to 'information societies' is that between those with informational capitals and those with economic capitals over the appropriate rates of exchange.

Arguments about the nature of value, like arguments about taste, cannot be resolved through rational argument, since they are arguments about hierarchies of ends, and since 'real' value is necessarily heterogeneous and contested. Walzer's argument serves as a reminder that, rather than simply being a vehicle for monetization, technological change can also call into question the power of money as a universal medium of exchange, a universal quantifier that breaks into every sphere of life. Instead the scope for arbitrary decisions, for strategies of blocked exchanges, for strategies of quality rather than quantity, is if anything greater in societies based on knowledge and communication.

9

Standardization and Flexibility

All communication depends on standards. Common agreement on words, grammars and formats creates the scope for infinite variety in the contents of communication. In art, too, rigid 'grammars' often turn out to be the precondition for the greatest achievements of imagination and creativity. A similar idea is gaining ground in economic life. Rather than pursuing ever greater standardization, the mass production of similar goods for similar markets, modularization and standardization are used to sustain flexible and differentiated products and services. Nowhere has this been more true than in communication, where the standard services of telegraphy and telephony have given way to differentiated services, networks and softwares that use standards as a tool for diversity.

Standardization is one of the things that makes industrial civilization work. It underpinned mass production of cars, clothes and consumer goods. Standardization and interchangeability of parts, standard measurements and statistical methods permitted greater control over the production process and the realization of economies of scale; without them the division of labour and the management of complex flows of materials would be impossible. Standardization is a form of preprocessing, a homogenization of heterogeneous things that makes them easier to manipulate. The same principle applies throughout the economic chain. Standard job descriptions and conditions simplify the task of organizing labour; standard package sizes simplify distribution and retailing. Standardization reduces the work the buyer has to put into judging the quality of the product: the problem of quality control is removed from the eye and judgement of the buyer and integrated within production, in the form of statistical quality-control methods to ensure that quality falls within a given range.

Standardization is a common tool of rational, control-orientated societies: it simplifies and brings order, releasing energies for other tasks. To this extent standardization is more than the dull agent of conformity: it is also essential for flexibility and diversity. Napoleonic decimal measuring systems, time zones, lines of longitude and latitude, and national currencies all made possible greater complexity in the organization of things. Within areas of rapid advance, such as information technology, standards also play an additional role. They become the means for organizing change as technologies change continuously in bursts of innovation and slower periods of modification. Some have used the Kuhnian model of scientific revolution to analyse technological change. In the early, 'pre-paradigmatic' periods of development of a technology varying solutions compete, until a single version, a Model T Ford, an IBM System/360 or PC emerges as dominant. Once this happens economies of scale and learning become more important than superior design. The cycle of competition and consolidation is particularly marked in network systems such as electricity and communications. Seen from this perspective standards, whether de facto or de jure, freeze change so that the complex, fluid reality of varying technologies can be telescoped into widely applicable forms.

Standards are public goods by Samuelson's definition: they are available for use by all, and use by one does not reduce what is available to others.[1] The economists' interest in standards first arose from the need to rationalize the incompatible electric and rail networks in the nineteenth and early twentieth century. According to Paul David, network technologies are characterized by technical interrelations and 'network integration effects', which make standards particularly important if the benefits that result from increasing the number of users are to be realized.[2] For all technologies there are some advantages to be gained from the economies of scale and the reduction of risk associated with a standard. With a standard light bulb, telephone or tape measure the user need not fear obsolescence and incompatibility. Conversely, standards lock the user into dependence on forces beyond direct control. There will nearly always be a cost associated with adopting a standard designed for the typical, rather than the individual user.

The earliest standards, even before those set by artisanal guilds, referred to money. Currencies provide a universal, interchangeable and standard medium for exchange, often with overt standards for the purity of metals. During the move from barter systems to systems using national or local currencies the trade-offs of power and autonomy are those of all forms of network: the benefits of widened access, choice and interchangeability come together with a loss of control as prices are now determined less by local custom, supply and demand conditions than by those of the larger economy encompassed by the currency.

Standards exist in many industries, covering everything from nuts and bolts to electicity outlets. An early example of network standards was the imposition of Stephenson's 4 ft 8 in. railway gauge in place of Brunel's alternative in the Railway Gauge Act of 1846. The standard is believed to have been designed to reflect the width of the rear end of a Norfolk mule used to pull coal wagons.[3] The Great Western Railway claimed its 5 ft gauge to be superior, offering a smoother and safer ride, and only finally yielded to the standard in the 1890s. In Australia, different states used their own incompatible gauges until the middle of this century, forcing most long-distance trade to use the sea. The particular importance of standards for network industries was also seen in electricity, where it was estimated that at the time of World War I, Britain had seventy electricity generating companies using fifty different systems of supply, twenty-four different voltages and ten frequencies. Cities and engineers chose their own specifications with pride, rather like architects. Competition in standards was one of the institutional factors that prevented Britain from building on its early lead in electrical power technologies. In the US, by contrast, Westinghouse and General Electric, having defeated Edison's DC technologies, together created a much more homogeneous system based on polyphase ACs; in tram networks too the US adopted a single overhead system.

Standards have never been innocent or purely technical. They have been used as a form of discreet (and indeed indiscreet) trade protection and became an important part of the 1970s 'Tokyo-round' of GATT negotiations. They have also served as tools of corporate strategy and governmental industrial policy. Because of this political dimension orthodox economics has proved ill-suited to describing the dynamics of standards processes; the economists' assumption of optimality offers little insight. Metaphors drawn from sociology or anthropology often seem more appropriate, with histories of crowd behaviour, leadership, tribalism, sabotage and subversion to describe the evolution of standards. Standards battles can be better explained with the language of politics, coalitions, battles, persuasion and cajoling.

The history of standards is not one of superior standards overcoming inferior ones. Rather it is one of small tactical advantages having a cumulative impact, an effect of positive feedback as costs fall and learning-by-doing increases demand for one standard rather than another. In determining which standards succeed control over markets has been more important than competition through price or quality. In this sense the history of standards parallels that of innovations in general. In a seminal paper on the history of innovations, David Teece[4] analysed why some firms failed to exploit their own innovations (EMI and the Computer Axial Tomography (CAT) scanner, R. C. Crown and canned cola, Xerox and office computers), and why other companies had succeeded through imitation, as IBM did with the personal computer. According to Teece, organizational superiority enabled latecomers to exploit the loose appropriability of the innovation even where the price and quality of their product was inferior. In the crystallization of standards, too, logistics have often proved more important than technical ingenuity.

It is not hard to understand why standards are particularly important to industries concerned with communication. Communication depends on reciprocity, on shared languages and modes of address. Demand for new services is interdependent.[5] As the density and dispersal of communications technologies has increased so the social irrationality of incompatible standards has become more apparent. Telecommunications organizations have long recognized this. In order to send a letter or telegraph across borders standard addressing, voltage levels, coding and charging methods are needed. Standardization, for example to permit international direct dialling, has been the main task of the ITU throughout its history. The more interconnections there are, the more standards are indispensable. Without standards the trend towards extending networks, and perhaps more important, towards linking different networks, is impeded. In the communications industry standards turn private goods into public goods. A telephone network has many of the characteristics of a public good. A personal computer, by contrast, is a private good whose benefits are directly realized by its user. A network of personal computers on the other hand, linked because of the existence of common standards, begins to take on the character of a public good.

The economic costs of non-compatibility and non-communication have become most acute in computing, with the proliferation of networks of smaller computers using distributed processing. According to Rob Wilmott of ICL, the world's computer industries made an 'illicit' annual profit of \$18 bn from incompatible standards which forced users to duplicate hardware and software. The social interest in interconnectivity clashed with the private interest in incompatibility. Medium-sized companies maximized compatibility within their own product ranges while minimizing the scope for interconnection with other brands. IBM, the dominant company, used its control of de facto standards to limit the scope for modular hardware. By selling, or rather renting, an interdependent system it was better able to control pricing: its resistance to standards such as ASCII (American Standard Code for Information Interchange) was designed to make it harder for competing companies to sell modular add-ons to IBM systems. The software industry is particularly notorious for its incompatible standards and for its 'angry orphans', those customers locked into use of an obsolete product. Some standards have been legislated – ANSI (American National Standards Institute) Fortran is one example – but by and large the computing industry has followed proprietary standards which are treated as private property controlled by copyright.

Communication between two or more computers is never simple. Any computer is itself a complex communications network, which passes information between memory, central processing unit, input and output devices, operating and applications systems. As such it depends on common rules for coding and decoding electronic information, for deciding which combinations of bits constitute a letter or full stop, an instruction to multiply or to store a piece of information. Hardware, operating systems and applications must be compatible with each other if they are to work. This complex interdependence is exacerbated when computers are networked.

The cost of incompatibility for users is that a machine or program is artificially constrained as to its possible uses. In the worst case, no more software can be bought to run on a piece of hardware. The costs of inadequate standards setting are highly visible in other areas, notably the video sector, where millions of consumers owning Sony Betamax machines have been left with an obsolescent new technology, increasingly excluded from rental markets. Owners of quadrophonic hi-fi are unable to buy quadrophonic records or tapes. In colour television three incompatible standards coexist, requiring expensive conversion procedures for anyone wishing to sell programmes overseas. High-definition television (HDTV), the current focus of standards setting in broadcasting, may be introduced with standards which are not 'downwardly compatible', so that those without special sets will be unable to watch HDTV broadcast programmes.

The classic strategy for companies involved in providing networks and networked services has been to use monopoly power to limit interconnection. Strategies of this kind have a long history. In the first decade of the twentieth century Marconi exploited its dominant position in radio systems by ordering its radio operators not to respond to signals from non-Marconi machines. The 1906 Berlin conference on international radio standards (which agreed the SOS distress signal among other things) was an early political response to this abuse of corporate power. In the early days of adding machines IBM used eighty-column punch cards with rectangular holes in competition with Remington Rand's ninety-column cards with round holes; both benefited from this limit on competition. In the second half of the century IBM, with roughly half the world market for computer hardware, overwhelmingly dominated standards setting and used its power to limit the scope for machine to machine connections. Only in the mid-1970s did IBM begin systematic work on encouraging compatibility between different machines within its own product range, and only in the late 1980s, under competitive pressure from customers and manufacturers, did it begin to design for interoperability with other brands.[6]

Standards and Externalities

The benefits of standards in communication are social. The joke about the person who bought the first telephone could equally apply to someone with a telephone incompatible with all others. In economics this value is described as a 'network externality' by which is meant the extra value conferred on the consumer by the fact that a computer can communicate with other computers, or that one VCR owner can swap tapes with another. Externalities are particularly important in networks as the value available to any node depends directly on the accessibility and compatibility of other nodes.[7] Centralized, organized standard-setting produces value for the end user which a fragmented market cannot, a socially produced value which is then privately appropriated through the market.[8] When standards are set for an industry a period of rapid growth often follows.[9] Standards also bring a series of parallel effects in supply such as low barriers to entry and enhanced competition as potential manufacturers are guaranteed a pre-existing market, economies of scale in production and lower costs through interchangeability of parts, and lower learning costs and higher value for any relevant skills learned; for example the skill of being able to use a qwerty as opposed to a Dvořák keyboard.[10] Standardization expands demand and allows manufacturers to make complementary products, such as VCRs, cassettes, portable cameras and prerecorded videos for a rental market. In their narrowest sense standards can also serve as shorthands in the manner of a dictionary defining the technical characteristics of a technology. Again, they preprocess a range of possibilities into a single form.

The benefits of compatibility and externalities came under theoretical attack in the late 1970s as part of the wider assault on bureaucratic and social forms of decision making which argued that they inhibit innovation and systematically make wrong decisions. These arguments have most force in sectors experiencing rapid technological change. By artificially freezing the flow of technological change standardization inhibits innovation and technological evolution. In place of the obsolescence faced by a consumer with an incompatible product, legislated standards can sustain whole sectors using obsolescent technologies. One famous example of the pitfalls of standards setting was the FCC's attempt to set standards for the new technology of colour television in the early 1950s. After a review of the available options a system was adopted which used a rotating wheel behind the screen. The intervention of the Korean War put the issue on ice, and by the time the FCC again considered it RCA had developed the far superior NTSC (National Television Standards Committee) system which had the added advantage of downward compatibility with existing monochrome standards. Had it not been for the war, millions of viewers would have been stuck with an obsolete technology. Later, when European countries came to set standards, they were able to opt for the PAL and SECAM systems, both markedly superior to NTSC.

Probably the most famous failed standard precedes the era of electronic communications. French revolutionary time, with twelve months of thirty days, ten-day weeks, and ten-hour days with 100 minutes to the hour survived for only two years in its pure form. Decimalization did, however, succeed, an indirect reflection of French political power just as the success of Greenwich Mean time and the US dollar standard are reflections of geopolitical domination rather than pure rationality and just as the export of NTSC, PAL and SECAM was shaped more by political than economic considerations.

Standards setting summons up an image of dull bureaucracy, caution and compromise. It exemplifies the classic bureaucratic function of fitting the exciting diversity of the real world into neat little boxes. This unattractive image was an important if unconscious factor behind the intellectual assault on standards setting. Instead of bringing order to chaos, it was argued, standards makers were forcing obsolete technologies onto unwilling consumers and constraining the process of technological innovation. Standards were a form of cartel, an anti-competitive practice fostered by regulatory agencies which had been captured by the industries they were meant to regulate. Standards setting was also seen to be extremely expensive, absorbing the time of ever more engineers and planners.

These arguments proved particularly influential within the FCC, which was itself one of the main objects of criticism. Traditionally, like similar bodies throughout the world, the FCC had set standards for all forms of broadcasting and telecommunications equipment, detailing the parameters within which the market would operate. When the FCC was called upon to decide between five different, and incompatible, standards with which to introduce stereo reception to AM radio it decided, after a five-year investigation, to let the marketplace choose. As in many other areas of regulation, it argued that the 'marketplace solution' was superior to bureaucratic decision making. Five years later two of the contenders remained in business. Only about 10 per cent of AM radio stations broadcast in stereo. Few radio sets were built with the capacity to receive AM stereo signals. By contrast, in 1961 a single standard had been set by the FCC for FM stereo, which resulted in the great majority of FM stations and receivers being redesigned to use the standard.[11]

While AM stereo may end up as an interesting historical footnote, the wider issues will not. The arguments against standards soon found a new target in ISDN, which was seen as a tool of mercantilist PTTs which would exclude US firms from European markets.[12] Conversely, in Europe OSI and ISDN standards have been justified as tools for reducing the anti-competitive dominance of IBM's proprietary standards. Throughout the communications industry standards have become a crucial weapon in the battle to control markets and technological change.

Politics of Standards

De facto and de jure standards are rarely the best available options: VHS video is technically inferior to Betamax, while many of IBM's standards (notably the PC) are inferior to those of their smaller competitors. Success depends on political and logistical muscle.

The French SECAM colour television standard offers one of the clearest examples of standards serving industrial and foreign policy. The French government's strategy was a response to an attempt by the ITU's CCIR (consultative committee for radio) to set a standard for European colour television. Many different standards had been used for black and white television, resulting in high costs for converting programmes from one to another. Three systems were available for colour television: SECAM from France, NTSC from the US and PAL from West Germany. NTSC uses 525 lines, PAL and SECAM 625. West Germany's PAL system had been developed from SECAM and combined its best qualities with those of NTSC.

The French government seized on SECAM as a means to develop its electronic industry. By offering financial inducements to communist and Third World countries France ensured that the CCIR failed to reach a consensus, despite the apparent technical superiority of PAL. Europe remains divided in two by incompatible television standards. Though French technicians might have been willing to compromise with PAL in the name of technological rationality, strategic industrial considerations were paramount. Using SECAM, France created markets for its own manufacturers and a large base for the broader *filière électronique*, while also protecting its own markets as there were now insufficient economies of scale for competitors to enter. In short, France's national interest conflicted with the wider interest of a single standard.[13] Any standard involves losses for someone, whether it be nations and manufacturers, coalitions which have invested in developing a technology, or areas of the world for which a standard is inappropriate (what is appropriate for Western Europe is often wildly inappropriate for Africa).

A similar set of struggles took place in the late 1980s over High-Definition Television (HDTV). Advances in TV technology made it possible to exercise much greater control over the television image, so that flickering and interference could be reduced and the gaps between horizontal lines minimized. Television sets began to take on the characteristics of computers, able to process and manipulate the raw signal they received, to combine images and data, to freeze frames, repeat, enlarge and simultaneously view several channels. Flat liquid crystal displays made the set less bulky. The nature of human vision favours more rectangular screens, shaped more like the cinema screen than that of the traditional television set. HDTV technologies combined these capabilities into systems capable of producing much higher-resolution images on large rectangular screens.[14]

Although there is a consensus on the general direction in which television technologies should go, there has been little agreement on the details. Any major advance in television technology is constrained by the need to reconcile the interests of manufacturers, broadcasters and viewers: each has different interests as to the amount of spectrum used for television channels, and the quality and cost of receivers. This poses substantial organizational problems. For a standard to succeed manufacturers must be persuaded of the benefits of a new market, broadcasters of the potential competitive edge a new technology can give, while users must be persuaded that the new sets represent a real breakthrough rather than a marginal one like quadrophonic hi-fi.

Japan's public service broadcasting company NHK led the way in promoting HDTV in collaboration with Sony. The NHK–Sony standard, named Hi-Vision, used 1,125 lines to produce a near-cinema-quality picture. The technology was very impressive, both as a cheaper and more flexible production medium than celluloid, and as a relatively cheap consumer item (the costs of the first generation of HDTV videorecorders and receivers were lower in real terms than the costs of black and white or colour television sets when they first went on sale). The barriers to the spread of Hi-Vision were primarily political and organizational. Manufacturers and planners in Western Europe feared another Japanese-dominated technology (by 1985 Japan had achieved an extraordinary 85 per cent share of world consumer electronics exports) and, led by Thomson and Philips and the European Commission, clubbed together behind the MAC (Multiplexed Analogue Components) series of standards, not strictly speaking an HDTV standard, but a considerable improvement on PAL and SECAM and easily upgraded to higher-definition forms. Western European countries successfully blocked its adoption as a standard by the CCIR in 1986 and again in 1990. In 1989 several firms in the US, significantly including AT&T, IBM and Apple, began to collaborate on their own HDTV standards, with the active backing of the Pentagon. The planned intervention in HDTV, though blocked by the White House, was proclaimed as a turning point, a return to overt industrial policy and cooperation as a response to the US's relative industrial decline.[15] The European and American industries repeated the SECAM arguments. Exclusion from the HDTV field would threaten exclusion from a whole range of new technologies, such as medical imaging, simulators and, perhaps most important, the chips and other components of HDTV.

Though widely used this argument has less force than it did in the 1960s. Whatever standards were set in Europe, Japanese, American and indeed Korean and Taiwanese manufacturers would remain able to produce equipment to meet them. The European offices of Toshiba and Panasonic ostentatiously committed themselves to supporting the European standards, while Philips and Thomson participated not only in the development of a US HDTV standard but also in alternative evolutons of PAL. Control of a standard does confer some leverage: JVC's decisions to withhold S-VHS licences from the newly industrialized countries mirrored the Philips/Thomson strategy to retain control through MAC patents. But it is no longer possible to use standards as a form of surrogate protection. Even with an earlier generation of technology, it is significant that RCA, which was primarily responsible for developing colour television technology, failed to capture the profits which accrued from manufacturing. The loose appropriability of the invention combined with uncompetitive manufacturing to cancel out the value of its technological lead.

Although the forces against Hi-Vision were predominantly economic and political, there were also strong technical arguments. These suggest just how hard it is to disentangle technical and non-technical issues. Perhaps the most telling argument was that any new television technology should be compatible with previous ones, so that existing television sets could be used to view HDTV broadcasts even if they could not benefit from its quality. Hi-Vision would depend on a single 'revolutionary' move. It could also be faulted for being an analogue technology (at least in part) in an era when all other forms of communications are becoming digital. It was also anachronistic in another sense. Developed before the widespread use of VLSI (Very Large Scale Integration) chips, it failed to exploit new techniques of signal compression: in its uncompressed form it needed around five traditional TV channels to carry a single channel. The use of computing to process television images (ultimately to make pictures rather than simply receiving a given image) suggested many more efficient and flexible ways of reaching the same end.

Although the CCIR had been working on HDTV standards since 1972, by 1990 it was clear it would be introduced with two or three competing standards, each reflecting a political and industrial bloc.[16] Even the Soviet Union briefly suggested that it might develop its own HDTV technology. Although there was some possibility of a common standard being agreed for production and programme exchange, broadcasters would still use incompatible standards.[17] This prospect led some to suggest that if the standards-making bodies failed to agree, the standards problem should be solved through the television receiver. An 'open architecture' receiver would use the computing power now available to television sets to convert incoming signals in any standard into a viewable form. With the evolution of artificial intelligence it would become possible to conceive of machines 'interrogating' their environment to enable them to use the appropriate standard for receiving or transmitting signals. This would be the ultimate technological solution to the failure of human institutions. It would be a solution with precedents. Where incompatible systems are in operation the use of a converter or 'gateway' technology can create compatibility for the user.[18]

The Web of Standards-setting Bodies

The task of agreeing communications standards is carried out by a tangled web of overlapping and conflicting bodies, the CCITT, CEPT (the coordinating committee of the European PTTs), ANSI and ISO, drawing on the work of thousands of experts meeting in an almost continuous stream of conferences from Rio and Geneva to Seoul. Together these bodies are taking power away from national state institutions as they prove a more efficient source of coordination.[19]

Arguably the most important is the ITU with its nominally independent organs the CCIR and CCITT dealing with radio and telecommunications standards respectively, and the International Frequency Registration Board (IFRB). The ITU is a treaty organization of 166 members (more than the United Nations) in which each country has one vote. It represents one of the most successful examples of cooperative planning on a global scale. Founded in 1865 at the instigation of Napoleon III to rule on telegraph interconnection and tariffing principles, it was a successor to the very earliest international bodies which oversaw the flow of trade along the major rivers of Europe, the Rhine and later the Danube. The ITU performed a similar function for telegraphy, guaranteeing the free flow of messages and organizing the system of tariffs and payments needed to sustain it. Radio was incorporated into its work in the 1920s.

The Third World has a nominal majority on the ITU, although in practice the economically advanced countries dominate. At the 1979 CCIR Plenary assembly, for example, nineteen out of the twenty-seven OECD countries took part, six of the ten Warsaw Pact countries and only thirty-six Third World countries out of a possible 117. In the same year, of the forty-four countries which took part in the seventeen regular

CCITT study groups only fifteen could be classified as Third World.[20] The standards process is simply too expensive for the great majority of firms and countries to participate.

In the past the ITU was dominated by the European PTTs. The US did not join for forty years, suspicious of a body made up of state-owned companies. As deregulation swept the world, however, the ITU was flexible enough to adapt to the new political economy. The private sector became increasingly influential, although it has no voting rights, and came to account for about half of the US delegation (which is much the largest). According to one trade journal, 'in the US, where this activity has been virtually completely privatized the CCITT . . . stands at the heart of the private sector infrastructure. Indeed . . . private bodies emulate the CCITT's decision making process . . . and have requested that the CCITT be the focal point for developing concepts and standards for private networks interlinking with public network facilities'.[21] This idea of the ITU as a service for the First World's private sector has never been uncontroversial: conferences on satellite and radio allocations were split down the middle between the Third and First Worlds.

While attempting to devise compromises between increasingly distant interests, the CCITT also had to speed up its sluggish bureaucratic methods. Its four-year decision-making cycles were devised in the leisurely climate of the 1920s. Just as the communications industries came to demand a faster rate of standards production, increases in the scale of the field made this harder to achieve, as it became more certain that some participants would have an interest in delay, mobilizing apparently technical arguments to retard approval of standards. By the late 1980s, the ISDN standards-setting process in the USA, for example, previously the job of one organization, AT&T, involved over 140 different organizations in the T1 committee of ANSI, the American National Standards Institute.[22] The volume of decisions also escalated. The size of the CCITT's coloured books, containing standards recommendations, doubled every four years: the 1988 Blue Book contained 16,000 pages and weighed 44 kg. The same regional and geopolitical pressures that undermined the progress of unified standards for colour television and HDTV also appeared in telecommunications. New regional bodies, the T1 committees in the US, the Telecommunications Technology Council and Pacific Basin standards group in Asia, and the European Telecommunications Standards Institute (ETSI) in Europe[23] all threatened to undermine the authority of the CCITT, recreating standards-making around regional blocs.

The second type of standards organization is explicitly based in the private sector. The International Standards Organization (based in the same Geneva road as the ITU) and the International Electrotechnical

Commission are both non-treaty organizations, again nominally organized on one member one vote principles but, in practice, dominated by private equipment manufacturers. According to *Le Monde* 'of the delegations of all countries, it is estimated that 30 per cent of the experts are employees of IBM. No other country is so well represented at the ISO.'[24] The web also includes professional bodies such as the Institution of Electrical Engineers (IEE), trade organizations, and INTUG, which represents large corporate users. As different industries converge these bodies collide. Just as different firms such as IBM, AT&T, the PTTs and manufacturers such as Siemens and NEC compete over the provision of integrated systems, so the standards bodies become strategic weapons in the struggle to define the terms of convergence. As in any negotiation they must both compete to advance the particular interest they represent and cooperate to produce the interconnectivity which all their industries demand.

Communications Standards and Convergence

Historically telecommunications and broadcast monopolies could set standards unilaterally, both de facto and de jure. This reflected the relatively closed nature of the systems they operated. Negotiation was only important to establish compatibility for international links. With the convergence of computing and telecommunications two different standards cultures collided. On one side were the highly standardized and regulated communications carriers concerned with network issues and universal provision and familiar with relatively unproblematic negotiations in the fora of the ITU. On the other was the unregulated, not to say chaotic, world of computing, massively dominated by IBM which by the mid-1970s was attempting to establish its Systems Network Architecture (SNA) as a de facto standard for data communications. Within each industry standards became tools of corporate struggle. Within computing, the conflict was that between IBM's SNA and the Open Systems Interconnect (OSI) model of the ISO; within telecommunications the struggle was between PTTs and the new competitors seeking to use standards to facilitate competition.

The dynamics of these processes are extremely complex. Market leaders like IBM traditionally used standards as a highly flexible competitive tool for sustaining market control. Alternatively, where there is no market leader the 'crowd behaviour' of an industry can take many forms: excess inertia when markets fail to shift despite evident benefits from a new technology and excess momentum when technologies are abandoned too quickly. These dynamics result from the large benefits available to those who pre-empt standards evolutions, enabling them to move up learning curves ahead of their competitors. The other side of the coin is the cost of misjudging such a move. To avoid this standards developers often license at little or no cost in order to spread standards and lessen the likelihood of being left behind. Computer manufacturers have done this by giving machinery away to universities; France successfully achieved it with SECAM; and the developers of both Betamax and VHS attempted it with the additional aim of creating a software base.

Market structures encourage complex games and strategies: large corporations act to crush superior innovations from small ones, and small ones gang up against larger ones. The most important recent example of these dynamics occurred as different parts of the industry have tried to define the terms on which it moves towards networking. This conflict was shaped by the overwhelming dominance of IBM and by its traditional use of standards as a tool of monopoly. These practices prompted two of the many anti-trust cases which have been levelled against it: one by the US Justice Department case, which was dropped by the Reagan administration in 1982; and a second by the European Commission, which was finally settled in 1985. A recent, unchallenged, example of IBM de facto standard setting is the MS-DOS software, designed by Microsoft for IBM's PC which became the effective standard for PC operating systems.

The cases against IBM focused on how it locked users into dependence: hardware and software were tied together, so that once a company had bought IBM equipment it could not switch to another manufacturer without writing off software. Those manufacturers which did produce 'plug-compatible' computers, which could operate with IBM software, both strengthened IBM's dominance and rendered themselves vulnerable to its strategic shifts. IBM was also accused of exploiting its dominance of de facto standards to announce new and non-existent models so as to confuse competitors and discourage buyers from investing in their models. In each case standards were an important tool for controlling the overall shape and direction of the computer industry.

IBM and SNA

IBM was for long criticized for the lack of compatibility between the machines it produced. This was partly a failure of internal organization. The Data Processing Division dealing with large mainframes and the General Systems Division dealing with small and medium-sized systems developed incompatible hardware and software. IBM's solution was to develop a set of standards which would allow different computers to be networked. SNA, Systems Network Architecture, was the first network architecture (and indeed coined the term), and in its earliest version was introduced in 1974, at the same time that SWIFT, SITA (Société Internationale de Télécommuncation Aéronautique) and other packet-switched networks were coming into operation. SNA was designed to help IBM's larger customers create their own private networks. It rationalized IBM's many different protocols and access methods into a consistent set of rules, logical structures, formats and protocols that is embedded in the hardware and software which IBM produces. Since 1974 the concept continually evolved. The original version permitted only centralized, tree-shaped networks with one host and terminals reflecting the rigid organizational hierarchies used by most of IBM's customers. After 1976 SNA was gradually developed to permit multiple hosts, moving in 1979 and after to more genuinely distributed arrangements.

As a standard, SNA is a classic case of an industry leader seeking to control the evolution of the industry and to maximize its own market by encouraging interconnection between different machines. SNA was designed as a proprietary standard, treated as the property of IBM, which could determine how it was used. It was also closely tied to the structure of IBM, which makes most of its profits from mainframe sales: SNA was designed before personal computers became widespread and involved sending messages up to a mainframe and back to terminals. SNA remains much the most complex and advanced network architecture, defining hardware, software, security and network management. Through its five-layer structure it is an all-encompassing model for communications, extended now to video and voice and seen by some as a possible starting point for IBM to expand to cover the whole field of communications.

The OSI Model

Despite its grip on standards, IBM failed to foresee most of the important developments in computing in the 1970s such as the importance of mini- and microcomputers, of wordprocessors and of networking. During the mid-1980s the market share of IBM competitors like DEC (Digital Equipment Corporation), which had stressed networking and interoperability, rose just as IBM's fell. Historically the computer industry had been vehemently hostile to common standards, which it viewed as constraints on imagination and innovation, inappropriate to a dynamic industry. All communications, however, depend on protocols and common languages: as computers came to resemble telecommunications systems, common languages would clearly become essential. These could either be imposed by a market leader, which could then manipulate the rest of the industry through tactical shifts, or be agreed by negotiation. The lack of standards was seen to be impeding moves towards networked automation of factories and offices. Some standards had been agreed before. During the

1960s, for example, the Cobol programming language was widely used, partly because the US government made it mandatory for government contracts. In practice, however, each company could fashion Cobol for specialized uses so that Cobol programs became incompatible.

In response to IBM's proprietary strategies the remainder of the computer industry chose the path of negotiation. In this it was backed by users wanting to share data and programs between machines and by European and Japanese interests seeking to counter IBM dominance. The chosen medium was the International Standards Organization (ISO); the task was that of developing an open, non-proprietary standard to enlarge the market for non-IBM products and to encourage the evolution towards networking. There was a widespread belief that electronic publishing had paid a heavy cost for its failure to develop common standards: the much-touted promise of easy access to all information, and easy transparent dissemination had failed to materialize. No one set of solutions developed within the market could achieve the critical mass needed to become a de facto standard. In telecommunications, ISDN was being used by the ITU as a tool for redefining and standardizing the whole range of telecommunications, which would include data communications. Rather than waiting for de facto standards to arise in the market, it was turning into a permanent planning tool acting ahead of the market, giving the standards making process an institutional, permanent form.

The Open Systems Interconnect model is the computer industry's attempt to come to terms with the convergence of computing and telecommunications. A general law of information technologies states that in design, assembly, testing and networking costs rise with complexity and complexity rises with the number of objects to be managed. This is equally true of networks (where the number of possible connections rises in proportion to the square of the number of nodes), of semiconductors and of computer systems. Coping with complexity depends on the use of hierarchy, modularity, competitive rules and standards, to bring order to an environment that continually threatens to run out of control. The OSI project, launched by the ISO in 1978, had the aim of achieving the interworking of any computer system irrespective of its manufacturer, operating system or location.

The first problem involved in setting standards is agreement on the functions needed. In computing, perhaps because the computer is essentially a universal machine, this is particularly difficult. The trade-offs and priorities of functions depend very much on the uses which are likely. This 'political' negotiating logic encouraged the technological logic of dividing the problem into layers, one physical and six logical, so that different groups could work in parallel. The seven-layer structure is a means of seeing communications as a hierarchy, a kind of theoretical preprocessing which made negotiation possible, and a reference model for standards. In principle, each layer provides its own functions and communicates with the layer below it.

Lower levels were specified first, mainly because these were needed for standardized packet-switching systems such as LANs, WANs and x.25 networks. Higher levels proved much more difficult to agree, and may never be fully standardized: instead a permanent dialogue of negotiation sets the parameters within which companies produce their own solutions. As standards are set for the higher layers, such as those for file transfers, messaging, rules of communications between terminal controllers and host computers, competing companies enhance them with optional or customized features. Progress in developing OSI has inevitably called into question its logical structure. There has been intensive debate about precisely how different functions are specified in each level and about likely uses and flaws. Real communications between computers do not neatly follow the OSI model (so that the second stage of standards setting has involved what can be called functional standardization: standardizing combinations of other OSI standards to meet particular needs).[25]

Nevertheless OSI rapidly gained ground. New institutions grew up to support OSI, notably COS (the Committee for Open Systems) in the US, SPAG (Standard Promotion Application Group) in Europe and POSI in Japan. The manufacturers and users mobilizing for consistent standards in factory automation used OSI as a model for the MAP (Manufacturing Automation Protocols) and CNMA (Communications Networks for Manufacturing Applications, used in building the European Airbus and BMW cars among others) and Boeing's TOP (Technical and Office Protocols) protocols for office automation. General Motors had found that half the cost of automating factories resulted from incompatibility. Each producer of program controllers and robots used different networking standards. Along with other large purchasers General Motors demanded that suppliers produce to common standards.

IBM was forced to revise its strategies. Its long involvement in the ISO, which in the past has been a subtle mixture of cooperation and subversion, became more positive. But though the strategies changed the purposes remain unchanged: what IBM could exploit was the relative fluidity of the ISO–OSI process. Even after they have been agreed, standards are continually revised in the light of technological change and changing uses. For any standard, there can be a number of different 'implementations'. COS and SPAG therefore organized 'conformance testing' to ensure that machines using OSI references could in practice communicate with each other. IBM's answer was to offer free testing facilities for other companies to determine whether their implementations of OSI were compatible with IBM's implementations. If they were incompatible it could be assumed that the other company would adapt, thus establishing IBM's version of OSI as the dominant standard. By joining the standards process, IBM naturally sought the maximum advantage.

By 1987–8 IBM, the traditional opponent of OSI, offered more products conforming to OSI than any other company and offered means of linking OSI and SNA networks. IBM also responded to the success of OSI with new product lines and a redefinition of SNA. Its SAA (Systems Application Architecture), announced in 1987, was designed both to incorporate the different principles of SNA and OSI and to ensure that software for any IBM computer was compatible. SAA was part of a long-term strategy, designed gradually to bring standards together and, equally important, to strengthen IBM's position in software markets. By making it possible for programs to cooperate with each other, the value of each would be enhanced. As in the past, the aim was to benefit from the creativity and innovation of small companies producing software within the SAA standards. Because of its size IBM was able to follow apparently contradictory paths. Both OSI and SNA architectures could be developed in parallel. Moreover, new coalitions could be built around competitors' standards. The Unix operating system, originally developed by AT&T at Bell Labs in the late 1960s became so successful that in 1988 IBM formed a coalition of companies, including competitors like DEC, to develop their own versions of Unix in opposition to those of AT&T.

OSI, Regulation and Standardized Interfaces

As the complexity of networks grows standards institutions may be forced to restructure to avoid being swamped with work. Rather than setting standards for every terminal, signal or transaction, as SNA did, they will, like OSI, concentrate on the interfaces, standardizing the points where the user connects to the network or where networks meet. The rest will be left to the market, with private networks developing standards and applications to meet their own needs.

The standards-setting process for communications networks reveals something of the interdependence of standardization and diversity. In a network a new set of standards will tend to foster greater diversity as more connections can be made and more services provided in new contexts. In this sense standards create markets. The relationship between standardization and flexibility can also be seen in production processes. Much has been made of the success of business organizations built on flexible specialization, non-dedicated machinery and production lines better able to respond to volatile markets. But many of the pioneers of flexibility soon reintroduced standardization into parts of the production line: if properly designed, standardization in one part of the productive chain facilitates flexibility at the next.

Standards setting is likely to gain in prominence as the trend towards integrating digital technologies continues. Battles are looming over High Definition Television, Digital Audio Tape, 8 mm versus half-inch videotape, recordable compact discs, broadband ISDN, electronic funds transfer and smart cards. Competing network standards – DECnet, SNA, OSI, operating systems – MS-DOS, PS-2, Unix, VMS, and presentation standards such as Apple Macintosh and Microsoft Windows, all remain in contention. Each will be bound up with geopolitical and economic struggles over who will control some of the most lucrative industries of the twenty-first century. Struggles of this kind raise again the fundamental tension between a private or partial rationality and a universal and public one. A gulf separates the rational ideal of neutral standards setting for the benefit of all from the reality of intensely competing firms and nations, formed into almost feudal gangs behind leading firms. Just as standards making becomes more permanent, more organized and more open, the fear of losing exclusive possessions becomes more acute. It has been estimated that between 1956 and 1978 Japan paid around $9 bn for American technologies that had cost $500–1,000 bn to develop.[26] Technological leadership carried a heavy price.

These costs of leadership and the experiences of OSI demonstrate that even the most powerful companies are no longer able to use standards as a straightforward tool for control. Instead, tactics and strategies become more subtle and more politically astute, orientated to influence as much as to domination, to the micropolitics of cooperation and coalition building as well as to competition. The organization of standards thus runs in line with that of the communications industries as a whole: a permanently shifting mosaic of international coalitions and tactical alliances combines with the most intensive competition to dominate markets and emerging technologies.

10

Electromagnetic Spectrum and Electronic Enclosures

The waves of the electromagnetic spectrum support an extraordinary range of activities. They are used to broadcast radio and television, to support microwave and satellite signals, radiopagers, military command and tracking systems, television and garage remote control devices, surveillance and espionage operations, cellular radio networks, marine and aeronautical navigation networks, as well as radio astronomy and amateur radio. Spectrum can be used to light and to cook. Animals use it to detect objects and enemies and to communicate.

As the uses of spectrum have proliferated, and as different uses have begun to compete for the same frequencies, the spectrum has come to be seen as an economic resource. In many respects it is like the air, a truly public and ubiquitous good that is vulnerable to pollution and interference. Unlike the air or the water of the sea it can be differentiated into segments and tranches and systematically planned. In the language of economics the spectrum falls into the category of 'common pool' goods, goods with many of the properties of public goods but which are exhaustible and subject to congestion. Anyone can in principle receive any radio signal, yet for communication to work it is essential that users of the spectrum respect each other's rights to non-interference.

Any modern society has to decide how it is to allocate access to the spectrum; how it is to judge between the competing demands of a mobile radio service, a television channel or an emergency service. This is by no means straightforward. The available approaches provide classic examples of the failings both of administrative bureaucratic systems and of markets, failings that are accentuated by spectrum's peculiar nature. Orthodox economics offers only limited insight into how allocation can best be achieved, since the very idea of spectrum as a commodity is vulnerable to changing technologies and since spectrum is a socially produced medium, dependent on the organization of systems of standards, transmitters, receivers, and rules of non-interference. At the same time those political principles which are invoked for their insight into problems of allocation, such as the US Constitution's First Amendment, offer necessary rather than sufficient conditions for fair, free and open use.

The peculiarities of spectrum communication have posed problems for governments and regulators ever since the first transmissions were made. Radio was inherently harder to control than communication over cable. The impossibility of containing radio signals first challenged legal and political sovereignties when, in 1918, the Spartacists issued calls for uprisings across Europe from their high-power transmitter in Berlin. In Britain, the Postmaster-General wrote that 'wireless communication admittedly cannot be kept secret but this seems no reason for making it easy for the general public to listen to everything that is passing in the ether'.[1] Similar comments have been made in the 1980s with respect to satellite broadcasting, seen as a potential threat to existing structures of social control. For many years the Soviet Union systematically jammed Western radio signals and the US attempted, albeit briefly, to jam Cuban radio signals, while in the UK the apparatus of the law has been directed against unauthorized pirate radio broadcasters. Concern for security and for the special power of broadcast messages has led to spectrum becoming the exclusive possession of governments in almost every country in the world, to be awarded by licence or decree to broadcasters, firms and armies, which became in turn beholden to governments for their renewal. The prerogatives of political control neatly dovetail with technical arguments for central planning of the spectrum. Electromagnetic frequencies provide a classic example of state planning to sustain efficient and equitable use of a common resource. Arguments for planning could also draw on older themes. As in the commons of history, the absence of enforcement would lead to the classic 'tragedy of the commons' where all users pursue narrow self-interest to use their space more intensively until the resource is destroyed: in the case of spectrum, until mutual interference reaches such a point that communication becomes impossible.[2]

The spectrum is a socially created medium which can be used to establish circuits of communication. On its own it has no value. What is valuable is the ability to communicate. The idea of the electromagnetic spectrum has its origins in Maxwell's equations defining radio waves and Hertz's work in the 1880s on frequency. It moved from the world of pure theory to practice when Marconi pioneered the transmission of radio signals in the 1890s (although earlier experiments had also succeeded in transmitting radio messages over considerable distances). Radio was initially seen as a medium for point-to-point communication, a wireless telegraph which would come to compete with undersea cables and telephones. Navies tended to be the first major users, so that questions of allocation were treated first as questions of military policy and security and secondly as questions of commerce. Among the leading civilian players was United Fruit, which needed to coordinate fleets of ships and plantations.

The organization of use evolved to reflect prevailing views of how the spectrum could be used. In the UK, for example, the basic regulatory framework, which placed spectrum under the central control of the Post Office, preceded the use of spectrum for broadcasting. Spectrum was seen as a resource for government and military use.

In the US, as early as 1912, the Navy Department had warned of 'etheric bedlam produced by numerous stations all trying to communicate at once', and amateur 'hams' deliriously communicating with each other, and had called for some form of central control. This became more urgent as radio's military role developed. Radio soon had a substantial impact on the nature of war, and between one-third and half of all spectrum in the US and Europe is still reserved for military uses. The *Dreadnought*'s order of battle required it to assemble beyond visible contact. In 1914 the Battle of Tannenberg was decisively affected by the German Army's success in intercepting unencrypted Russian radio signals. In World War II the German army's use of tanks was wholly dependent on radio communication. The idea that spectrum is a security resource continues to be reflected in regulations. In the UK, the 1949 Wireless Telegraphy Act, still in force in 1990, makes it an offence to listen to radio signals which are not public broadcasts on the grounds that this threatens national security.

The idea that radio could be used as a mass medium, a medium of culture, broadcasting from one point to many, developed in the early 1920s and was promoted by manufacturers searching for a market for their vacuum tube or valve receivers. Arguably the first use of radio as a broadcast medium was that of the rebels of the 1916 Easter rising in Dublin, who broadcast a Morse message in the hope that ships would relay the message on to the world. Early radio stations experimented with different programming formats, unsure of how the medium would evolve, and of what radio was really for. At first the medium was parasitic, feeding off concerts, talks, stars and established news services. Cultural experiment coincided with economic experiment as different funding structures – toll radio, sponsorship, advertising and licence fee finance – were all tried.

The root problem for any service offered over the spectrum is that charging is very difficult. Once broadcast, a signal can be picked up by anyone with an appropriate receiver. The control that can be exercised over a physical commodity is no longer viable unless signals are either scrambled or in some way addressed. Neither solution was either technically or economically viable in the 1920s. Instead, alternative solutions were found. In both the UK and the US manufacturers initially financed radio programmes as a loss leader to encourage people to buy sets. It was widely believed that programmes should be financed out of a levy on sets. Advertising was opposed both in Europe and the US (by

Herbert Hoover and David Sarnoff among others) as threatening to ruin and degrade the new medium.

Public broadcasters sought support through taxation: in the UK the radio manufacturers formed themselves into the BBC which was given a royal charter and monopoly access to the spectrum, alongside the military and the Post Office. Funding was secured through a licence, a form of hypothecated tax, which could be justified by the public good nature of the radio service. Within a few years commercial broadcasters in the US bypassed the problem of selling a service to their audience by instead selling their audience to advertisers. The basic commodity of the broadcasting industry was to be neither a cultural service nor access to the spectrum (as in toll experiments) but rather a portion of the consuming public, rigorously measured by companies like Nielsen. Other countries chose direct finance by government. More recently a wide range of solutions have been devised, particularly by community radio and television stations, ranging from voluntary subscription, through various forms of sponsorship to soft subsidy from educational institutions.

While the BBC's monopoly solved the problem of spectrum planning in the UK, the adoption of advertising as a solution to the problematic nature of the broadcasting commodity only exacerbated 'etheric bedlam' in the US. Anyone could broadcast on any frequency, prompting radio amateurs and entrepreneurs to rush to secure suitable frequencies, to sell advertising and to reap the rewards of the new medium. According to one American commentator, by 1922 there were '21,065 transmitting radio stations. Of these, 16,898 were amateur stations, 2,762 were ship stations, 569 were broadcasting stations, thirty-nine were coast stations, twelve were transoceanic stations'.[3] It was soon clear that some form of regulation or oversight was needed to bring stability to the industry, to prevent interference between signals and the practice of using higher-powered transmitters to eliminate a competitor's signals. The problem was to define who should or should not be given rights of access to the spectrum. Despite widespread fears of censorship and violation of free speech, a regulatory system was eventually set up in the US, first in the 1927 Radio Act and later in the 1934 Communications Act, which remains to this day the defining legislation for communications. The Act established the Federal Communications Commission, mixing executive, legislative and judicial functions in a body whose duty was to manage the electromagnetic spectrum in the name of the 'public interest, convenience and necessity'. The problem of allocation was solved conservatively: the status quo of frequency use was legitimized when eighty-nine broadcasting channels between 550 and 1,500 KHz were licensed.

Several points are worth noting. A number of years before the two Acts were passed an historic agreement had been reached between RCA,

AT&T and Westinghouse, an agreement that was to underpin the network structure of American broadcasting. RCA had been set up in 1919 largely at the instigation of the Navy Department, which wanted to free the US from dependence on British cables and from British technological domination in the form of Marconi and its subsidiaries. To this end AT&T, United Fruit, Westinghouse and General Electric pooled several thousand key patents in the new company, and soon seemed set to dominate the sudden growth of broadcasting in the early 1920s. Within a few years the partners fell out. AT&T was pioneering the development of networks with its toll broadcasting stations in which 'anyone who had a message for the world, or wished to entertain was to come in and pay their money as they would upon coming into a telephone booth, address the world and go out',[4] a model not unlike the broadband common carriage systems being suggested for the 1990s and beyond.

AT&T was also seeking to enter the receiver market, claiming that radio receivers were an integral part of the toll service. AT&T argued, in other words, that it was offering a system of communications. In response to this threat the other participants engineered a new demarcation of spheres. The agreement led to the formation of NBC as a subsidiary of RCA, and the removal of AT&T from active broadcasting. In exchange AT&T won exclusive rights to link different stations through its cables. The first broadcasting networks, NBC's red and blue networks, were thus established. AT&T's monopoly of network links also applied to CBS, which was built up in the 1930s, and to ABC in the 1940s.

Networking was essential to the economics of broadcasting: few small stations could afford to make their own programmes, to maintain news staff or to buy the services of the most popular orchestras or bands. The nature of spectrum implied that an additional listener, and in principle additional advertising revenues, could be reached at zero marginal cost. This provided a powerful incentive to maximize audiences. The network is a natural solution to the economies of scale inherent in broadcasting.[5] In Britain the various local stations of the early 1920s were soon consolidated into a single national network. In the US, of the eighty-nine frequencies originally licensed, forty were reserved for only one station. Nearly all of these were held by network affiliates. In terms of transmitting power the networks were even more dominant, with CBS and NBC controlling 88.4 per cent of total transmitting power. Later, in television, the networks also proved dominant. In 1987, 637 stations were affiliated to the three major networks, 300 to the public broadcasting network, while the 283 independents were largely dependent on syndicated, nationally produced material. The tendency towards networking, driven by economics, remains apparent in all forms of broadcasting. Deregulation in Italy, which followed the Supreme Court's judgement that the state had no privileged rights of access to the spectrum, very soon saw the creation of dominant networks by Silvio Berlusconi's Fininvest group (linked by dispatch riders carrying tapes to circumvent restrictions on networking). More recently, radio liberalization in France soon resulted in the formation of a handful of Paris-based networks. The use of satellites to distribute signals to local transmission centres, pioneered in the case of television in the USSR and by Home Box Office and the Public Broadcasting System in the US, has further reinforced the pressures towards linking apparently local media into national and transnational networks.

In most countries the state's right to control the spectrum was unquestioned. The interests of the state and of the public were officially seen as identical. In Britain spectrum allocation grew out of the functions of the Post Office, which was organized as a government department. The coincidence of political and technical arguments was spelled out by the 1923 Broadcasting Committee (Cmd 1951): 'We consider that the control of such a potential power over public opinion and the life of the nation ought to remain with the state . . . the regulation of the power and wavelength of each transmitting station must necessarily be undertaken by the Government in order to avoid chaos.' Control was vested in the Postmaster-General, accountable to Parliament. Today licences to use spectrum are awarded by the Secretary of State for Trade and Industry alongside licences from the Home Secretary in the case of broadcasters. Decisions over allocation are made in a closed process, very different from the formal and public procedures of the US. Instead there is a small number of large users, the BBC, BT, IBA (the Independent Broadcasting Authority) and Mercury, each of which is granted an omnibus licence leaving to it the routine tasks of managing the spectrum and coordinated assignments. Allocations are negotiated with government departments and the military with the aim of reaching consensus. In practice, respect for 'squatters' rights', especially those of the military, makes it hard to dislodge existing users.[6]

The US is distinctive in that the constitutional tradition of a balance of powers, the ideological commitment to markets and the culture of free communication crystallized in the First Amendment combined to make the question of who owned the spectrum much more problematic. Government control over the spectrum could be held to infringe rights of free communication. In contrast to most other countries, broadcasting was carried out by private, commercial companies rather than by public service, state or quasi-state institutions. While framing legislation, however, the public-good nature of spectrum was generally accepted, and with it the notion that it would be impossible to conceive it as a form of property. Regulation was further justified in terms of the special scarcity of spectrum (Herbert Hoover, then Secretary of Commerce, spoke of it being a 'simple physical fact that we have no more channels') and the pecular power of broadcasting as a medium. Congress was concerned not to create property by right of use, rights deriving from the de facto possession of frequencies, but it was never made clear whether the Congress or the Executive, as representative of the people, possessed the spectrum. It seems that the prevailing view was that the nature of spectrum precluded the possibility of ownership.

The FCC's role was to further the 'public interest' in some ill-defined way and to plan the use of the airwaves, the allocation of bands of spectrum for future use according to categories of service (a process analogous to land zoning), technical standards relating to transmission, modulation and operational rights. The production of useful spectrum depended on active planning both of the uses of spectrum and of the standards used for making equipment. Although this procedure was taken on by the public sector and although a usable form of spectrum was produced by a procedure of socialized allocation, the spectrum was awarded free of charge to be used as a tool for private appropriation. Once awarded, licences have effectively granted rights in perpetuity: they can be bought and sold on the market and are always by far the most valuable asset of private TV and radio stations.

States versus Markets

In the US and elsewhere, two main sets of arguments have been used against state allocation of spectrum. One is essentially political. It argues that broadcasting is now no different from printing or for that matter any other economic activity. If spectrum was ever scarce in some special way (which is doubtful) it is now as abundant as any other resource. Just as printers have the right to publish anything in any form subject only to laws of copyright, obscenity, official secrecy and libel, so should broadcasting be freed from the paternalistic or oppressive embrace of the State. The prerequisite for this is the existence of a free market in spectrum. Just as the free market in printing has sustained a diverse marketplace for ideas, so will it in broadcasting and all forms of electronic publishing. Two texts are often cited in support of these arguments. One is Milton's *Areopagitica*, written in 1644 to denounce the imposition of licensing laws on printing. The second is the First Amendment to the US Constitution which guarantees freedom of speech and freedom of the press from state or religious intervention. Deregulators have sought to reapply this amendment to broadcasting. In the US their main target has been the regulation of content by the FCC, such as rules for fair reporting of politics, and rules governing educational and children's programming. By invoking the First Amendment, the broader goal is to remove the constitutional premise for any form of state intervention in broadcasting. A free market in spectrum is held to be the precondition for a free market in programmes and a free and responsive broadcasting system: according to the then Chairman of the FCC, 'instead of defining public demand and specifying categories of programming to service this demand, the FCC should rely on broadcasters' ability to determine the wants of their audiences through the mechanisms of the marketplace.'[7] In other words, the public interest is what the public is interested in.

Economic arguments have bolstered the libertarian, political ones. Most of these fall within the scope of longer-running arguments about the relative virtues of state bureaucracies and markets as means of allocating resources. One version of the argument attacks the bureaucracy, for its failure to allocate resources to the most efficient uses, or to encourage innovations. In an extension of arguments developed first by Hayek, the virtues of markets as discovery procedures and information processing systems are stressed. Free markets, it is argued, are more efficient at spotting new uses and reallocating resources than centralized administrations; if markets make incorrect decisions investors lose money. If an administration makes a major mistake a whole country can be left with an obsolete technology or a misuse of spectrum. Bureaucracies are also inevitably subject to political pressures. The phenomenon of regulatory capture, whereby the regulating agency, supposedly acting in the public interest, comes to identify with the interests of the industry it is meant to regulate, is common in the communications industry. In the US, incumbents, notably broadcasters, successfully used their political muscle to squeeze out newcomers. One example was their success in dislodging the infant FM radio service. Another led to the maintenance of a mixed VHF–UHF TV system when a technological rationality would have favoured a long-term shift to a uniform UHF system as in the UK and elsewhere. In the UK similar pressures discriminated against mobile users and radiopaging services. If decision making is located within the political structure such decisions, often running counter to the public interest, are inevitable. An equally important result is that decision making is bound to be slow. Regulatory agencies in the US are bound by fixed procedures for rule-making and consultation (laid down in the Administrative Procedures Act) which lead to long delays in granting approval to new technologies. New enterprises commonly have to invest more heavily in the legal and political task of changing regulatory rules than they do in the technology itself. Such manifest inefficiency seems inappropriate in industries which see themselves as the cutting edge.

A second, related, line of attack argues that the provision of spectrum as a free good leads to inevitably inefficiencies. Those who are awarded the use of spectrum by the state have no incentive to use it efficiently. On the contrary, it is in their interest to use as much as possible, so as to minimize the threat of new competitors for business or advertising, and to provide a free resource for future expansion. In most forms of communications there are fairly simple trade-offs betwen spectrum use and investment in devices to compress signals or multiplex. Similar considerations apply to land use. Investment in skyscrapers (or fertilizers) increases the productivity of the resource. Where spectrum is available free there is little incentive to invest in technologies which use it more efficiently.

This argument has much to commend it. It is important because the quantity of spectrum available for use can be greatly increased. One approach is to develop technologies which use virgin spectrum at higher frequencies. Since the regulatory apparatus was established in the 1920s as a response to spectrum scarcity, the 'frontier' beyond which frequencies are largely unusable has risen from around 1,500 KHz to 30 or even 300 GHz. World War II brought what has been described as a 'forced march' into the higher reaches of the spectrum as radar and microwave came into use. Alternatively spectrum already in use can be used more intensively. This can be achieved by processing signals to minimize redundancy or by improvements in reception and transmission technologies. Examples include single sideband technologies, voice compression techniques such as Linear Prediction Coding which reconstructs fricative and voice sounds, and the more common compression technique, Digital Speech Interpolation (DSI). Colour television signals can be reduced from 90 mbs to 1.45 mbs using 'codec' techniques or even 64 kbs where images are relatively static. Satellite antennae using gallium arsenide are fifty times cheaper and more spectrum-efficient than the equivalents of the mid 1980s which used cryogenic amplifiers. Using Time Division Multiple Access (TDMA) several different earth stations can share satellite capacity. In cellular radio, spectrum can be used more intensively by splitting cells. In all cases, higher spending on research, development and production means that less spectrum is needed to send a given message. The comparison between broadcasters, who felt no incentive to improve efficiency and use the same bandwidth they used thirty years ago, and mobile radio equipment manufacturers whose demand was constrained by spectrum limitations is instructive. The mobile industry's solution was progressively to reduce the bandwidth their equipment used from 240 KHz in 1940 to 12 KHz in 1990.[8]

Spectrum as a Resource

Spectrum is an unusual resource. It is inexhaustible, and non-containable yet shaped by the physical environment, by buildings and clouds. More than any other resource its very value derives from its public nature. Its value is its capacity to communicate signals: once transmitted these can be easily intercepted. For a radio transmission to be in any meaningful sense private, messages must be encrypted. Spectrum use also has the characteristic of a public good in which, if one ignores the costs of receivers, the marginal cost of reaching an additional consumer is zero, and of goods involving interdependencies such that the way one person uses it affects others. In this respect it has similar characteristics to fishing, which is regulated by international and national agreements to avoid exhaustion and maximize long-term output. Clear boundaries or property rights are hard to define. Instead rights are defined in terms of allocated output quotas which can subsequently be traded. Rights to fish off the coasts of Alaska and Canada, for example, are sold by auction to encourage the most efficient fishing techniques.

Whereas fish are an exhaustible resource, spectrum, at least in theory, has no limits. Advances in processing and compression techniques, combined with intensive research on the frontiers of usability (generally underwritten by the military) have gone well in advance of new uses. This may seem a surprising conclusion. In the 1920s spectrum was seen as an unusually scarce resource, although, according to de Sola Pool, there was 'vague awareness of possible future technological solutions to spectrum shortage'.[9] This is no longer the case. Although there are shortages of the capital needed to use spectrum, of audiences to finance uses, and of receptive capacity in television sets or radios, there is now no peculiar scarcity characteristic of spectrum. Arguments for regulation which derive from spectrum scarcity (as opposed to a scarcity which arises from a large sunk investment in certain kinds of television receiver) are no longer relevant.[10] For most uses of spectrum there are also straightforward substitutes: cable, whether twisted pair, copper or fibre optic.

Scarcity is relative. Like land, spectrum is not a homogeneous resource since different frequencies have different properties. Medium- and high-frequency signals are reflected by the ionosphere and can travel great distances, making them suitable for national broadcasting systems, or point to point communications in sparsely populated regions. Signals at VHF and higher frequencies lose the ability to go around objects and exploit reflections. Transmissions tend to be line of sight and over short distances. UHF and VHF are probably the most congested areas of the spectrum, being suitable both for broadcasting and for mobile communications. The primary advantage of higher frequencies is that they can carry more information: 1 GHz has a thousand times as much bandwidth as 1 MHz, which in turn has a thousand times as much as 1 KHz. There are also other advantages. Microwave, above 1 GHz, can be directed into narrow beams of energy which help to minimize interference and errors. At these higher frequencies, however, the atmosphere begins to interfere with signals. Above 6 GHz raindrops begin to act as antennae, absorbing and dissipating energies. The higher the frequency the more relay stations are needed, and systems need to be built to assume periods of downtime such as storms. Microwave frequencies are generally used for fixed links for oil companies, utilities, or railways, as satellite links in the C and Ku bands and as elements within broader telecommunications networks. The spectrum also has special properties which give rise to new techniques. Citizens' Band (CB) radio benefited from temporary sunspot behaviour carrying signals over long distances. The US military has developed techniques for bouncing signals off meteor showers, and the spread spectrum technique, now widely used, whereby a signal uses a rapidly changing, pseudo-random sequence of different frequencies.

Markets for Spectrum

Limited markets for spectrum have existed in the US since the 1920s, when the courts and the FCC began to acknowledge the sale of licences. While the issue of new licences was organized administratively, resale was effectively liberalized. The most influential theoretical case for fully fledged markets in spectrum was made by the economist R. H. Coase in 1959.[11] Coase argued that the spectrum chaos and 'etheric bedlam' of the early days of radio resulted not from the absence of administrative regulation but rather from the absence of adequately defined property rights which could have sustained a market. The apparent scarcity of spectrum in the 1920s was not a technological fact but an economic result of pricing below equilibrium and the absence of incentives to use it efficiently. A properly functioning market would remove the problem of interference and spectrum 'pollution'. Coase also believed that in an ideal world environmental pollution could be 'solved' by the market; but for the transaction costs involved those affected by pollution could band together to pay the pollutant to stop.

Coase's successors have concentrated on defining the property rights that could sustain a market in spectrum. Spectrum is often compared to land, being subject to zoning laws, different uses for different regions and virgin territories. Defining an unambiguous and, most important, enforceable property right for spectrum demands a far more complex set of specifications than the drawing of boundaries on a map. Any viable property right needs to operate in several dimensions. In 1969, writing in the Stanford Law Review,[12] A. S. De Vaney defined a three-dimensional property right involving time, the area covered by a transmission and frequencies used. To be viable a right of this kind would be supplemented by a set of legal attributes including rights of use, admission and transfer, and, most problematic, emission. Emission rights would be defined by power levels not to be exceeded at the boundaries of the area concerned, and involving controls on spurious radiation emitted on adjacent or harmonic frequencies.

De Vaney's scheme described property rights in terms of the output of a transmitter. Alternative approaches which start from inputs or rights of non-interference are no simpler. Any viable system needs to take account of the variability of signals due to natural phenomena, the unconfinability of signals and, perhaps most serious of all, intermodulation effects from services on other frequencies.

During the 1980s the FCC tried to define property rights in terms of rights to non-interference. Felker and Gordon used the concept of 'protected contours' of reception and (larger) contours of interference, with rights being defined in terms of parameters of out-of-band and out-of-area emissions.[13] In 1985 the FCC committed itself to using a market mechanism to allocate a part of the spectrum which had been reserved for land mobile but which was by then sought by seven different kinds of user ranging from air telephones to the military. In the end only a very small band, 2 MHz, was allocated by market mechanisms, as the FCC came up against apparently insuperable political and practical obstacles. Nevertheless the economic literature on spectrum has multiplied. Some have argued that administrations should seek to mimic the market, charging fees for spectrum to encourage efficient use,[14] while others have questioned the market approach altogether.[15]

In principle there are a multitude of ways in which resources can be allocated: fiat, force, chance, custom, fraud, competitive or oligopolistic markets, auctions, sealed bids, voting, bargaining and contract are all options. State regulatory systems have used most of these in one form or another: voting, albeit indirectly mediated through parliaments and assemblies; custom in the tolerance of incumbents; contracts in the form of licences; competitive markets for resale; and so on.

Proponents of deregulation favour the use of sealed bids, auctions and chance in the form of lotteries. In the late nineteenth century local governments often auctioned telephone and electricity franchises, subject to commitments to low prices and a high quality of service. In the US state-owned oil fields have also been auctioned. In the UK, the 1990 Broadcasting Act introduced an auction process for awarding commercial television licences. Economists favour auctions because, in theory, they sell goods at the 'correct' price to the most efficient user.[16] In practice, where fairly similar bidders must guess the real value of the good they are seeking on the basis of inadequate information, the winner suffers from the famous 'winner's curse': by virtue of winning the auction, the winner knows that too high a price has probably been bid. Collusion can also be a problem: this already happens in competitive bidding, when applicants minimize risk by forming a single consortium to bid for a franchise, a phenomenon particularly prevalent in local cellular radio franchises in the US. An extreme and highly unstable form of the auction is the system proposed by the Hungarian economist Liska, and used in some sectors of the Hungarian economy: groups of people or companies can at any time outbid the present user or provider of a publicly owned resource and take control.

Hitherto lotteries have been more widely used than auctions, notably for the award of Low Power TV (LPTV) and radio licences in the US. The FCC argued for the use of lotteries on the grounds that there were few real differences between applicants and that these could not be 'rationally measured against a public interest standard'.[17] As it turned out several large firms made multiple applications through ostensibly local organizations with the intention of setting up LPTV networks.

To sustain a market the ideal property right must be both flexible enough to cope with technological changes and rigorous enough to minimize the costs of administrative and judicial arbitrations which arise from ambiguities. If a new system simply moves the necessary regulatory role from the state to the courts, little is gained. This ideal may prove unachievable. Definitions of property rights are bound to become obsolescent. The problem is that any definition of rights is inevitably embedded in prevailing technologies and prevailing ways of understanding the nature of spectrum. There can be no simple, unchanging definition of rights of property. Much simpler problems of a similar kind have had to be faced in the definition of land property rights: when boundaries were first set no one had anticipated aeroplanes flying in the sky or oil wells miles beneath the surface. Recent developments such as spread spectrum and spectrum hopping would have undermined any pregiven definitions. The limited viability of any property right means that pure markets are probably impossible in the sense that they exist for orthodox commodities with clear boundaries. Given the spectrum's properties, if the state is not to regulate and allocate spectrum, and to retain the right continually to redefine rights of access, the only alternative is to locate regulation in the private sector.

This emerged as the favoured route in the late 1980s, as the British government took the lead in investigating market mechanisms with a Department of Trade and Industry (DTI) report on deregulation of the radio spectrum.[18] Viewing spectrum as an intermediate good, important for the coordination of business and the provision of services, the report argued that there was substantial allocative inefficiency. This could be gauged by the different prices that could be charged for different uses of the spectrum. According to the study, an additional MHz of spectrum would be worth £75 k for fixed services, £1–4.6 m. for mobile uses and £4 m. for television. These figures were taken to prove that substantial sums could be raised by a government which was prepared to sell spectrum. A 1986 estimate for the US similarly suggested that the auction of 50 MHz between 800 and 900 MHz could raise up to £2 bn.

Rather than recommending pure markets, the DTI report recommended licensing private Frequency Planning Organizations (FPOs) with 20-year licences to manage and sublet large bands of spectrum for profit. These bodies, which would be administratively chosen, would play an active role in developing new standards and in assisting their clients to design networks. Instead of deregulating spectrum itself, the task of regulation would be privatized, passed on to private sector bodies whose task it would be to manage and sell access to the spectrum.

Despite this retreat from pure markets, the more radical route remains an option, and was taken by the New Zealand government, which decided in 1988 to auction tranches of the spectrum, including those used for radio and television, in the form of twenty-year licences. Successful bidders would be able to switch frequencies from broadcast uses to, for example, data.[19] Rules would be imposed to prevent the sorts of monopoly, speculation and hoarding familiar in parallel areas like land. The dramatic decision to take market theory at face value may show whether it really is possible to treat spectrum as a commodity or whether the problems endemic to the definition of property rights and the political problems likely to arise if the new system disrupts a well entrenched broadcasting economy will prove fatal.

Competing Economies

At the core of all these debates is not spectrum per se, but rather communicability, the system of technologies, competences and frequencies that makes communication possible. As one element in systems of communication, spectrum does not exist as a resource or a virgin territory analogous to a piece of land or sea, but is socially produced through the combination of technology with legal and economic structures. It is dependent on standards, rules on interference and emissions, and on structures for arbitrating and redefining rights in the light of changing technologies. This systemic nature combines with the fact that spectrum is public in a way that no other resource is. As a result there is wide agreement that neither the State nor the market is adequate either to the philosophical needs of free communication or to the logistical task of managing the evolution of systems of communication. In recent debates about new ways of allocating spectrum, however, its public nature has been subordinated to questions of instrumental efficiency. This emphasis on efficiency, productivity and the need to remove barriers to change is common to the whole communications field and represents the most fundamental shift from earlier times when debates about spectrum use were couched in the language of culture and quality, national security and order.

Arguments based on economic efficiency and competitive, equilibrating markets frequently run into contradictions. One derives from the fact that commercial broadcasting, the most lucrative use of spectrum, is financed by advertising, rather than by the sale of programmes to audiences. In their seminal article arguing for spectrum deregulation Fowler and Brenner wrote that 'in a sense the advertiser acts as the representative for consumers, sometimes for all consumers, sometimes for demographic sub-groups'.[20] In practice, however, spectrum is being used to sell audiences to advertisers, rather than a service to viewers. There is no direct market expression of demand and no direct relationship between viewer demand for programmes and advertisers demand for time. Within a strict neoclassical framework this makes it impossible for equilibrium to result in allocative efficiency. By contrast with a cable system in which viewers pay for programmes, viewers of broadcast television cannot pay more in order to receive more. One study in the US suggested that the benefits viewers receive from television exceed television revenues by a factor of seven: if there was a market relationship between broadcasters and viewers they would probably be willing to pay much more than they pay indirectly through advertising.[21] The existence of a non-market relationship between broadcasters and the public removes the incentive to use spectrum efficiently. Advertising finance also brings with it a series of other barriers to allocative efficiency: the bias against small audiences and against programming that undermines the power of advertisements.

The example of commercial broadcasting, one of the most important users of the spectrum, illustrates the two general weaknesses of market approaches. The first is that fragmented markets are ill-placed to organize the kinds of systemic change needed to improve broadcasting's use of spectrum (in the future perhaps to move broadcasting out of UHF altogether). The second is that exponents of unified spectrum markets implicitly place different economies onto a single plane. The advertising economy of maximizing impact on certain kinds of audience, the video economy of providing services for paying customers, that of a public service mission to inform and educate, to bind a nation or community; that of the vision of a pluralistic society in which access to spectrum is provided to major social groups (as in the Netherlands); and those of corporate communication, switched telephony, and emergency service are all treated as directly comparable. The analytical rigour of neoclassical economics is won at the cost of losing any sense of the different kinds of value which function in different communications economies.

Arguments for spectrum markets implicitly call for a removal of control from the political sphere to the economic one. They draw on deeper beliefs about social organization, in particular the influential view of Hayek and Friedman that the political realm, the realm of collective action and public power, is necessarily oppressive and clumsy and that liberty can only be secured through the economy. Ultimately spectrum markets have the mission of removing politics from the organization of communications. Control passes from the State to the consumer, whose power is expressed through the market.

This perspective offers at best a partial truth. Free markets in spectrum no more guarantee freedom of communication than do free markets in the press: public libraries, subsidized newsprint and distribution, grants and subsidies, Press Councils and statutory rights to reply are all responses to the failure of the market to guarantee reasonably open access to the means of printed communication. Ironically it was R. H. Coase, the original proponent of spectrum markets, who gave one of the most coherent accounts of why transaction costs led to the creation of permanent political and administrative structures; why, in other words, transaction costs hinder citizens from collaborating in the market, perhaps to buy spectrum for a community service.

The crude dichotomy between state and market is misleading. For there are many possible models which reconcile public ownership with limited markets and rules to guarantee access. Dispersed public ownership could offer an alternative to centralized, nationalized state control. Much of the regulatory role for local uses of spectrum could be passed to local authorities; while as in the EC, coordination of spectrum moves to the transnational level. Tranches of spectrum could be awarded to quasi-public bodies, at one remove from the state, with rights to charge for use of spectrum and to spend on research or on public interest uses. Trusts could oversee the uses of broadcast spectrum, again with powers to redistribute funds within the broadcast economy. Looser rules on how spectrum is to be used could combine with fees or auctions for fixed-length licence periods.

All would meet many of the valid criticisms made of bureaucratic mechanisms while preserving the general principle of public rights over a public resource. Spectrum would become more like the land, which is controlled not just through the market but also through a plurality of structures, ranging through national and local parks, trusts and federations of non-profit bodies, to authorities protecting planning rules and rights of way.

11

Transnational Corporate Networks

In a famous speech, Jacques Maisonrouge of IBM argued that the 'world's political structures are completely obsolete' and that 'the critical issue of our time is the conceptual conflict between the global optimization of resources and the independence of nation states'.[1] The maximalist view was summarized by Martha Buyer: 'As technology advances, the importance of national boundaries will decline and the communications network of the multinational corporation, developed in form by the banks, will have the potential to become the guiding force for the development of world political and economic policies'.[2]

The description of the communications network as a political and economic force would have seemed extraordinary even a few decades ago. Now, as unprecedented sums of money move electronically day by day, beyond the control of national governments, and as data and images cross borders and oceans, it seems less far-fetched; the sheer reach and logistical power of the largest corporate networks is matched only by the military networks of the superpowers. This chapter examines just what kind of force the communications networks of the transnationals represent; what their relationship is to sovereign governments and national network operators; how communications are used within the structures of the firm or its relationships with other firms; and, above all, how we are to understand the economy of control within which the corporate network is used.

Like the increasingly global economy, the modern transnational firm is a creature of the age of satellites, transoceanic cables and computers. It is inconceivable without them. With each advance in technology the scope for global, centralized organization appears to extend.[3] Instant and transparent control over factories, warehouses and offices in every corner of the world becomes a compelling and apparently achievable goal for the central offices of any transnational corporation. The world can become a single office and factory, without the need for delegation and intermediaries. Each unit can be 'run by numbers' through data flows carried over satellites, public data networks like Telenet, Tymnet and Euronet, and through lines leased from telephone companies.

The increasing centrality of communications, especially of structured data, has implications well beyond the boundaries of the firm. As companies like Ford, American Express, Mitsubishi and Unilever develop their systems of command and control, they also play a part in shaping the world's telecommunication infrastructures which were once the exclusive province of common carrier telegraph and telephone companies. Roughly half of all information flows across borders now take place within transnational corporations, which operate increasingly sophisticated private networks. These networks, linking mainframes and small terminals, telephone and VSATs, have taken on many of the functions previously provided by the public networks, and are gaining access to the heart of public networks through the Intelligent Network and open network models. Seen from this perspective the global network is less a McLuhanesque village where the world congregates than a series of private, separate and competing nervous systems overseeing and commanding flows of goods, people and money at one remove from the public gaze. With deregulations and liberalizations, themselves in large part a response to pressure from the transnationals, public investments in new infrastructures are increasingly centred on the key business centres, while private investments contribute nothing to the common infrastructures that preceded them.

The growing role of communications networks in business has prompted new ways of thinking about the nature of the firm and the market. The scope for enhanced control has focused attention on its limits, on when transparent communication is unable to achieve its promise. Thus alongside interest in automation and data networking there is a new interest in the limits to globalism and global Fordism, the barriers to achieving economies of scale in research, product design and manufacturing, limits which parallel those of other types of excessive control. There is also a concern for the informal networks that shadow the physical and formal ones, an interest in the organization of creativity, of milieu, of horizontal communications and of more flexible and 'soft' structures than those analysed by Chandler, Williamson, Coase and Penrose.

The advent of more open networks poses fundamental questions about the nature of the firm. The firm is a form of closure, a bounded organization that insulates itself from certain kinds of volatility, movements of prices and of labour. Its very structure is a form of positional control that cannot be simply reduced to the immediate, purposive calculus of minimizing transaction costs. More open networks continually cut across the boundaries that preserve closure, encouraging greater use of contracts, internal markets and joint ventures. They allow firms to benefit from greater flexibility but also render the firm more vulnerable to the external environment, locking it within a larger matrix.

The Ambivalence of Communication

The relationship between communications technology and organizational form has been studied for over a century. The telephone was soon seen as the agent of greater centralization, allowing a central office to control its factories. Skyscraper headquarters could relocate in city centres, as the telephone replaced messengers. A single manager could oversee huge corporations. De Sola Pool refers to Morgan's partner George W. Perkins who used a system of 'rapid transit telephony' to call ten or thirty bankers in a row to raise capital.[4] Yet it was soon recognized that the impact of technology on organization is rarely straightforward. At the same time that centralization became feasible the telephone also permitted greater decentralization and equality, as the Chief Executive could speak directly to the overseer, and as the paper hierarchies of bureaucracy and middle management could be more easily bypassed. Operations could be decentralized or subcontracted while remaining under central supervision.

More recent technologies raise similar issues in new forms. Advanced communications technologies appear to be creating a global, transparent economy in which the centre can monitor and command people and machines in real time. In principle, transparency allows multinational corporations to become genuinely transnational, exploiting an international division of labour, and using the same brands, the same production and research to serve a truly global market. But just as the telephone favoured both centralization and decentralization, so more recent technologies have ambiguous effects. Control can prove costly. Although technologies create the space for novel solutions, they alone can solve neither the problems inherent in large organizations nor the instability of the world outside.

This instability is itself in part an effect of communications technologies. The very systems designed to enhance control, particularly in the financial sector, have themselves contributed to chaos, vastly increasing the volumes of footloose money. Volatility in exchange rates, interest rates and share prices are direct products of networks which make it possible to move money and assets from market to market instantaneously. By 1986 it was estimated that annual international foreign exchange transactions had risen to around $87 trillion, less than 10 per cent of which was concerned with trade. In the mid-1980s it was estimated that the West's banking transnationals were electronically transferring around $4,000 bn each day so as to exploit tax and interest rate conditions. Instability has in turn fed the corporate demand for more machines to restore predictability and to enhance their ability to respond more quickly than anyone else. What appears as a rational strategy to the individual corporation becomes highly irrational at the level of the system as a whole.

The new volatilities reflect a world in which distance no longer acts as a barrier to competition. The Soviet trade ministry receives information from economic data banks in Canada about Eastern Europe's imports from the West. The Polish airline LOT keeps operational information in Atlanta. The Swedish furniture company IKEA manages all distribution and retailing information in a single centre.[5] Technologies extend the geographical extent of markets, so that more functions can be specialized and made available over wider distances. Knowledge, information and assessments can be transported and used away from their point of production. Processing power, memory and data bases can be concentrated. According to one study in Canada, for example, the networks used by large multi-locational companies have approximately 90 per cent of their computer capacity concentrated at or near head offices.[6] The concentration of knowledge tends to gather its own momentum. The world's largest data bases, such as the 'Chemical Abstracts System' or Lockheed's Dialog in the USA, which are available on-line throughout the world, have rendered their competitors virtually irrelevant. Meanwhile the global division of labour becomes more fluid and more open to choice. Within the communications industries themselves, for example, offshore production in Taiwan or Malaysia can be rapidly located in more automated factories in the US or Europe. Information processing can be sent out to China or Barbados (the phenomenon of 'telecolonialism'), software writing and editing to India or Pakistan. Within a country low-grade processing work can be removed to non-union regions like South Dakota in the US. Even the task of monitoring closed-circuit security systems in New York or London can be removed to cheap labour countries.

The dispersal of activity, following the geography of educated populations and low wages, is matched by new concentrations of high value added activity around the key nodes of the information economy. New service economies based on producer services such as advertising, insurance, consultancy, marketing and law are growing up around the key metropolitan centres in Japan, South-East Asia, Europe, the US and South America, serving the transnational corporations, and seeking out the best communications services and the most liberal regulatory regimes.[7] Within countries, too, the new information services are equally concentrated around a few cores, linked by high-capacity fibre-optic cables. In the UK, for example, 75 per cent of all value added services are located in and around London. In the US, 30 per cent of all international telephone calls are made from New York or Los Angeles.

Internationalization of the Economy and the New Visible Hands

The idea of an evolution of national and regional economies into a single global economy has become something of a cliché. The spread across boundaries coincided with transformation in communications: the real price of telecommunications fell by a factor of 3.5, while the volume of computer communications rose by nearly 30 per cent each year during the 1970s and 1980s. Satellite terminal prices fell by a factor of 10 between 1982 and 1987, fibre-optic prices by a factor of 20 in seven years. A proliferation of new technologies and services, satellites, LANs, private microwave and VANs transformed telecommunications from the status of a simple cost, like buildings or energy, into a tool for defining the structure of a corporation and its relationships with suppliers and markets. Communications systems became the defining architecture of the corporation. Private corporate investment in telecommunications equipment rose by 400 per cent between 1980 and 1987, from $15 bn to $75 bn. The private networks that result from this spending are the epitome of what Alfred Chandler described as the 'visible hands' of capitalism, the organizational systems which substituted for markets at the time of the birth of the modern corporation in the late nineteenth century to solve the problems of coordinating complex operations. These control mechanisms operate largely outside the market: whereas 70 per cent of the total goods trade of OECD countries is carried out between firms, between 80 and 90 per cent of data trade is carried on within firms. This data provides corporations with fast and accurate information about prices, financial conditions, output and trade so that resources can be flexibly deployed to meet objectives, the 'C3I' of corporate strategy. Networks can also be used for more direct control. The MAP automation protocols being developed by General Motors and other manufacturers will make it possible directly to control automated factories across national boundaries.

These intracorporate networks run alongside an intricate web of intercorporate networks, linking manufacturers, traders, financial companies and distributors. Networks of this kind are evolving as a parallel track to the traditional trade of physical goods. Within Europe, for example, much of the reinsurance trade is carried out through IBM's Rinet network. Airline reservation systems such as Galileo shape the structure of competition in air travel. Within all kinds of trade the boundaries between the physical and the informational are blurring. According to GATT (General Agreement on Tariffs and Trade) between 3.5 and 15 per cent of the value of all traded merchandise is accounted for by paperwork. A substantial proportion of the value of a shipment of wheat or cars is accounted for by insurance. Similarly, the informational value of a floppy disc or cassette may far exceed its physical value. Trade, the original task of the transnational corporation, is turning into something quite new, a mix of informational and physical goods, of physical links and electronic networks.

Paradoxically, however, the internationalization of economic activity over the 1970s and 1980s coincided with the partial breakdown the apparatus built up to regulate trade and exchange. The collapse of the Bretton Woods system, together with recession and extremely volatile exchange and interest rates, drove some out of the world money system altogether. Just as the global economy has taken physical form in private networks it has shown signs of falling apart. The debt crisis is one example. Another is countertrade, which has grown enormously, to as much as 20 per cent of all trade and 40 per cent of all Third World trade. Transnationals have become heavily involved, ironically using their high technology networks to facilitate the most ancient forms of exchange: General Motors and Chrysler exchanging cars for Jamaican bauxite, and General Electric exchanging steam turbines for Romanian nails.

Informational Sovereignty

As privately controlled networks spread they inevitably impinge on the sovereignty of national governments. Historically the tension was exemplified in the cavalier approach governments took to commercial communications. In the early days of transoceanic cables, the British government was notorious for listening to all relevant diplomatic and commercial messages. Today the American National Security Agency (NSA) routinely scrutinizes commercial traffic both on public and international leased lines at such listening stations as Menwith Hill in England. Governments also systematically restrict the flow of data across borders. Restrictions cover the content of data, privacy and data protection laws. They include requirements to purchase data and transmission equipment locally, to make use of public networks, rules denying access to national reservation systems and restrictions on the use of leased lines. Banks and financial institutions tend to be most vulnerable to these restrictions as information is a prime component of the products and services they market. Canada, for example, requires that all data generated by banks in Canada is maintained in Canadian data bases. The Brazilian government, which has pursued a comprehensive policy of building up its domestic computer industry, holds a monopoly of access to foreign data bases through Embratel's gateway. Japan, France and

West Germany are often criticized by the transnationals for their restrictive rules, which, according to a Vice-President of Continental Illinois: 'erode centralized decision making, hamper global management and curtail the creation of new financial services'. A 1986 survey of thirty transnationals on the subject of barriers to further globalization showed the two most important to be restrictions on service industries and on the flow of data across boundaries.[8] The underside of control is a hidden economy of transgressions: illegally used leased lines, physical movements of tapes and discs across boundaries and smuggling of hardware all take place on a vast scale.

All governments face difficult choices as networks threaten their ability to exercise control over their economies, and over the distribution and processing of information about their resources and citizens. Network-induced changes in the velocity of circulation of money have effectively demolished all previous theories and practices for the application of national monetary policy, and networks provide routes to bypass any structural barriers designed to limit the flow of money. Walter Wriston, formerly of Citicorp, has written that, 'the enormous and instantaneous flow of data from all over the world has created the "Information Standard" which has replaced the gold standard and the Bretton Woods agreement. Today with new technologies, no-one is in control; rather everyone is in control through our collective valuations.'[9] This collective control can be deeply destabilizing, as when a rumour on the Tokyo Stock Exchange resulted in the rapid collapse of the Continental Illinois bank on the other side of the world.

Finance and communication have always been closely linked. One of the first European newspapers, produced in sixteenth-century Augsburg, was published by the Fugger banking family. The nature of money, a form of information that draws its value from scarcity and credibility, makes financial transnationals unusually dependent on communication. Some predict that the intermixing of data will make it impossible to make laws restricting the transmission of one kind of information without impinging on all others, on the grounds that attempts to impede the flow of capital must inevitably lead to restrictions on the flow of information and vice versa. The competitive deregulation of telecommunications during the 1980s was mirrored in finance: it is no coincidence that the leading deregulators, the USA, UK and Japan, were also competing for position in financial services. Transparency of trading became the key to the competitiveness of major financial centres. As money flowed more quickly and more easily government control became harder to achieve. Rules and traditions were breached and innovative abilities directed towards inventing techniques such as off-balance sheet financing which escape banking regulations. Banks evolved from their traditional role as lenders into general providers of financial services, their profits less dependent on interest rates than on the ability to provide customized services. Communications technologies served to make it easier to enter neighbouring sectors, eliminating the role of frontiers in demarcating markets as it became possible for banks to internationalize without heavy investment in buildings and branches. In all these ways communications technologies allowed the monetary economy to resist the powers of sovereign governments.

Edward Ploman has written that the impact of communications technologies 'has been a decisive factor in transforming traditional views of sovereignty which have been understood and expressed in geographical and territorial or spatial terms into a new kind of concern ... about communications or informational sovereignty and integrity'.[10] This concept of information sovereignty has focused attention on trans-border data flows. Many countries have struggled to gain control over natural resources only to find that the real terrain of control has shifted to information resources. The structure of communications links in many countries undermines control, since external links are both more numerous and efficient than internal ones, and used more intensively by foreign companies. In the Philippines, for example, 65 per cent of international circuit use is accounted for by British, US and Japanese companies. There is also another dimension to this erosion of informational sovereignty. The US Landsat and French Spot (Satellite Pour l'Observation de la Terre) satellites export images of the world's resources, of crop patterns and minerals, without regard to any traditional notion of sovereignty.

The Evolution of Private Networks

One hundred years ago the global economy, such as it existed, was run by large trading companies. These would purchase goods from local manufacturers or wholesalers and invest their capital in exchange rather than production (although there are numerous examples going back to medieval times and beyond of merchants vertically integrating from production through trade to distribution). Communications were generally crude. As in medieval times, an international economic presence depended on autonomous intermediaries, commission merchants or factors empowered to act on a merchant's behalf, buying, selling, shipping, negotiating insurance and discounting bills. Without the information flows necessary for direct control there was no alternative. Limited control over long distances could best be ensured by using family members rather than strangers. Each exchange was a *salto mortale*, a death leap, as Marx described it. The movement from money into commodities was always risky, and each party would try to minimize the number of transactions through which its assets were illiquid. In the mid-nineteenth century, for example, the movement of cotton from a plantation in the US to Liverpool and London 'required at least three commercial exchanges: between planter and factor, between factor and manufacturer's agent, and between the agent and the manufacturer. With each separate movement of cotton towards England, an advance against its sale moved in the opposite direction so that the total voyage generated at least four commercial transactions and four different bills of exchange.'[11]

The opening of the transatlantic cable in 1866, the Pacific cable in 1903, transatlantic wireless telegraph in 1907, transatlantic telephone in 1927, transatlantic air mail in 1937 and commercial jet travel in the 1950s empowered traders to establish tighter control and to integrate more elements in the economic chain. When the American corporations spread across the world in the wake of the American army in the 1940s and 1950s, a control infrastructure was developing around them. A new era opened in 1963 when Honeywell used a terminal in Britain to control a computer in a plant in Massachussets with signals sent by the standard telex line. The promise of this experiment is being made operational in the 1980s and 1990s, as monitoring and oversight give way to the potential for real-time control over production on the other side of the world. The huge expansion in international capacity brought about by successive satellite generations, and by the fibre-optic transoceanic cables of the 1980s, has greatly enhanced the scope for central control. By 1990 it is estimated that there will be 2,500 civilian transponders in orbit in the West, compared to 1,400 in 1985; combined with competing fibre links, the effect will be a sharp drop in costs. The cost per circuit on the transatlantic cables will have fallen from $243,000 on TAT-5, (a generation of transatlantic cable) to an estimated $17,000 on TAT-9.

In principle, private networks on short-wave radio or leased telegraph or telephone circuits would have been possible from an early date. After the first transatlantic voice service was set up in 1927, there were three decades of 'rudimentary radio telephone ... plagued by chronic atmospheric interference and interminable queuing'.[12] Apart from the regulatory and technical barriers there were strong economic disincentives: leased circuits only become viable once a certain density of traffic can be guaranteed between two nodes. This in turn depends on production being genuinely international: most transnationals grew as multi-domestic operations, using local production to service local markets. Communication with other branches and with the parent company was limited. The early transnationals like Unilever managed overseas subsidiaries as microcosms of the parent company. More recently the forms of the transnational have become increasingly global, as according to Chris Bartlett and Sumantra Ghoshal,[13] the early multi-national forms have been succeeded first by the 'international' corporation, driven by standardized procedures and management practices, and more recently by the global corporation, exploiting global economies of scale and reducing overseas offices to distribution centres.

The three forms each have their own advantages, in terms either of responsiveness to local market needs or of cost reduction. But one effect of the overall trend from the first to the third has been a massive increase in the volume of intracorporate communications, primarily data about production, finance and other operational issues. It was this that made private networks viable. The significance of data is not primarily a question of volume. Even the computer industry's private networks are still largely used for voice traffic. Hewlett Packard, which operates one of the most advanced, spent 82.5 per cent of its transmission costs on voice telephony in 1985, compared to only 12.6 per cent on data. But data requires a different kind of transmission, involving more reliability and security, a higher degree of error control and architectures appropriate to rapid, sporadic bursts of computer data. Transnationals also have a special need for data communication: with the growth of data communication 'the ambiguity of the written and spoken word shrank dramatically. The elimination of ambiguities, which is important for all business operation is especially important for business conducted over long distances where error and distortion can go undetected for long periods.'[14] Data networks allow for preprocessing, and bring everything within the homogeneous plane of financial accounts and statistics, a precondition for tight control.

PTTs, brought up in an environment of voice telephony, circuit switching and universal service, were slow to adapt to business demands for data communications. Instead it was the computer and electronic companies, notably IBM, General Electric (and GEISCO) and Control Data, which led the way in designing private data networks and the novel architectures they demanded. The first private international networks were put together around services such as hotel and airline reservation, stock market quotations, banking and insurance transactions. SITA, serving the airlines, originally used a network of telex links before moving to a network of leased lines linking nodes in over 100 countries. These networks are cooperative ventures: SWIFT is a cooperative of banks, SITA a cooperative of airlines. Other examples include the VISA and Mastercard networks, and airline reservations systems such as SABRE, APOLLO and System One in the US, Amadeus and Galileo in Europe. All can be used both to assist coordination and to control the terms of market entry: airline reservations systems, for example, were able to exclude smaller carriers schedules.[15]

The transnationals own networks were generally built somewhat later as a response to deregulatory decisions. In the USA, private microwave networks spread after the FCC's Above 890 decision in 1959–60. These could then be internationalized by leasing lines from AT&T and foreign PTTs. The deregulation of satellite communications in the US after the 1972 'Open Skies' decision gave private networks a new opportunity to bypass the public network: By 1988 there were 143 private satellite networks in the US.[16] Examples include Federal Express, which uses a satellite to coordinate the routeing of packages, and K-Mart, which uses its network for inventory control and product information.

Bartlett and Ghoshal have argued that the world is now seeing the emergence of a fourth type of transnational, structured to manage intensive change in which it is essential simultaneously to cope with varying demands, innovation and global economies of scale. This emerging model, exemplified by companies like IBM and NEC, is held together less by structure than by common vision and experience. Such a model requires a new kind of communication to go alongside the flows of voice traffic and data. This is communication, usually in the form of video and magazines, that instils corporate loyalty and identity. By 1989, corporate television, the favourite medium for communicating values, was a rapidly growing sector worth around $150 m. in the US alone.

The varying needs of private networks explain their use of a mix of different technologies to serve different purposes. LANs and WANs linking workstations and computers, high-capacity links between mainframes and head offices, satellites to serve dispersed operations or for internal broadcasting, all overlap. Some networks integrate their different functions into ISDNs, while others maintain separate voice and data networks. Some are wholly owned, some leased; others use the public network in 'virtual' private networks. Many of the networking technologies used by private systems were originally pioneered by the US Air Force in the 1950s in the SAGE (Semi-Automatic Ground Environment) project, which coordinated in real time the surveillance data of a series of radar stations stretched across North America. IBM used its experience in SAGE to develop the IBM 305, which permitted distant access and the SABRE systems developed with American Airlines for flight reservations. The Department of Defense also developed ARPAnet, which became the prototypical international distributed network and the base for the first transnational packet networks. More recently leased capacity on satellites has been used for corporate television. In general, as private networks have developed, their technologies have tended to diverge from those of the public network; in particular their use of computers, and their orientation towards radio technologies of microwave and satellite, have led many away from the technical solutions of the PTTs.

Telecommunications technologies transform the structures of corporate life. The boundaries of the individual firm blur as its tasks are redefined. Networks such as SWIFT, SITA and ARINC were originally used as vehicles for sharing and coordinating information, subsequently developing transactional services in which the network acted as a market. ARINC's use of its network to provide a brokerage service for aircraft parts is one example. The transnationals use their private networks in much the same way, branching out from internal communication into the provision of services to other customers. This is turn creates problems for the affinity networks. SWIFT, which manages much of the world's international banking communication with a daily traffic of 950,000 messages, now faces competition from its own members, such as Citicorp, which sell access to their private networks to other banks. The pattern is familiar from the deregulation US telecommunications industry. As networks proliferate bypassers are themselves bypassed.

Bypass is a phenomenon with implications beyond telecommunications. Networks can be used to circumvent established relationships with banks or suppliers. By using telecommunications links investors can be reached directly without the mediation of commercial banks. A network can itself be used to sell banking services. As the interrelationships and boundaries of the corporation become more fluid the network permits multiple forms of bypass: internal divisions, for example, may choose to reject central services, instead providing their own processing or finance. The role of managing networks can be contracted out to companies like IBM, GEISCO and EDS which offer specialized network management services for transnationals throughout the world. IBM has operated SNA networks for eighty of the world's top 100 transnational corporations; its long history of involvement in running management and accounting systems gives it a depth of understanding of control and communication issues within the corporation that no other company can match. Where Intelsat functions as a 'carrier's carrier', the networks run by IBM, EDS and GEISCO have evolved into the private networks' private networks.

The Crisis of the Public Network

The evolution of bypass is one factor explaining why public telecommunications operators have experienced the spread of private networks as a profound and destabilizing crisis. The crisis is also in part a crisis of scale. National networks operate under a national jurisdiction, serving a national economy, while most of the important entities in the economy, and most of their largest clients, operate globally. Disjunction between the two is a source of many tensions. It creates costs for transnational operators which must deal with large numbers of different regulatory regimes and pricing policies, with differing standards and rules of interconnection. Tariff structures also heavily penalize communication across borders.

The need to increase functionality and reduce costs was the primary reason for building private networks. By using up to date technologies designed for the special needs of the company, telecommunications costs could be substantially reduced. Intensive use of leased lines is cheaper than use of the public network. The other factor has been control. The greater responsiveness afforded by a private network could speed up product development, reduce inventories or improve security. Privatization of networks was part of the long-term move away from standardized provision to increasing specialization and customization. Transnationals wanted to be able to choose the shape of their communications to meet their special needs and reflect their particular mix of finance, CAD/CAM, the extent of centralization or dispersal in marketing, research and management. The capacity to manage networks, to control the allocation and make-up of channels and the security of messages have all taken on a high value. Control also has other dimensions: independence of monopoly telecommunications companies, the flexibility to redesign the network, to restructure relationships with suppliers or retailers, are all important parts of the promise of private networks.

Just as the demands of data communication were ill understood by PTTs, so was the idea of specialized communication. The universal public network serving households and business alike was generic and standardized. The diverging needs of the two have forced PTTs fundamentally to re-evaluate their priorities. During the 1980s this had the apparently contradictory effect of making them simultaneously resist and serve the fragmentation and privatization of networks. In most countries PTTs argued against liberalization, usually in the name of the technical integrity of the network and the danger of 'cream skimming'. The political arena was used to constrain the growth of private networks. At the same time the PTTs sought to appease their largest customers.

In the US the Above 890 decision permitting the establishment of private microwave networks was a turning point. AT&T responded by offering discounts for bulk leasing of private lines and the WATS, which discounted bulk use of long-distance telephony. According to one commentator, private line provisions have 'consistently failed to cover their directly attributable embedded costs',[17] so that other users in practice subsidized the private networks. The pattern established by Above 890 has continued ever since, both in the US and elsewhere: legal concessions to large users have prompted PTTs to reorientate tariffs and services to their needs. Autonomy is used both as a means to control and as a lever on public networks. The ratchet effect of deregulation has been amplified as transnationals move data processing and other functions to the most loosely regulated countries. Its parallel effect has been to encourage the PTTs to develop cooperatively an array of specialized services aimed at transnationals. Managed data network services (MDNS), Centrex, x.25 networks, ISDNs, forms of electronic data interchange are all examples, often developed in collaboration with competitors like IBM and CSC.

The transnationals face a dilemma. On the one hand they are bound to oppose anything which could be used to prevent bypass and re-establish the position of the PTTs. On the other hand, they could not help but be attracted by the potential for high speed, compatible data flows across borders, and for services which may be provided below cost. Their dilemma is a universal one, the conflict between immediate improvements in the price and the functionality of services and strategic position in the long run, a trade-off between purposive and positional forms of control. All institutions want choice and control, but equally they do not want too much control, and neither do they want control with an excessive opportunity cost.

Thus the rise of private networks was followed by their (partial) fall. Having successfully altered the behaviour of PTTs and established their legitimate role in standards bodies like the ITU, ISO and ETSI, and having encountered serious barriers, skill shortages and inefficiencies in network management, many firms preferred to focus on their core business rather than operating and reselling capacity on their own networks. The open network and intelligent network models were also offering a 'control compromise'. In exchange for going back into the public network, large firms would be allowed much greater flexibility as to the terms on which they used it. Having achieved its purposes, bypass would become redundant.

The Changing Form of the Corporation

During the 1960s all the advanced countries experienced a rapid growth in the size of firms. Buoyant sales meant that tight centralization and monitoring were unnecessary, and subsidiaries could be left as relatively independent profit centres. Since the early 1970s volatility and uncertainty have forced all large corporations to reappraise themselves from top to bottom. An early response was conglomeration to spread risks. Between 1950 and 1980 the proportion of conglomerates amongst the top 500 US industrial companies rose from 4 to 34 per cent. The fundamental weakness of conglomerates was their failure to integrate disparate activities and exploit fluidities in the boundaries between different sectors and products. This was in large part a failure of communications. By the 1980s the lurch towards conglomeration had been replaced by a widespread commitment to integrating operations and to the use of communications as a means for tightening coordination. Communications networks which were initially used to rationalize resources and cut costs became instead a means of offering new services and redefining the nature of the value being sold. In this way a resources-based corporation, a bank or car company could sell information or financial services over its private network. Sears Roebuck used its network to become a major credit company. BP and Volvo extended their networks to set up in-house banks. Eastman Kodak offered VANs services. Networks could be used to encourage interlinking across previously separate activities, sharing R&D, product ideas and marketing, emulating Japanese practice.

These relationships between technology and organizational form have never been easy to delineate. There has been a long debate over causal priorities, between those for whom technology shaped control, and those like Braverman for whom control imperatives shaped the choice of technologies. Somewhere in the middle is the view that technology and organizational form evolve together, each defining the other's limits. Rather than technology causing organizational change, organizational change comes to be seen as an attempt to improve the congruence of an organization's technology and its control system. Thus, communications technologies raise the threshold at which divisional forms and the dispersal of control are needed while also limiting the scope of decentralization when it does appear. Tendencies towards both decentralization and centralization evolve in tandem: the tendency is towards decentralization of decision making because control is easier.[18]

In the past transnationals followed a conventional wisdom going back to Adam Smith that favoured the use of scale to extend specialization. As the firm grew, functional divisions would proliferate: corporate planning would be organized separately from top management; within each division specialized workers would be responsible for quality control or industrial relations. In design a similar logic led to sharp demarcations between research, development and production engineering. On the shop floor or within an office a rigid division of labour would go alongside tightly defined job specifications and close supervision. These were the organizational analogues of Taylorism on the shop floor. Intellectual, control and design functions were separated from production itself and the division of labour was used as a means of maintaining basic relations of power within the enterprise.

These techniques are now widely recognized as inefficient. Each is being transformed. At the top corporate planning returns to senior management. Design and engineering are reintegrated using computer-aided design, manufacturing and engineering so that products can be quickly designed for easy manufacture. Quality control is reintegrated into line work using semi-automated machinery and more flexible job definitions. In all of these cases excessively mechanistic ideas of control have proved too inflexible for the rapid turnover of ideas and products which corporations need.

Changing organizational forms have often been explicitly copied from Japanese practice (described in one account as Fujitsuism, a deep linkage of production and innovation[19]). The integration of design and production, which is in part a reflection of Japan's early experience of reverse engineering, and the emphasis on horizontal flows and more general training are characteristic of the most successful Japanese firms. Japanese 'just-in-time' supply systems have also been widely emulated (even by SWIFT, whose 24-hour banking system can be seen as a kind of financial just-in-time: by abolishing the 16-hour float it saved an estimated $1 bn each year). Although each of these approaches depends on communication none depends on sophisticated technology. Just-in-time systems can be run with telephones. The emphasis on structure rather than technology explains why Japanese approaches to automation have been much more gradualist than those of the West. In the most successful Japanese practice the communicational structure precedes the implementation of technology: technology is adapted to the existing network forms rather than being imposed in a 'big bang' restructuring.

New thinking about corporate organization stresses the significance of horizontal communication as opposed to the vertical communications of the classic corporation. Multiple lines of accountability in matrix structures replace the single line of accountability flowing up to a chief executive. A recent exposition by Peter Drucker, one of the world's leading business theorists, argued that 'the typical large business 20 years hence will have fewer than half the levels of management of its counterpart today, and no more than a third the managers' and will resemble not the typical corporation but rather 'the hospital, the university, the symphony orchestra'.[20] It will be based on knowledge, and its problems will be those of coordinating groups of specialized workers, under relatively small top managements, of motivating and rewarding specialists, of managing task forces and sustaining a unified vision. Drucker describes it as the replacement of the 'command-and-control' corporation, based on the model of the army, with the information-based organization structured on the mobilization of knowledge: control is largely decentralized to self-regulating units, leaving to the chief executive a task of coordination more like that of the orchestral conductor than the army commander. This model has implications for how the architectures of communications networks are to be organized. The emphasis is on open links within and between small groups of specialists rather than on a vertical command and control structure: vertical links are used more for overseeing than for command. Individual units become more responsible for their own use of computers and intelligence, less dependent on centralized processing power.

Masashiko Aoki has described the difference between US and Japanese-style management as a difference in the ways that information is organized.[21] In the US jobs tend to be specialized; integration of tasks is a specialized function of management; control is vertical, while worker mobility tends to be interfirm rather than intrafirm. In the latter, decision making is relatively widespread; the on-the-spot knowledge of workers, shops and subcontractors tends to be used and neighbouring units are encouraged to share information. Learning-by-doing mobilizes that economically useful knowledge, emphasized by Hayek, that does not take the overt form of the blueprint, manual or patent. In the US knowledge tends to spread across firm boundaries as people leave, while in Japan it remains within. Clearly each model requires a different structure of communications network. In the Japanese model much of the communication need not take an electronic form and is indeed unsuitable for formalization. This suggests the importance of informal network structures in promoting flexibility and efficiency, structures that are rarely found when the corporation is seen as a system of command-and-control.

Despite experimentation with new conceptions of control, more mechanistic and hierarchical notions of control continue to survive within the context of integrating strategies. Some would argue that the more flexible models outlined above are fundamentally inefficient: that they lead to horizontal duplication of resources and that they fail fully to exploit economies of scale. Instead they argue for a reformation of the traditional pyramidal corporation, in a more global and technology-intensive form. This alternative strategy has been bound up with automation technologies and with the use of technology as a solution for organizational problems. The classic example is probably General Motors, which took over EDS, the software company it bought in 1984, with the aim of creating an integrated information system that would link the factory floor with the chairman's office in a twenty-five nation network of over 500,000 terminals.

The idea of global automated factories linked by telecommunications and controlled by a handful of computers has a long and unhappy history. GM saw technology as the solution to the gradual erosion of competitiveness it has experienced during the 1970s. Automation with EDS (and Hughes) would exploit the parallels between cars and aircraft built in automated factories and structured around electronic control systems.

The first problem encountered by GM was the incompatibility of automation standards, which increased the already enormous costs of automation (it is estimated that $2 bn of GM's $5 bn Saturn Car project went on computer hardware and software). Successful automation depends on machines being able to communicate with each other. GM's solution was to participate directly in the process of developing the new technologies of manufacturing automation, forcing its suppliers to cooperate in developing the MAP set of protocols.

Although MAP gained ground as a family of automation standards, technology proved to be only a partial solution to the problems of competitiveness. By 1988 GM had installed 7,000 robots, over 1,000 machine vision systems and hundreds of 'robot trucks'. Because technology had been seen as a panacea, less attention was given to the problems of educating people and allowing them control over the use of machines, despite traumatic earlier experiences such as the secretly automated Vega project in the early 1970s in Ohio. The hard solutions of technology and systematic control ignored the soft contexts within which they must operate. It was no coincidence that by 1986 the joint GM–Toyota NUMMI plant in California, based on Japanese management styles and relatively low-technology equipment, outperformed the more advanced plants in terms of both productivity and quality.

The Limits of Globalism

Learning the virtues of decentralized control seems to be particularly hard when technologies promise ever greater control at the centre. This can be clearly seen in the experience of the global car strategies of General Motors and Ford. The global car strategy was one of a number which extrapolated from the mass-production practices of the past to the global reach of transnationals. It was anticipated that transnational production of similar cars, modified for national markets, would reap the benefits of a new level of economies of scale. Globalization strategies aimed to take advantage of what were perceived to be the growing similarities between different parts of the world: similar levels of communication, transport and energy infrastructure, similar distribution, credit and retailing systems, widespread television advertising and falling tariff barriers. The world created by global corporations and global culture seemed to demand global industrial strategies to benefit from economies in everything from research to advertising. The benefits of globalization were particularly associated with Harvard's Theodor Levitt,[22] who offered three main arguments: that needs and interests were becoming more homogeneous; that customers were prepared to sacrifice specialized preferences for lower prices; and that substantial economies of scale in production and marketing could be achieved.

Each of these assumptions proved flawed. Increasingly sophisticated market research has shown much greater heterogeneity, suggesting that Rolex and Dior at the top end of the market and McDonald's at the bottom cannot be taken as harbingers of the future. Instead, for example, Findus continue to market fish cakes and fish fingers in the UK, *boeuf bourguignon* in France and *vitello con funghi* in Italy, while in Japan Coca-Cola markets 'Georgia' cold coffee in a can and a tonic drink 'Aquarius' alongside its global products. Lifestyle approaches have revealed complex regional and subcultural differences that show no signs of diminishing over time. The evidence 'suggests that the similarities in customer behaviour are restricted to a relatively limited number of target segments, or product markets'.[23] Product quality rather than price has emerged as the determinant factor in marketing strategies, suggesting that customers were not prepared to forego distinctiveness for lower prices. Considerable differences also persist in the avilable marketing and distribution structure (e.g. the availability of television advertising, the relative position of small stores and supermarkets), making it hard to devise truly global marketing strategies.

The weakness of the global reasoning in relation to production became apparent almost as soon as the strategies were put into practice in the late 1970s. For the global car, the end of multiple sourcing quickly rendered firms vulnerable to national governments and trade unions which now had the leverage to disrupt a global production line. Inventory and quality control costs proved immensely high. Because of the distances involved, a just-in-time system could not be used: faults were often not noticed until many batches had been produced. Lead times became a problem as the global system proved too inflexible for volatile markets.

Despite the benefits of globalization in exploiting the economies of scale of a Sony Walkman or Coca-Cola, the world remains resistant to sameness regardless of the technologies used. Companies like Sanyo and Sharp design for particular lifestyles in different parts of the world where ten years before they would have made one global product; the most astute transnationals have learnt the virtues of 'diversity from above', where diversity is contained within a highly flexible organization, able to standardize some features of organization and production the better to promote flexibility and difference in end-products.

Some authors have seen in the barriers to global strategies symptoms of the larger crisis of Fordism, the system of mass production based on large corporations, standardized products aimed at mass markets and rigid divisions of labour. As Fordism reached its limits, strategies which sought to extrapolate from the past would be bound to fail. Charles Sabel and

Michael Piore in their influential book on industrial policies, *The Second Industrial Divide*,[24] argued that the grain of change was coming to favour quite different forms of organization: flexible, specialized, small companies, often linked by cooperative forms of organization which minimize competition through price and encourage sharing of technology. In their paradigm case, the industrial district, informal links between local government, business, banks, universities and trade unions proved better able to cope with volatility than the hierarchies of the transnational. These informal networks have had more success than the more advanced communications networks tying together large hierarchical organizations, though they are themselves threatened by cheaper communications.

These lessons have not been lost on the more perceptive firms, which have sought to combine control with flexibility in ways analogous to the 'planned spontaneities' that Walter Ong has seen as characteristic of the era of electronic communication.[25] IBM, for example, has always limited the degree to which it globalizes despite its commitment to a global division of labour. Conscious of its unusual market domination and the danger of government retaliation, IBM has tended to distribute research and development functions in subsidiaries while balancing exports and imports in each country. During the 1980s it tried to bring some of the organizational flexibility of Silicon Valley into its own structures, setting up independent business units in education, robotics and biomedical systems. Each of these strategies reflected awareness of the dangers of excess control, particularly where creativity and ingenuity are being mobilized. The trend towards flexible specialization is also as much a social policy as an economic one. The break-up of mass, standardized production is paralleled in the break-up of traditional welfare systems. These are replicated within the structures of corporations, providing insurance, health care and recreation. The move away from rigid hierarchies towards more flexible and networked structures tends to be accompanied by an emphasis on values and corporate culture as the glue that binds the corporation together.

The industrial district model and the IBM model suggest that corporate forms may be moving in a parallel direction, exploiting the properties of communication so as to evolve into networks of firms and network-like firms, with some strategic centralization and operational devolution.[26] This evolution raises some problems for the transactions cost theory of the firm, according to which activities are brought inside the firm when the coordination costs of carrying it out within a bureaucracy are lower than the transactions costs of purchasing the same goods or services within the market. Communications technologies reduce both transactions and coordinations costs. Interorganizational networks blur the boundaries between markets and bureaucracies as do organizational innovations around the joint venture, the licensing agreement, contractual arrangements, franchises and federations, which all mix elements of market and intra-organizational relationship. What makes these work is a dynamic accumulation of trust or loyalty that is not captured by the transactions cost approach.

The erosion of regulations and trade protection has been an important factor in this tend. The need for corporate allies to hasten development of a new product, to enter a new market or to resist a rival lies behind the rapid spread of ventures that spread across corporate boundaries. Cooperation can take many forms: cross-distribution and cross-licensing (such as between Eli Lilly and Yamanouchi Pharmaceutical), arrangements (such as that between Celltech and Boots) where the established firm takes its dividends in the form of new products, or pooling of technical knowledge (such as Siemens and Corning Glass cooperation on fibre optics). In the military industries second sourcing rules lead competitors to agree to produce each other's products, as National Semiconductor and Motorola do in semiconductors. Sometimes cooperation takes the forms developed by Esprit (the European high technology research fund) and RACE (orientated to advanced communications technologies), and is limited to the 'precompetitive' stage of technological development. The crucial point is that in all these cases some degree of trust and reciprocity is necessary: not all contingencies can be contracted for; informal links become as important as formal ones. Similar considerations apply in another modern business form, the franchising system. According to one commentator, 'at the core of most successful franchise systems we find mutual interdependence and trust based on standing relationships and an entire web of linkages between system members'.[27]

Similar patterns are visible in trading. Logistical control remains crucial to effective trade, and Mitsui, the world's largest trading company, reportedly spends as much as 10 per cent of sales revenues on communications.[28] But this type of control over prices and flows of goods has to be rooted in continuing relationships. This has become particularly clear to Western companies seeking to enter the dense networks of Japan's internal markets. Pilkington Glass, which supplies the glass for two-thirds of Japan's sunglasses, found it necessary to 'tie itself closely to the intricate network of subcontractors which do the cutting, edging, hardening and polishing of the glass', realizing the importance of showing 'a company at each point of the chain that they can rely on us to help them if necessary'.[29] Relationships of this kind allow a trader or a supplier to ride out temporary volatilities.

In this more complex environment with its dependence on soft power and trust relationships the assertion of central control can become difficult. The clothing company Benetton, which was highly successful at organizing a flexible network of suppliers, found it impossible to tighten its control over the private communications network it had built up with its suppliers. Suppliers were not prepared to make full use of a network that gave Benetton too much operational information about production and distribution conditions. Instead, Benetton was forced to move the network outside its direct control, to GEISCO, so as to allay fears of excessive control and encourage greater use of communications between points of sale, manufacturers and the headquarters.

In both network-like firms and networks of firms there are strong pressures towards specialization. Within the transnational, specialized functions such as data processing, trading or financial control can be efficiently provided from one point for the whole company. Within federations and networks of firms, specialization is attractive because it minimizes conflict and maximizes the scope for productive cooperation.[30] Strategic interests can also be served by maintaining boundaries. Although the pressure towards common standards in such things as EDI remains strong, there are equally strong pressures towards building incompatibilities into the network, so that suppliers or distributors become dependent on a dominant firm.[31]

This emphasis on soft controls, on the network rather than the hierarchy, has been predominantly confined to the First World. The use of softer structures in the advanced countries has often been accompanied by the use of harder ones elsewhere, described by one writer as primitive or 'bloody Taylorism',[32] the subcontracting of unskilled tasks, acceleration and superexploitation of labour.

Paradoxes of Control

Problems of control are as old as power itself. It is inevitable that they become particularly critical in organizations dispersed across the world, caught between conflicting loyalties to the local country or affiliate and the parent. Cross-cutting lines of communication between top management at the centre and on the periphery generate a wide range of different patterns. The French business theorist Yves Doz has written of the problems that arise when local managements are 'more preoccupied with seeking corporate approval of all actions than with taking actions that were appropriate for the subsidiary',[33] and of the more general tensions between fragmentation and unity in transnationals, in particular the tension between the 'economic imperative' of survival and success and the 'political imperative' of adjusting strategy to the demands of host governments. As more subtle strategies evolve simultaneously to achieve global coordination and local flexibility, the structures of communication become more complex. According to the work of Bartlett and Ghoshal, which has already been cited,[34] the Japanese company Matsushita provides an exemplary case of how this can be done: 'rather than trying to limit the number of linkages between headquarters and subsidiaries, or to focus them through a single point, as many companies do for the sake of efficiency, Matsushita tries to preserve the different perspectives, priorities and even prejudices of its diverse groups worldwide'. Centralization of some activities coincides with decentralization of others. Another example cited by Bartlett and Ghoshal[34] is Ericsson's development of the AXE telephone exchange, which combined the standardization of core elements with sufficient flexibility to allow modification to local conditions: structurally this was achieved by linking people in different subsidiaries through job transfers and task forces as well as through more formal intersubsidiary boards. Effective control was achieved through a judicious mix of the formal and the informal, the soft and the hard.[35]

This new dependence on softer structures which are rooted in a locality or a culture qualifies that vision of the transnationals as a vast spaceship able to choose when, where and if to descend to earth. 'Equidistance' and proximity to markets are as important as a strong base in the home country. The centralized surveillance power of the communications network is not unambiguous. The strategic problem is that the transnational corporation seeks both predictability and that degree of change and responsiveness that can only come from a loosening of control. Equally fundamental is the problem of volatility. Even the most highly attuned strategies will be uncertain and fragile in a volatile world. The spread of communications and control systems has been as much a response to increasing uncertainty as a clear strategy to enhance control, but the proliferation of highly responsive systems creating more interconnections and more transactions tends to undermine predictability rather than enhance it. In the same way more widespread access to information can actually reduce knowledge and certainty if everyone else is also acting in the light of improved information. Aggregated across a system of competing organizations, ever-larger investments in interconnected control technologies feed uncertainty and chaotic behaviour. This is why pressures to increase transparency, through standards for computer communication or such things as EDI (Electronic Data Interchange), are matched by pressures to reduce it, to lock a chain of supply and distribution into dependence on a dominant company. This is also the diseconomy of all open systems: openness and transparency bring dependence and vulnerability as well as the benefits of greater scale.

12

Rethinking Public Control

For most of the twentieth century the majority of telecommunications and broadcasting networks were under some form of state or public control, accountable to governments, parliaments and various forms of 'arm's length' body. Organized in this way they built up vast telegraph, telephone and broadcasting networks reaching across continents. They helped to transform complex communications technologies into everyday household goods. In many ways the state-organized communications sectors, together with their international institutions, the ITU and Intelsat, represent extraordinary success stories of rational planning, fair allocation and steady progress.

But the incorporation of communications within a sphere of activity defined as public, committed to a public interest or public service and controlled in one form or another by the state, is no longer as unquestioned as it once was. The idea of collective solutions, of a general public interest that is more important than individual interests, has found it hard to make the transition from the relatively standardized services of telegraph, telephony and television to the more complex worlds of the fax, electronic mail, videotex and high-definition television. For alongside more widespread social and political winds there were also factors special to communication that called into question the legitimacy of state and public control.

The public good properties of communications came under attack from the professional economists; the supposed scarcity of spectrum looked much less credible in the age of the satellite and the cable; and fears that technologies could become tools of moral contamination or political destabilization came to seem anachronistic in an era of media saturation. Meanwhile, in many societies, an assumption of the state's right to control communications in the name of national security or development had withered, too often revealed as a bare excuse for tyranny and deception. The critics argued that public controls are neither feasible nor legitimate in the age of digital networks, of almost limitless technical capacities and (perhaps equally limitless) moral relativism. Public control came to be seen as ultimately indistinguishable from state coercion, a reflection of the self-interest of regulators and politicians. The critics drew on a long tradition of principled opposition to state controls, invoking Milton's *Areopagitica*, the First Amendment of the US Constitution, and John Stuart Mill's seminal work *On Liberty*. This powerful tradition, which continues to occupy a central place in the self-image of the Western world, has argued for freedom of the press and communications as the precondition for moral choice and virtue, as the indispensable defence of natural rights, a precondition for good government or for the emergence of truth.

As the older traditions of public and state control lapsed into crisis, alternative visions of the future appeared, visions which take for granted some basic freedoms but which draw very different conclusions as to how they are to be protected. Both are problematic and only half-formed but, in their flaws as well as their appeals, they provide a useful starting point for considering the political choices for the future. In one the new media and networks are to be like the public spaces of the modern city, the parks and streets, theatres, pubs and cafés where all the classes and groups of society mix and jostle, learn about and respond to each other's lives. They are to be a common property. Access to entertainments and to society's discourse with itself is to be universal, rather than determined by the market, the major channels a common property subject to public regulation and accountability. The state's role is either to promote and run communications networks or, at the very least, to preserve balance between the networks and to subsidize certain kinds of service. Social solidarity and the common good are emphasized over diversity and fragmentation. In one version, which stresses civil society rather than the state, networks assist in communication across borders: global communication allows communities to form across East and West, North and South, under the aegis of non-governmental civic institutions. Above all communication is conceived as open and inclusive, rather than as a commodity that must be rendered exclusive.

In the second vision the networks become more like private clubs, with exclusive entry and segmented and separated entertainments for each class or each lifestyle, akin perhaps to the medieval cities in which people kept to their own quarter or caste oblivious to the life of those in the next neighbourhood. Rather than being a common property the various networks become the strictly private property of corporations, accountable only to their shareholders. Communication and culture are governed by the rules of commodity production and exchange. Regulation is left to the marketplace, growing organically upwards out of the relationships of companies, cartels, clubs and free associations rather than down from a sovereign state. Plato believed that the size of cities should be limited to the number of people who could be addressed by a single voice. With extensive digital networks any number of 'invisible cities' can be formed, microcosms of social solidarity that need bear no relation to the physical facts of where people share the same spaces. Above all the second vision stresses the value of continual innovation and change in the provision of services and its dependence on individual choice rather than state determination.

Each vision has different implications. The first stresses collective access to the externalities of the network, the second their private appropriation. Neither has an unambiguous moral advantage over the other, although the first is often couched in a language that emphasizes the good and the virtuous over the immoral, the shallow and the subversive. In its purest forms, however, the totally public world can be as oppressive and alienating as the totally privatized world, one reason why each new generation of communications technology has raised the profile of privacy as a political issue. The public space is that of social distinction, violence and shame as well as that of community and solidarity, the private world that of loneliness and introspection as well as autonomy. Each model also has very different implications for the organization of political life. In the first, political life is focused on common institutions, issues and debate, and on an ideal of fair and balanced treatment of competing positions. Ideally there are only a small number of common fora, so that communication can take place across social boundaries. In the second model political ideas take on some of the properties of commodities in a free market. Providers of broadcasting, news services or videotex are free to offer any news, any bias or prejudice and, arguably, any standards of truthfulness, subject only to the response of the market. Public service controls to guarantee 'fairness', balance and equal access are swept away in the name of freedom. Public communications systems become like the press, free to editorialize at will. Consumer sovereignty takes on the role of moral regulation. Public, statist control is replaced by the control exercised by a discriminating consumer, mediated through the market. This market need not be wholly orientated towards profit. In principle any number of 'micropublics' – trade unionists, methodists, racists or football hooligans – can form themselves into free associations providing their own non-profit communications systems. Minitel in France provides an embryonic example of such a system, open to political parties, campaigning organizations and newspapers to sell or give away their services subject to none of the rules that constrain broadcasters.

As will be clear from earlier chapters, neither model can guarantee economic stability. The first depends on public subventions that are always vulnerable politically if the public channels cease to be used by a substantial part of the public, while the second is vulnerable to the forces that threaten any form of informational commodity. Nor can either make an unambiguous argument as to the superiority of its methods of relating the economic structure of communication to political openness. Forty years ago the first UK Royal Commission on the Press expressed a widespread view when it declared that 'free enterprise is an absolute prerequisite for a free press'. This is widely accepted, yet it is equally clear that although market mechanisms may be a necessary condition for openness they are by no means sufficient. There remain strong reasons for doubting whether private ownership and markets can guarantee the quality and diversity of information needed by active citizens participating in a democratic society. Any structure that ties communication too closely to private capital will inevitably skew the messages it broadcasts to the interests of capital. There are also concerns, expressed most forcefully by Neil Postman,[1] that commercial electronic media bring an unstoppable tendency to reduce all issues to the metalanguage of entertainment.

Similar arguments appeared as the press entered the era of mass circulation and advertising-financed newspapers around the turn of the century. Graham Murdock quotes a writer of 1910: 'Just as the moment came when it was seen that private schools, loan libraries, commercial parks, baths, gymnasia, athletic grounds and playgrounds would not answer, so the moment is here for recognising that the commercial mass media does not adequately meet the needs of democratic citizenship.'[2] Walter Lippman wrote in 1920 that 'a great newspaper is a public service institution' an approach reflected in the trusts established to protect newspapers' editorial independence in an age of takeovers and conglomeration. In each case public controls were seen as a necessary countervailing force to the tendencies to monopoly of the market, the downgrading of truth or goodness when the pursuit of profit becomes the primary motivation for communication.

Public and Private

Attitudes to the two models are inevitably coloured by the histories of public control on the one hand and markets on the other. Public controls have never been simple expressions of a public interest. The history of public regulation of broadcasting and telecommunications networks has often been one of narrow interest (whether of cultural elites, of private corporations or civil servants) parading in the guise of universal interest. Public service broadcasting has often reflected the views and interests of unrepresentative, metropolitan elites while public service in telecommunications took shape in monopolies which often failed to provide any service at all to the majority of the public. In communications, as in other spheres, the interests of the public became identified with those of the state, expressed in unresponsive and inefficient organizational forms, classic examples of strong power systems largely devoted to reproducing themselves.

There is also a sense that the technologies of communication may have made it harder to articulate a sense of a coherent public interest. For Richard Sennett, an influential historian of public life in the West, 'electronic communication is one means by which the very idea of public life has been put to an end. The media have vastly increased the store of knowledge social groups have about each other, but has rendered actual contact unnecessary'.[3] The private, atomized, consumer, receiving messages on a screen, is a member of the public only in the sense of sharing with others a passive role of reception. There is a widespread sense that the virtue of public life, of the *civitas*, has been severely eroded. In most of the visions of the information society, networks end up in the living room, and relations with the outside world pass through the television screen: cable and satellite TV replace the cinema, telework replaces the office, teleshopping the high street. Within the home family members pursue their own interests at their own electronic terminal. Rare attempts to reverse the trend towards an 'immobile privatization', such as the Community Information Centres movement in the US in the 1970s, or the Scandinavian electronic village halls of the 1980s, have been marginal. Others maintain that electronic networks can support new forms of community, such as Special Interest Group networks on videotex, and the 'virtual' communities of a Minitel.[4] The network becomes a means of maintaining public life against the pressures of a mobile society.

The debate between the two positions is not new. Carolyn Marvin, a historian of the early years of the telephone, quotes Judge Robert S. Taylor a patent attorney and counsel to independent telephone interests, claiming that the telephone had ushered in the 'epoch of neighbourship without propinquity',[5] a theme echoed in the 1980s advertisements proclaiming 'telecommunity'. Marvin notes the irony that the age of the public, the municipal and the civic was when the city's inhabitants for the first time spent much of their time watching strangers in streets, cafés and newspapers, when, in other words, the idea of a shared space was already fatally compromised. The nostalgia for an earlier and more authentic age straddles the divide between the private and the public. Harpers in 1893 commented that 'public amusements increase in splendor and frequency but private joys grow rare and difficult, and even the capacity for them seems to be withering'.[6]

The contest between the two alternatives, the one of publicness, social solidarity and collective provision, the other of specialization, segmentation, fragmentation and private worlds, runs parallel to the more overtly political clash between the public and the private as social organizing principles. During the 1980s the relationships between states, private sectors, markets, bureaucracies and what is sometimes called 'civil society' have been deeply questioned and contested in advanced capitalist societies and socialist ones alike. This historic shift has been particularly marked in communication. Yet the benefits of a fresh look at old structures have been limited by the fact that much of the debate about communications policy has been posed in terms of simple dichotomies between regulation and deregulation, monopoly and competition, public and private, state and market. In practice each of these dichotomies serves to obscure as much as it illuminates. Deregulation has tended, ironically, to demand more oversight and vigilance on the part of the state and its agencies. Competition has, paradoxically, often served to strengthen monopolies. State and market interpenetrate more than ever before. In modern industrialized countries the boundaries of traditional categories have eroded beyond repair; states are massively implicated in all areas of the economy, as regulators, financiers of research and education and providers of infrastructure. Within state bureaucracies market systems spring up, while market sectors create their own quasi-state organizations.

These considerations apply with particular force in communications, where the public sector has created diverse forms of quasi-state organization in broadcasting, in culture and in regulation and where private sectors have their own 'regulatory' organizations to set standards, to act as buffers to a complaining public, to organize cartels or jointly to fund research and development. The communications industry is largely dominated by institutions which occupy the grey area between the state and market, the endless alphabet soup of BT, BBC, IBA, of the PTTs, CEPT, ETSI, EBU in Europe, of AT&T, ANSI, Sematech, COS and MCC in America, of POSI, NTT, NHK and MITI in Japan. The most successful entrepreneurs have been those best able to make political alliances and win the backing of governments rather than the ones who have sought success in the market alone. In both broadcasting and telecommunications global competition between transnational corporations is closer to medieval jousting for territorial control than the classic vision of atomistic markets. Politically too, neither state nor market has any monopoly of efficiency, innovation or responsiveness: at different times and under different conditions both have acted either as liberating forces, opening communications and dispersing power, or as constraints and fetters.

The Public Sphere

Use of the words 'public' and 'private' is particularly problematic in the field of communications. The word 'public' originally referred to the common good, before taking on the more modern meaning of making something manifest. Such words as 'publishing' and 'publicity' are bearers of this underlying link between communication and the common. The idea of a common good can never be politically or economically neutral. Whether the common refers to the city, the nation or the race profoundly shapes what it means. In Aristotle's writings the common good of the *polis* was based on the common good of the family, the household or *oekonomia*, which shared things in common and was concerned above all with needs rather than wants. The realm of the economic was bound up with commonality and value was inseparable from justness. Similar ideas of the common, the public and their links to needs were effectively mobilized by some of the builders of the first communication networks: these would serve to bring people together, to satisfy psychic needs for social intercourse and for information about a rapidly changing world. Indeed, Anthony Smith has argued that 'tele-communications became a very early theatre for the rehearsal of modern arguments concerning public interest and society equity' and that the 'history of the telegraph and its offspring acts as a kind of commentary on the history of modern ideas about the nature of the public interest'.[7]

Yet this apparently simple idea of a public is in fact beset by contradictions. Perhaps the most basic contradiction in our notion of the public arises from the sociological and political divide that accompanied the birth of the modern state and civil society. This was well described by Daniel Bell, who wrote that the distinctive feature of the modern market economy, sociologically, is that 'it has been a bourgeois economy. This has meant two things: first that the ends of production are not common but individual; and second, that the motives for the acquisition of goods are not needs but wants'.[8] It was this same bourgeoisie which came to define much of what we now mean by a public space in its struggle in the eighteenth century to create what Jürgen Habermas has called a 'public sphere of discourse'. Habermas defined this as 'a realm of our social life in which something approaching public opinion can be formed . . . a portion of the public sphere comes into being in every conversation in which private individuals assemble to form a public body'.[9] In his characterization (which has been much criticized by historians) the public sphere, which came to mediate between state and society, was born out of the struggles of a new and confident middle class, able to defend its gains by mobilizing economic power against the repressive powers of Church and

State. Basing its means of communication in the market, the middle class could provide itself with the time and material resources for discourse. This base was essential if the new class was effectively to generate strategies for growth and survival, a binding philosophy and in the longer run an all-embracing world view. Equally important to the workings of this public sphere were the rules of discourse based on relatively equal access and a commitment to rational argument. In the Kantian tradition these rules implicitly assumed that the best and truest argument would prevail. The class therefore had a material interest in preserving free and equal discourse. Such freedoms were the prerequisite for developing the best arguments and the most effective strategies. It was a public space which of necessity was not controlled by the public or by public institutions except through the choice of the consumer to buy or not to buy. It was public by virtue of the ideology of the providers and the rules of discourse.

The public sphere also counterposed the principle of supervision, of making things public, to the traditional principles of existing power. The public sphere implied public control (in French the word *contrôle* carries this meaning of inspection). Parliaments and assemblies were required to debate in public, overseen and criticized by independent newspapers, following a principle which found its purest expression in the first extensive freedom of information act adopted by Sweden in the mid-eighteenth century. According to Habermas, this world of free and rational discourse was undermined by its own success. As the bourgeoisie grew and capital began to move into communication, the structure of the media changed and with it the nature of public discourse. Advertising became the primary source of revenue for newspapers and magazines. Ownership became concentrated. Newspapers were increasingly seen as indistinguishable from other business activities, their goals commercial rather than political. Newspapers changed, too, from being retailers of news to becoming dealers in public opinion and ultimately a medium of consumer culture. Yet the bourgeoisie remained committed to the principles which had served it well and which seemed threatened by evolving mass media. The market had ceased to be guarantor of the public sphere and had, instead, become a threat. This, Habermas argues, was the logic which led to the state being called in as a bulwark against the encroachment of commercialism. Public education and public libraries were mobilized as the bearers of the principles of rational public discourse, of a space insulated from the logic of the marketplace under the aegis of the state. Later public service radio and television, and in some countries subsidized arts and cinema, would play similar roles.[10]

In this way a fundamental split was created between a political being and an economic being. The first was, and is, taught to have opinions, to vote, to participate and to debate within the community's accepted rules for arriving at decisions and furthering the public good within a discourse of needs. The second is brought up to be private in outlook, to consume, maximize and calculate as an individual pursuing individual wants. The idea of the economic, originally born out of the common commitment to the needs of the household, was made to stand in opposition to the public. The public sphere, originally embedded in the market, came to stand against it, and the idea of multiple economies was subsumed by the idea of a single economy of interchangeable commodities and prices.

Habermas's account of the origins of state public service leaves out crucial elements: in particular it ignores the alternative public spheres of other classes, most importantly the working class organized in clubs, libraries, corresponding societies, trade unions and nonconformist church organizations. When governments introduced compulsory universal education, public libraries and later broadcasting, it was clear to many that beneath the rhetoric of benevolent liberal reform these were also deliberate attacks on an autonomous realm of working-class activity, with its own material base, its own networks of exchange and its own meanings. The self-education movements and subversive literary cultures of subordinate classes were effectively pre-empted and coopted, as governments and ruling classes learned to use access, rather than the denial of access, as a tool of power. This assault on the independent public sphere and 'social literacy' of the working classes was also a defence of the divide between economic and political life. For if one idea can be singled out as common to the working-class movements of the late nineteenth century it was that political and economic being should be reconciled, and that production and politics should be the subjects of needs and the common good.

When modern public institutions began to emerge in the first decades of the twentieth century it was the bourgeois conception of the public that proved dominant. As Daniel Bell has argued, there never was a very coherent theoretical foundation for the 'public household' producing public goods, nor a clear set of criteria for making decisions. The public space as it emerged was to serve an abstract public, to be insulated both from economics and from direct political control. Since the decline of cooperative, guild, syndicalist and anarchist movements in the 1920s and 1930s, alternative visions of how public or socialized enterprises should be run have been scarce. When states brought economic organizations into public ownership they rarely had any coherent and distinctive philosophy of how they should be run: arguments for universal service and security, for example, gave little indication as to how accountability should be organized. As a result state-run post offices, telegraph and telephone companies followed other models, organized as government departments, as quasi-military bodies or as independent public corporations required to make a profit.

The Principles of Public Service

Public service in communications had two dimensions. One was an ethos of selfless service, rationality and an elevated and rather abstract idea of the public good involving a concern for the national identity and detachment from vested interests. The second was a set of principles about provision: geographical and social universality and the provision for minorities as well as majorities. What has always been missing from these definitions is any sense of public control or direct democratic accountability between public servants and their public. Instead control has rested with managers and specialists, intellectuals and engineers. Democracy in the form of accountability to a parliament or assembly has, of necessity, been at one remove: the service of the public must be above party, faction and interest, the task of the wise, the disinterested specialist and the expert commission. In the UK, which pioneered many of these ideas, two kinds of structure took shape: a public service broadcasting organization under the control of an independent board, the precise ideal of the Habermasian sphere of public discourse, that is to say public in ethos rather than control; and a public telephone company originally under the Post Office, a pioneer in the new forms of management but one that took many of its organizational forms from the Civil Service and defined its publicness in terms of rules of provision. The Labour politician Hugh Dalton wrote of the BBC as a mode of public ownership, public accountability and business management for public ends and it did indeed become a model for the many industries nationalized in the UK after World War II. One writer described it as a social invention 'no less remarkable than the invention of radio in the sphere of practical science'.[11] In one form or another these structures have also been widely exported. After the war, the BBC model was widely adopted in Europe as a means of avoiding the twin evils of commercialism and state manipulation, while in Germany it was actually imposed, in a regionalized variant, by the allied occupying forces.

Most countries have run telecommunications under the direct control of government in PTT (post, telegraph and telephone) monopolies. Government control was reflected in the heavy concentration of telephones in capital cities and administrative districts. In most cases political regulation tended to be very weak, although the PTTs continuously complained about short-term political interference and pressures to contribute to the national exchequer. The loose nature of traditional control has meant that deregulation has, paradoxically, tended to lead to much stricter regulation by newly formed bodies such as Oftel in the UK. Despite 'regulatory capture', probably the most actively regulated telephone company was AT&T, the only fully private system among the major industrialized countries,[12] and also the one that arguably did more to promote genuinely universal service than any other, with the single exception of Sweden. Strikingly, too, the US more than any other country defined universal service in telephony not only in terms of geographical spread and common prices but also in terms of the affordability of services. In most European countries no contradiction was seen between a philosophy of public and universal service and a reality in which large sections of the population had no access. Even today, between 20 and 25 per cent of households in most European countries are not connected to the telephone network.

Broadcasting has come much nearer to being a universal service, but this has in no way solved the problem of defining the nature of its service to the public. The BBC structure, for example, owes much to the peculiar history of British politics: the dominance of a clearly defined 'national' culture, identified with a close-knit ruling class, and with a confidence and cohesion which continue to be manifested in the wide use of delegation and the arm's length principle. Public service could thus be both independent and controlled through what Raymond Williams has called a 'preexisting cultural hegemony',[13] and through the informal networks of power and friendship that cut across state, culture and the private sector. Democratization, either through elections or control by broadcasting workers, has always been vigorously opposed.

The BBC, like the telephone and broadcasting networks of most advanced countries, was formed at a time of widespread faith in the powers of rational, public organization, a time of Fabian dominance in Britain, progressivism in the US and corporatism in Europe. There was a widespread faith in technology, and rationality in debate and organization. There was also a belief in the virtues of scale, at least when it brought order to the chaos of the untrammelled market. Both RCA and the BBC are products of this period: centralized corporations, each with a national purpose, and each a creation of collaboration between State and private sector.

The period was also one in which a new relationship between the State and the population at large was being forged, born of universal suffrage and the experience of a 'mass war' and exemplified in broadcasting both in Hitler's piped propaganda and in ritualistic mass celebrations around Empire, armistice, monarchy and presidency. The idea of the public as mass played a critical role both in the ways governments organized communications and in how it was perceived in academia and literature: the sociology of mass society, the cultural pessimism of the Frankfurt

School, the dystopias of George Orwell, Aldous Huxley and Zamyatin, all share a belief in the unparalleled power of communications and the vulnerability of an undifferentiated, passive mass. Even for the most liberal outlook the mass society demanded what Walter Lippman described as the manufacture of consent.

Each polity shaped public service according to its own traditions. In the UK the tradition was that of Matthew Arnold as redefined by Reith, Grierson (for whom the state was 'the machinery by which the best interests of the people are secured'[14]) and others, committed to responsibility, impartiality, education and active citizenship.[15] The role of public service was to educate and inform as well as to entertain. It straddled Left and Right in its opposition to the ravages of industrial civilization and its paradoxical faith that technology could serve enlightenment. In France, the tradition was that of a Kantian, anticlerical rationalism. Its ideal was perhaps best represented in Leon Blum's famous initiative as Popular Front prime minister in 1936. Blum, an intellectual and journalist, proposed to create a public space for the discussion of ideas that would be free both from the pernicious logic of the market and from the dangers of outright state control.[16] In his plan the State would act as benign enabler, providing presses, printing material and editorial costs, ensuring distribution and collecting advertising. Beyond this the system would be left to the free play of idea and opinion, and to the free choice of the public. Implicit in the plan was the old idea that, given free rules of discourse, truth and the correct argument would ultimately prevail. This 'utopian vision' (in Blum's own words) was destroyed by the conservative Senate but emerged again after the war as a key idea in the reconstruction of the media. In certain respects Blum's ideas did foster diversity: the French system of guaranteed distribution of newspapers compares well with near-monopoly control in other countries. But his ideas, which in practice left the State to define the public interest and the terms of discourse, were also used to bolster what became one of the most centralized and propagandist broadcasting services of the Western world.

Traditions of public discourse in the US are markedly different from those of Europe. It is arguable that the War of Independence was the delayed outcome of the attempt to impose the Stamp Tax in 1765, a tax which struck at every form of communication, commercial transactions and documents such as licences and insurance contracts, together with newspapers and pamphlets. The tax at a stroke united commercial interests with the political struggle to defend an American public sphere from the attacks of a tyrannical state. The commitment to free speech that grew out of the struggle against the British and earlier religious conflicts was crystallized in the First Amendment, which prevented Congress from making any law 'abridging freedom of speech or of the press', and it was given greater substance in the form of subsidies to cover the cost of posting newspapers. When broadcasting emerged in the twentieth century its relationship to the First Amendment was ambiguous. For, while the Amendment constrained the State from interfering in the press, the State found itself heavily involved in broadcasting, both as a user of electromagnetic spectrum and as the source of licences. From the start, however, the dominant powers in US broadcasting were the manufacturers, which established the first networks and agreed to regulation as a means of bringing order to the chaotic airwaves only when it legitimated the existing status quo of spectrum allocation. The close relationship between regulation and private commercial interests followed the pattern established in telephony.

Herbert Hoover had spoken of radio as a public concern 'impressed with the public trust' in 1925, and David Sarnoff of RCA had spoken of it as a public service, but the precise meaning of these words was never made clear. The first systematic attempt to regulate communications was the 1934 Communications Act, which committed the Federal Communications Commission, originally conceived as a Commission of independent experts, to act in the 'public interest, convenience and necessity'. This Act, which remains in force in the late 1980s, laid down the ground rules for regulation of telecommunications and broadcasting. Yet it does little to clarify the definition of the public interest. Instead its articulation was left to successive FCCs which for many were the very epitome of the captured regulatory body, weak and ineffective against the industries they were meant to control.

During certain periods the FCC did carve out a more independent course. The FCC of the 1960s and 1970s attempted to advance the concept of public service in broadcasting and to articulate the public morality that broadcasters should follow to enrich what Newton Minow, Chairman of the FCC in the early 1960s, described as the 'vast wasteland' of American broadcasting. The 'fairness doctrine', guaranteeing balance in political reporting, and support for non-profit public broadcasting and educational channels operating under a similar ethos of public service to the BBC and its European counterparts were evidence of the FCC's commitment to an ideal of public service. But in the absence of any wide agreement about what broadcasting was about or for (social improvement, profit, cultural diversity), or about its relationship to a public interest, all of the reforms proved to be vulnerable to the deregulatory winds of the 1980s.

Despite the apparent localism of US broadcasting (licences are awarded to local stations not to national networks), the US shared with public service in almost every country a sense that the great networks should contribute to building and binding the nation. The same years which saw the spread of the telephone and radio also brought national corporations, distribution networks, retailing, advertising, national parties and movements. In Europe, public service was often an explicitly nationalizing project, imposing the national language and the culture of a 'national' ruling class, erasing regionalisms and backwardness in the same movement. In Europe as in the US, the communications networks would create a single social organism. The project was famously described by AT&T's Theodor Vail in 1910, in a comment which belies the myth of a myriad of small local networks. The ideal was rather 'one system with a common policy, common purpose and common action; comprehensive, universal, interdependent, intercommunicating like the highway system of the country, extending from every door to every other door'.[17] In almost every country public control over telecommunications was exercised through national, governmental institutions. Indeed it can be argued (following Gellner) that the emergence of national communications systems, strongly committed to national culture and education, mobility and growth, was an automatic corollary of industrialization.[18]

The Contradictions of Public Service

Public control and public service have never been a single object or movement; rather they have served as prisms through which nationalizing projects, rationalisms and a vague notion of progress have become crystallized. As ideology they often bear the unmistakable marks of interests parading in the guise of disinterestedness. In telecommunications they have served as a veil behind which states maintain control over communications and private corporations sustain their monopoly. Penetration rates for most European PTTs have varied between 30 and 75 per cent. In most Third World countries, almost no PTTs have achieved penetration rates greater than 15 per cent, with huge waiting lists for extremely unreliable services. Universal service has rarely been either universal or a real service, sustaining instead the interests of PTTs, equipment manufacturers and Treasuries which have seen the telephone network as a source of easy revenue.[19]

In the media, the nature of public service has always been particularly ambiguous. There has always been doubt as to whether the media should be by, of or for the public. The special social position of media workers, employed within State or public institutions rather than the market, makes this question inherently unanswerable. As the modern State evolved it took over many of the roles previously played by the market as guarantor of public discourse. As the State moved to control education and research, to promote the dissemination of knowledge and public service in broadcasting it became itself a key site for struggle between different factions and fractions, a site for shaping what Pierre Bourdieu describes as the rates of exchange between the symbolic capital of the intellectual and knowledge worker and the economic capital of the commercial and industrial elites.

Superficially, the commitment to public service in communications appears as part of the historic compromise between classes with which states restructured to provide universal education, welfare services and to guarantee full employment and economic security. A more considered analysis suggests, however, that public service has been caught up in more complex struggles. For although they have often invoked democracy and the public as aids in the continual struggle for autonomy from direct commercial or political pressures, the interests of knowledge workers often seem to preclude any real opening of the 'sphere of public discourse' or any real democracy as this would undermine the value of their own capital and their position as part of a dominant class which shares in its economic rewards. This interest in sustaining status and autonomy has played a significant role in shaping the norms of public service. The intellectuals and technocrats, those whom Sartre described as the technicians of practical knowledge, systematically used the idea of disinterested and elevated public service as a platform to win a privileged position as mediators of society's knowledge of itself and as beneficiaries of its economic rewards. This project was not without its contradictions: to sustain the political legitimacy of public broadcasting systems concessions have always been made to public tastes and to the commercial pressure to sell programmes or advertising space. Yet this use of the public has been remarkably consistent throughout the Western industrialized countries. It has identified 'the public sphere' and public service with an educated, intellectual and therefore, by definition, exclusive class. For these very reasons advocates of the free market, grounded in the free choice of the sovereign consumer, have consistently been able to counterpose its populism to the restricted, abstract public of public service. This history, in which socialist parties and labour movements have usually been complicit, not least because they contained within themselves similar tensions, has often made it hard to defend a public sphere of discourse, unsullied by the logic of profit and commodities.

Within socialist thought, which one might expect to provide some answer to this problem of the public, there is an almost complete silence. The dominant Leninist model followed in the socialist countries, in which the media are organs of the party, runs against all the traditions of independence, disinterestedness and intellectual autonomy that have shaped Western public service. An alternative and popular position draws on Brecht's famous phrase about radio, imagining every receiver to be a transmitter. In this view, more recently promoted by Hans Magnus

Enzensberger among others, the privileged power of the intellectuals is dissolved by a dispersed technology and by subversive strategies to undermine the encroaching power of the 'mind industry'. The utopian vision of communicational abundance, of perpetual free discourse, however, begs most of the important questions about how communication is to be organized within limits of time, interest and material resources. The 'right to receive and impart information' is contained in many modern constitutions and in the European Convention of Human Rights. It is, however, a minimum position, which offers no insight as to how access to satellite transponders should be organized, or whether spectrum should be privatized; it also offers little help to a world in which the problem is no longer a deficit of information but rather an overabundance. The third socialist position by contrast is very practical, a modern echo of the early bourgeois media: it supports small-scale and diverse media or videotex special interest groups, supported by the purchasing power of socialist and radical people and movements, produced and distributed through a mixture of voluntarism and the market. It is suited to those media, like the early printing press, which have low barriers to entry and grow in the interstices of the market system, thriving in the cracks.

The Future of Control

Public service, in communication has traditionally been associated with the nation state. In the past, the rules of provision were also the rules of limitation. With exceptions in radio, such as the BBC, Radios Luxembourg, Cairo, Moscow or Free Europe, signals respected the jurisdiction of states and rarely transgressed national boundaries. Because of the propagation characteristics of VHF and UHF, television signals only marginally spilled over into neighbouring countries while telephone systems were unambiguously under the control of national authorities. What the State licensed or directly provided was the beginning and end of electronic communications. Nowadays, however, signals spill much more easily, making it harder to define the public by means of political boundaries, in Ernest Gellner's words to endow a culture with its own 'political roof'.[20] Low-powered satellites broadcast signals to cable headends and medium- or high-powered satellites have the capability to broadcast signals directly to antennae attached to homes. Pirate radio or television stations can broadcast from the sea. Thriving markets for videos bypass censorship and quotas aimed at the cinema. In telecommunications private networks and competition have expanded ahead of the law. One of the factors forcing deregulation in the UK was the illegal but uncontrollable existence of competition in telephone equipment. In all of these areas public service under the national State has become, de facto, just one element in the organization of communications rather than its guiding principle. There is now no real prospect of a return to simplicity, to the situation where a State could easily control what its citizens see or hear or who they speak to. A degree of openness thus exists, whatever policies governments attempt to pursue and despite persistent 'neomercantilism' in industrial policy.

This erosion of restrictive controls inevitably raises the philosophical and political question of whether this is a good thing, whether there should be any room for public powers, either identified with the State or with some notion of civil society, to influence the shape and contents of communications media in the name of decency, cultural values or political balance. Doubts as to the right of any State to determine the contents of communications reflect the general suspicion of absolute truths and values associated with a postmodern culture. The older view that there is an extrinsic value in a free press or a public sphere, whether it be to ensure good government or to assist a community in coming to rational decisions, is increasingly hard to articulate, as is the traditional distinction between freedom and license, freedom to do good and freedom to do anything. Instead freedom, like openness, becomes an intrinsic good.

But this apparent trend towards freedom is never as one-dimensional as some commentators would claim. The public nature of most communications continues to make it possible to mobilize political coalitions on issues of communications content. Neoliberalism continually creates its own countervailing forces. Historically, faith in the redeeming powers of the market has tended to go in cycles, reduced when its flaws become too apparent. As Karl Polanyi pointed out, in nineteenth-century Britain, the classic *laissez-faire* society, the movement to remove regulations from the free market had hardly run its course when the reaction was already in full flood, in the form of a wave of new interventions and regulations. Moreover the economic realities of new concentrations around transnational firms operating in all media and all markets serve as a reminder of the need to protect spaces from the market and, where the market is seen as an appropriate means of exchange, carefully to structure competition to limit the abuse of monopoly power. It should therefore come as no surprise that support for alternative communication economies, for unbiased news, for locally produced cultural material organized at one remove from the market, or for moral censorship shows no signs of diminishing; the realistic question to ask is not whether there will be forms of public intervention in the future, but rather what form they could and should take, and how collective freedoms can be reconciled with those of individuals and minorities.

At least three types of regulation and public control seem likely to survive in most conceivable societies. Each is not only compatible with a basic commitment to individual freedom and diversity, but also a necessary condition for their realization. Together they help to amplify that negative sense of freedom implied by a removal of restrictions into a positive notion of freedom that recognizes that there may be communicational needs as well as communicational demands expressed through the market. The first type of control that seems likely to survive in some form is a traditional contents regulation of the core mass media: regulators, governments and other public institutions will retain some role as a medium for public opinion, standards and values, albeit probably in a looser form than in the past. The publicness of communications and its centrality, particularly to the political process, and prevailing attitudes to childhood, together make it hard to conceive of a wholly uncontrolled set of mass audience communications channels. Whether channels are privately or publicly owned, the need is to protect against bias towards the interests of their owners. Rules governing the contents of any service that reaches beyond a small minority seem set to persist. Elsewhere, however, in the sorts of minority service conceivable in broadcasting or videotex, contents control looks increasingly unachievable, both technically and morally, despite the extensive pornographic uses of value added services, the early video recorder, Minitel, phone services and cable.

The second set of controls will focus around access to networks. The issue of universal access to the basic networks of a society such as the ISDN seems likely to gain prominence. The relatively low penetration rates offered by most communications technologies will come to be seen as inadequate, potentially divisive and economically costly as large sections of the population are excluded from learning familiarity with advanced technologies. Achieving universal access and connectivity will depend on infrastructure policies to ensure that outlying regions are connected, on social policies to ensure access to the poor, the elderly or disabled, and on safeguards against disconnection. Alongside this positive commitment to access will come the continued devotion of resources to information and communication outside the market, to news, cultural experiment and the preservation of identity, all in the name of a positive rather than a negative conception of freedom.

The third set of controls will also concern the terms of access. Whether with common carriage networks or more fragmented, dedicated ones, public institutions will still be called to play a role in organizing common menus and directory information services to guarantee easy access and competition between information providers; common standards to allow for interconnectivity, and the provision of a substantial base of free, public services alongside more specialized ones sold through the market. Open network forms of access will need to be guaranteed through laws and regulations to ensure that the communications infrastructure is a genuinely public resource: fair competition will need to be carefully structured.

In each of these examples public controls would come to be used both to preserve openness against the tendency of the market towards closure, vertical integration and monopoly, and to preserve a degree of closure so that some collective control is maintained over the broader communications ecology. What remains unclear is which institutions are now the best vehicles to guarantee basic requirements of this kind. The traditional vehicle for guaranteeing public service, the nation state, is diminishing in importance. Transnational institutions like the European Community and the ITU are gaining in significance but are generally too distant to be effective democratic media. In place of the nationalizing projects of public service, what may evolve is a much more differentiated picture of local powers and regional powers that enable a balance between different interests on communications networks; alternatively, local public control over infrastructures may be combined with open access to its bandwidth. In general, the hope must be not that all regulations and restrictions dissolve but rather that the states' roles can shift to accommodate the benefits of technology while mitigating some of its dangers. Their roles would shift from that of policer and provider to that of the guardian, preserving the balance between different economies of communication, competing and parallel systems, market driven, public service and community orientated, each with its own economic roots and legitimacies, and each acting as a countervailing force to the others. Paradoxically, the maintenance of some degrees of closure, of some separation between systems, may be the only way of preserving diversity in increasingly open systems. Such an approach, recognizing the coexistence of parallel economies and spheres, each with its own hierarchies of ends, would also reflect a philosophical acceptance that there is no one economy of communication sovereign over all others.

Glossary of Acronyms and Technical Terms

Analogue   Direct representation in another form: one example is the use of electric currents representing voices on telephone wires, which directly correspond to the sound waves they represent.

ARPAnet   Network run by DARPA (see below).

ATM   Asynchronous Transfer Mode, a model for fast packet switching which breaks all signals into discrete packets of information.

AT&T   American Telegraph and Telephones, the dominant US network operator, divested of its local networks in 1983.

Bandwidth   The range of frequencies that can be conveyed over a channel, more easily understood as its capacity to carry information (for example, UK television uses a bandwidth of 5.5 MHz).

Bitrate   The speed of operation of a digital transmission channel (e.g. a 64 kbs channel can carry 64,000 bits each second).

BT   British Telecom, the UK's main telecommunications operator, privatized in 1984.

C3I   Command, Control, Communications and Intelligence, a widely used military catchphrase.

CAD/CAM/CAE   Computer-aided design, manufacturing and engineering.

CCD   Charged Couple Device, the digital imaging technology used by many satellites.

CCIR/CCITT   Consultative committees of the ITU concerned with radio and telecommunications respectively.

CEPT   Coordinating organization of European PTTs.

CPU   Central Processing Unit of a computer.

DARPA   Defense Advanced Research Projects Agency, run by the US Defense Department.

DAT   Digital Audio Tape, digitized minicassette tapes first marketed in Japan in the late 1980s.

DBP   Deutsches Bundespost, the West German PTT.

DBS   Direct broadcast satellites; satellites whose signals are strong enough to be picked up on a small domestic receiver.

DES   Digital Encryption System: widely used technical standard for encrypting messages.

Digital   Principle for organizing communication (or the operation of a computer) based on sequences of signals at two levels, representing 0s and 1s.

DOS or **MS-DOS**   Computer operating system developed by Microsoft Corporation for IBM.

EDI   Electronic Data Interchange; set of protocols for transferring such things as invoices.

EFT/EFTPOS   Electronic Funds Transfer (and EFT at Point of Sale used in shops).

ETSI   European Telecommunications Standards Institute, established 1988 under aegis of EC and CEPT to develop Europe-wide standards.

FCC   Federal Communications Commission, the body responsible for regulating telecommunications and broadcasting in the USA.

GATT   General Agreement on Tariffs and Trade; organization responsible for multilateral trade agreements.

GEM   A set of graphics facilities developed by Digital Research.

IBA   Independent Broadcasting Authority, regulator and broadcaster for UK commercial TV and radio. To be disbanded in 1991/2 and replaced by an Independent Television Commission and Radio Authority.

INS Information Network System, Japan's plan for developing the telecommunications infrastructure.

Intelsat International Telecommunications Satellite Organization, agency based in Washington with large PTT membership which operates the world's main satellite network.

ISDN Integrated Services Digital Network, the model for integrating voice and data on a single network. Most of the PTTs plan to upgrade existing telephone networks to become ISDNs.

ISO International Organization for Standardization; the agency based in Geneva, which is responsible for setting and promoting many technical standards.

ITAP UK Cabinet's 'Information Technology Advisory Panel'.

ITU The International Telecommunication Union, the body affiliated to the United Nations which is responsible for overall coordination of frequency allocations, standards setting and investment in development projects (generally through its two committees the CCIR (for radio) and the CCITT (for telecommunications)).

JANET The UK Joint Academic Network linking colleges and universities on a telecommunications network.

JIT Just-in-time, Japanese method of organizing delivery of parts and other goods, widely emulated during the 1980s.

Kbs Kilobits per second, a measure of bitrate.

LAN Local Area Network; specialized, high-capacity networks used for communication between computers, generally within a single building or site.

LSI (and **VLSI**) Large Scale Integration and Very Large Scale Integration; the integration of large numbers of components on a single microchip.

MAC Multiplexed Analogue Components; family of television standards developed by the IBA and supported by the European Community. Includes DMAC, D2MAC, and HDMAC.

MAP Manufacturing Automation Protocols; set of OSI compatible standards developed for automating manufacturing systems.

Minitel French videotex terminal given away in large numbers to telephone subscribers and making use of the Télétel network of services.

Multiplexing Technique for combining a number of different message signals on a single channel through the various techniques of Time Division Multiplexing (TDM), Frequency Division Multiplexing (FDM) and Wave Division Multiplexing (WDM).

NSA US National Security Agency, responsible for wide range of communications technology applications in military and espionage.

NTIA National Telecommunications and Information Administration, responsible for policy in these areas in the USA's Executive branch.

NTSC National Television Standards Committee, a television standard developed by RCA for 525-line sets and in general use in North America and Japan.

NTT Nippon Telegraph and Telephone, Japan's main telecommunications operator.

ONA Open Network Architecture, regulatory proposals which emerged out of the FCC's third Computer Inquiry in 1985/6.

ONP Open Network Provision, set of proposals first devised by European Commission in 1987 to allow for open access to the communications infrastructure.

OSI Open Systems Interconnect, the reference model for standardizing computer communications under the aegis of the International Organisation for Standardisation (ISO). Backed by the various bodies such as SPAG, POSI, COS.

Packet-switching The technique for transmitting data signals in discrete packets, a technique distinct from the circuit-switching common in voice telephony.

PTT   Post, Telephone and Telegraph authority, a generic name for the public telecommunications and postal systems in existence in most countries. Confusingly, the term is also used to include such private companies as British Telecom and AT&T which have no postal functions.

QUBE   Widely publicized experimental interactive cable system established in Columbus, Ohio, in the early 1980s. Interactive services now discontinued.

RACE   European Community research initiative on advanced communications technologies, launched in the mid-1980s.

RBOCs   Regional Bell Operating Companies, the divested local companies formerly part of AT&T (such as Nynex, Pacific Telesis).

SNA   Systems Network Architecture, IBM's set of technologies and protocols for linking its computers into networks.

SPOT   French commercial imaging satellite.

SWIFT   The worldwide satellite based banking network for transferring funds.

VANS   Value Added Network Services, value added and data services and enhanced services, all descriptions for the various complex uses of telecommunications networks to provide specialized, computer-based services.

VLSI   See LSI.

VSAT   Very Small Aperture Terminal, a satellite receiving (and transmitting) dish which is considerably smaller than previous models.

WAN   Wide Area Network; extension of LANs to cover large numbers of sites.

WINDOWs   Graphics-based system for personal computers and other workstations.

X.25   Set of standards for packet-switching networks, part of the x series of recommendations of the CCITT relating to the interfaces between user terminals and networks.

X.400   Parallel set of standards for electronic mail.

Notes and References

Introduction

[1] The average cost of processing information has fallen from around $75 per million operations in 1960 to less than a hundredth of a cent in 1990.

[2] Jean Baudrillard, 'The implosion of meaning in the media and the implosion of the social in the masses', in Kathleen Woodral (ed.), *The Myths of Information* (Coda Press, Madison, 1980), p. 139

[3] National Telecommunications and Information Administration, *Telecom 2000* (NTIA, Washington DC, 1988).

[4] Gregory Bateson, *Mind and Nature: A Necessary Unity* (Wildwood House, London, 1979).

[5] Friedrich Hayek, *Law, Legislation and Liberty* (Routledge & Kegan Paul, London, 1982).

[6] See, for example, Walter Benjamin's critique of the SPD's slogan 'Knowledge is Power' in 'Eduard Fuchs, collector and historian', in *One Way Street and Other Writings* (Verso, London, 1979), pp. 349–87.

Chapter 1   Networks and Post-industrial Societies

[1] Alfred Chandler, *The Visible Hand* (Bellknap, Cambridge Mass., 1977), p. 98. Subsequently productivity rose rapidly, as the railways benefited from new organizational forms, training, standardization and new equipment.

[2] Quoted in I. de Sola Pool, *Forecasting the Telephone* (Ablex, Norwood NJ, 1983), p. 26.

[3] Milton Mueller offers a penetrating analysis of why attempts to use more labour and apparatus failed, and why organizational innovation proved to be the only solution to the diseconomy of scale: 'The switchboard problem: scale, signalling, and organization in manual telephone switching, 1877–97', *Technology and Culture* 30 (1989), p. 534.

4   Shoshanna Zuboff, *In The Age of the Smart Machine* (Basic Books, New York, 1988).

5   Krishan Kumar, *Prophecy and Progress: The Sociology of Industrial and Post-industrial Society* (Penguin, Harmondsworth, 1978).

6   Yoneji Masuda, *The Information Society as Post-Industrial Society* (Institute for the Information Society, Tokyo, 1980).

7   For the most influential account, see Daniel Bell, *The Coming of Post-Industrial Society: A Venture in Social Forecasting* (Basic Books, New York, 1973). Innumerable other books make similar arguments, such as Christopher Evans, *The Micro Millenium* (Pocket Books, New York, 1979); James Martin, *The Telematic Society, A Challenge for Tomorrow* (Prentice-Hall, Englewood Cliffs, NJ, 1981).

8   Parallels between the hierarchy of needs and sectoral changes are analysed in a study by Martin Ernst, discussed in W. Russ Neuman, *The Future of the Mass Audience* (Harvard University Press, Cambridge Mass., forthcoming).

9   Krishan Kumar also points out the crucial role of the Cold War in escalating expenditure on research and development, and the evolution of communications technologies: *Prophecy and Progress*, p. 229.

10   Charles Jonscher, 'Information resources and economic productivity', *Information Economics and Policy*, 1 (1983), p. 17.

11   J. Gershuny and I. Miles, *The New Service Economy* (Pinter, London, 1985).

12   Ian Miles, *Services and the New Industrial Economy* (Science Policy Research Unit, Sussex University, UK, October 1988).

13   See Jean Voge, 'Communication society: a network for a crumbling pyramid', paper presented to the Thirteenth Annual Telecommunications Policy Reseach Conference (Airlie, Virginia, April 1985).

14   James Beniger, *The Control Revolution: Technological and Economic Origins of the Information Society* (Harvard University Press, Cambridge Mass., 1986).

15   Marc Uri Porat, *The Information Economy: Definition and Measurement* (Office of Telecommunications, Department of Commerce, Washington DC, 1977).

16   Fritz Machlup, *The Production and Distribution of Knowledge in the United States* (Princeton University Press, Princeton NJ, 1962).

17   G. Dosi et al., *Technical Change and Economic Theory* (Pinter, London, 1988).

18   Peter Hall and Paschal Preston, *The Carrier Wave: New Information Technology and the Geography of Innovation 1846–2003* (Unwin Hyman, London, 1988).

19   See R. Hayes and T. Erickson, 'Added value as a function of purchases of information services', *The Information Society* 1 (1982),

pp. 307–38; H. Engelbrecht, 'Information resources in US manufacturing: a reassessment', *The Information Society* 5 (1988), pp. 147–59.

20 Jean Voge, 'The political economics of complexity', *Information Economics and Policy* 1 (1983), pp. 97–114.

21 Jean Voge, 'Information and information technologies in growth and economic crisis', *Technological Forecasting and Social Change* 14 (1979), pp. 1–14.

22 Simon Nora and Alain Minc, *The Computerization of Society* (MIT Press, Cambridge Mass., 1980), p. 126.

23 A. R. Bennett, speaking to the British Association in 1895, quoted in Carolyn Marvin, *When Old Technologies Were New* (Oxford University Press, New York, 1988).

24 'Communism is the Soviet Government plus the electrification of the whole country.'

25 John Naisbitt, *Megatrends* (Warner Books, New York, 1984).

26 Alvin Toffler, *The Third Wave* (Pan Books, London, 1980), p. 444.

27 Nora and Minc, *The Computerization of Society*.

28 Starr Roxanne Hiltz and Murray Turoff, *The Network Nation: Human Communication via Computer* (Addison-Wesley, Reading Mass., 1978).

29 Jessica Lipnack and Jeffrey Stamps, *The Networking Book* (Routledge & Kegan Paul, London, 1986).

30 For Ewen much of the power of modern capitalism derives from its ability to feed of utopian images and aspirations: Stuart Ewen, *Captains of Consciousness: Advertising and the Social Roots of Consumer Culture* (McGraw-Hill, New York, 1976).

31 A range of articles on satellites can be found in G. Bugliarello et al., 'Commercial remote-sensing satellites: adding transparency to the Information Age' and succeeding articles, *Technology and Society* 11 (1989).

32 E. Rogers and D. Lawrence Kincaid, *Communication Networks: Toward a New Paradigm for Research* (Free Press, New York, 1981), p. 218.

33 For example B. Markovsky, D. Willer and T. Patten, 'Power relations in exchange networks', *American Sociological Review* 53 (1988), pp. 20–235.

34 Everett Rogers and Judith Larsen, *Silicon Valley Fever: Growth of High Technology Culture* (Basic Books, New York, 1984).

35 Janos Kornai, *Economics of Shortage* (North-Holland, New York, 1980) and other writings.

36 John Killick quoted in James Beniger, *The Control Revolution* (Harvard University Press, Cambridge Mass., 1986), p. 127.

37   Janet Abu-Lughod, *Before Hegemony* (Oxford University Press, New York, 1989).

38   Fernand Braudel, *Afterthoughts on Material Civilization and Capitalism* (Johns Hopkins University Press, Baltimore, 1977).

39   Lewis Mumford, *The City in History* (Peregrine, London, 1961), p. 474.

40   Emile Durkheim, *The Division of Labour in Society* (Macmillan, London, 1984), p. 370.

41   The effects of a change in scale and density on the form of social organization have provided an explanation both for the evolution of property rights and, alternatively, of medieval communalism. See H. Demsetz, 'Towards a theory of property rights', *American Economic Review* 57 (1967), pp. 347–59; Barry C. Field, 'The evolution of property rights', *Kyklos* 42 (1989), pp. 319–47.

42   Kenneth Arrow, *The Limits of Organization* (Norton, New York, 1974).

43   N. Luhmann, *Trust and Power* (Wiley, Chichester, 1979).

44   Robert Axelrod, *The Evolution of Cooperation* (Basic Books, New York, 1984).

45   Jean Marie Charon, 'Videotex: from interaction to communication', *Media, Culture and Society* 9 (1987), pp. 301–31.

46   Michael Piore and Charles Sabel, *The Second Industrial Divide* (Basic Books, New York, 1984), p. 287.

Chapter 2   The Dynamics of Electronic Networks

1   John Carey, 'Technology and Ideology' in John Carey (ed.) *Communication as Culture* (Unwin Hyman, London, 1989), p. 202.

2   Richard B. Du Roff, 'The rise of communications regulation: the telegraph industry 1844–80', *Journal of Communications*, Summer (1984).

3   NTT's capitalization was 24.2 trillion yen in March 1989, with 67.5 per cent of shared held by the Japanese government, according to the 1989 annual report.

4   I. de Sola Pool, *Forecasting the Telephone* (Ablex, Norwood NJ, 1983), p. 6.

5   Most accounts stress the government's bias against telephony, as it sought to protect its investment in telegraphy. This resulted in significantly lower penetration rates in the UK compared to other industrialized countries.

6   Hull, which operates (under the name 'Kingston Communications') its own telephone network, remains the only descendant of the many municipal systems operating at the beginning of the century.

7 Gerald W. Brock, *The Telecommunications Industry: The Dynamics of Market Structure* (Harvard University Press, Cambridge Mass., 1981).

8 Raymond Williams, *Television Technology and Cultural Form* (Fontana/Collins, Glasgow, 1974), p. 147.

9 This designation is becoming increasingly inappropriate as telecommunications operations are separated from postal services. However, it continues to be more widely used than the alternative designations such as Public Telecommunications Operator (PTO) and Telecommunication Administration (TA).

10 See Gerald Brock, *The Telecommunications Industry: The Dynamics of Market Structure* (Harvard University Press, Cambridge Mass., 1981).

11 By the 1980s it was estimated that 75 per cent of surplus in the USSR was taken by the state, thus contributing to chronic underinvestment. See O. Kuznetsova, 'Telecommunications in the USSR', paper presented to International Telecommunications Society, Budapest, 29–30 August 1989.

12 James Martin, *Future Developments in Telecommunications* (Prentice-Hall, Englewood Cliffs, NJ, 1977).

13 T. Darmaros, 'Beyond the sales pitch: realising ISDN in the US, Japan and Europe', Working Paper 5, Centre for Information and Communications Technologies, Science Policy Research Unit, University of Sussex, 1989.

14 W. J. Blyth and M. M. Blyth, *Telecommunications: Concepts, Development and Management* (Macmillan, New York, 1985); H. S. Dordick, *Understanding Modern Telecommunications* (McGraw, London, 1986).

15 Eli Noam, 'The public telecommunications network: a concept in transition', *Journal of Communication* 37 (1987), pp. 30–48.

Chapter 3 Communication and the Limits of Control

1 Gregory Bateson, *Mind and Nature: A Necessary Unity* (Wildwood House, London, 1979).

2 Quoted in Daniel Bell, *The Winding Passage* (Basic Books, New York, 1980), p. 17.

3 Some mention should also be made of the English toolmakers and designers of the eighteenth century. See Peter Drucker, 'The knowledge economy', in A. E. Cawkell, (ed.), *Evolution of an Information Society* (Aslib, London, 1987).

4 See Pierre Levy, *La Machine univers: création, cognition et culture informatique* (Editions La Découverte, Paris, 1987).

5   Jacques Ellul, *The Technological Society* (Knopf, New York, 1964).
6   Norbert Wiener, *Cybernetics* (MIT Press, Cambridge Mass., 1948), pp. 28–9.
7   Joseph Needham, *Science and Civilization in China, vol. 2: History of Scientific Thought* (Cambridge University Press, Cambridge, 1956), p. 475.
8   Ian Hacking, 'How should we do the history of statistics?', *I&C* 8 (1981), p. 15.
9   Michael Mann, *The Sources of Social Power*, vol. 1 (Cambridge University Press, Cambridge, 1986).
10 Harold Innis, *Empire and Communication* (Clarendon Press, Oxford, 1950); *The Bias of Communication* (University of Toronto Press, Toronto, 1951).
11 For a fuller account, see G. Mulgan, 'The power of the weak', in S. Hall and M. Jacques (eds), *New Times: The Changing Face of Politics in the 1990s* (Lawrence & Wishart, London, 1989), pp. 347–63.
12 W. R. Ashby, 'Self-regulation and requisite variety' (1956) in F. E. Emery (ed.), *Systems Thinking Volume One* (Penguin, Harmondsworth, 1969), pp. 100–20.
13 Jan Tinbergen, *On the Theory of Economic Policy* (North-Holland, Amsterdam, 1952).
14 I. Prigogine and I. Stengers, *Order out of Chaos* (Heinemann, London, 1984), p. 187.
15 Bernard Mandeville, *The Fable of the Bees*, first published 1724 (Penguin, Harmondsworth, 1970).
16 For the latter view see Kevin G. Wilson, *Technologies of Control: The New Interactive Media for the Home* (University of Wisconsin Press, Madison, 1988).
17 Friedrich Hayek, 'The mirage of social justice', in *Law, Legislation and Liberty* (Routledge & Kegan Paul, London, 1982), pp. 108–9.
18 Karl Marx, *Grundrisse: Foundations of the Critique of Political Economy* (Penguin, Harmondsworth, 1973).
19 See Oscar Gandy, 'Information privacy and the crisis of control', in M. Raboy and P. Bruck (eds), *Communication: For and Against Democracy* (Black Rose Books, Montreal and New York, 1989).
20 See Alfred Chandler, *The Visible Hand* (Bellknap, Cambridge Mass., 1977) and *Strategy and Structure* (MIT Press, Cambridge Mass., 1962).
21 Oliver Williamson, *Markets and Hierarchies* (Free Press, New York, 1975).
22 Oliver Williamson, *The Economic Institutions of Capitalism: Firms, Markets, Relational Contracting* (Collier-Macmillan, London, 1985).

23 Jonathon Gershuny, *After Industrial Society? The Emerging Self-service Economy* (Macmillan, London, 1978).

24 Alvin Toffler, *The Third Wave* (Pan Books, London, 1980).

25 See Bill Nichols, 'The Work Culture in the Age of Cybernetic Systems', *Screen* 29 (1988), pp. 22–48.

26 R. Loveless (ed.), *The Computer Revolution and the Arts* (University Press of Florida, Gainsville, 1986).

27 Stewart Brand, *The Media Lab: Inventing the Future at MIT* (Penguin, Harmondswoth, 1988).

28 See Ian Miles, *Home Information: Information Technology and the Transformation of Everyday Life* (Pinter, London, 1988).

29 S. Moores, 'The box on the dresser: memories of early radio and everyday life', *Media, Culture and Society* 10 (1988), p. 23.

30 For a sophisticated analysis of these issues, see D. Morley and R. Silverstone 'Domestic communications – technologies and meanings', *Media, Culture and Society* 12 (1990), pp. 31–57.

31 Tessa Morris Suzuki, 'Communications and the household', *Prometheus* 6 (1988), pp. 237–48.

32 M. Douglas and B. Isherwood, *The World of Goods: Towards an Anthroplogy of Consumption* (Penguin, Harmondsworth, 1980).

33 Toffler, *The Third Wave*.

34 National Academy of Sciences, *Office Workstations in the Home* (National Academy Press, Washington DC, 1985).

35 For example D. Jones, 'Must we travel? The potential of communications as a substitute for urban travel', PhD thesis (Standford, California, 1973) and others quoted in Jean Walters, *The Telecommunications Impact* (Papers in Planning Research, Dept. of Town Planning, University of Wales, Cardiff, July 1983).

36 Frances Kinsman, *The Telecommuters* (John Wiley, Winchester, 1987).

37 Thomas Cross, 'Telecommuting – future options for work' *Oxford Surveys in Information Technology* 3 (1986), p. 255.

38 Robert E. Kraut, 'The Trade-offs of home work', *Journal of Communication* 39 (1989), p. 26.

39 See, for example, David Morley, *Family Television* (Comedia, London, 1987).

40 T. Kotera, 'Past, present and future of intelligent buildings in Japan', *Journal of Asia Electronics Union* 6 (1987), pp. 79–84.

41 Benjamin Barber, *Strong Democracy* (Basic Books, New York, 1984).

42 W. Russell Neuman, *The Future of the Mass Audience* (Harvard University Press, Cambridge Mass., forthcoming).

43 F. Christopher Arterton, *Teledemocracy* (Roosevelt Center for American Policy Studies/Sage, New York, 1986).

44   P. Bourdieu, *Distinction* (Routledge & Kegan Paul, London, 1984), p. 397.

45   Josaine Jouet, *'L'Ecran Apprivoisé: télématique et informatique à domicile'*, (Réseaux/CNET, Paris, 1987).

46   Steven Levy, *Hackers: Heroes of the Computer Revolution* (Anchor Press/Doubleday, New York, 1984), p. 284.

47   Carolyn Marvin, *When Old Technologies Were New* (Oxford University Press, New York, 1988).

48   Paul Beaud, *La Société de Connivance* (Editions Aubier-Montaigne, Paris, 1987).

49   Vincent Mosco, *Pushbutton Fantasies: Critical Information Technology* (Ablex, Norwood NJ, 1982).

50   For one of the best accounts of the coercive properties of networks, see Frank Webster and Kevin Robins, *Information Technology: A Luddite Analysis* (Ablex, Norwood NJ, 1986).

51   Quoted in Kevin Robins, *Capital and Cable* (Greater London Council Economic Policy Group, London, 1983).

52   Oscar Gandy, 'The surveillance society: information technology and bureaucratic social control', *Journal of Communication* 39 (1989), p. 61.

53   Frank Donner, *The Age of Surveillance* (Knopf, New York, 1980); Kenneth Laudon, *Dossier Society: Value Choices in the Design of National Information Systems* (Columbia University Press, New York, 1986).

54   US Congress, Office of Technology Assessment, *Electronic Records Systems and Individual Privacy*, OTA-CIT-296 (US Government Printing Office, Washington DC, 1986).

55   Under the name 'GOSIP': Government Open Systems Interconnect Protocols.

56   Vannevar Bush, 'As we may think', *Atlantic Monthly* (July 1945).

57   Quoted in Frank Barnaby, *The Automated Battlefield* (Oxford University Press, Oxford, 1986), p. 1.

58   Ibid., p. 38.

59   Quoted in Vincent Mosco, *Computers, Communication and the Information Society* (Garramond, Toronto, 1988), p. 190.

Chapter 4   Control Economies

1   John Carey, *Communication as Culture* (Unwin Hyman, Boston, 1989), p. 215.

2   For a detailed analysis of the conflicting control imperatives of different interests, see F. R. Fitzroy, 'The modern corporation:

efficiency, control and comparative organisation', *Kyklos* 41 (1988), pp. 239–62.

3 Alfred Chandler, *The Visible Hand* (Bellknap, Cambridge Mass., 1977).

4 A parallel argument underlies Michels, 'Iron Law of Oligarchy': increased scale engenders specialization and a permanent differentiation between managers and managed, leaders and followers.

5 The classic exposition is to be found in D'Arcy Wentworth Thompson, *On Growth and Form*, ed. and abridged J. Bonner (Cambridge University Press, Cambridge, 1961).

6 Janos Kornai, *Overcentralisation in Economic Administration* (Oxford University Press, Oxford, 1959).

7 N. I. Kovalev, quoted in T. D. Sterling, 'Democracy in an Information Society', *Information Society* 15 (1986), p. 17.

8 Robin Murray, 'Fordism and socialist development', Institute of Development Studios, University of Sussex, mimeo, p. 28.

9 O. Lange, 'The computer and the market', in C. Feinstein (ed.), *Socialism and Economic Growth* (Cambridge University Press, Cambridge, 1967), pp. 158–61.

10 F. Hayek, 'The use of knowledge in society', *American Economic Review* 35 (1945); L. Hurwicz, 'The design of mechanisms for resource allocation', *American Economic Review* 63 (1973).

11 Clausewitz, *On War* (Princeton University Press, Princeton, 1976).

12 James Beniger, *The Control Revolution: Technological and Economic Origins of the Information Society* (Harvard University Press, Cambridge Mass., 1986).

13 Chandler, *The Visible Hand*, pp. 27–8.

14 An unforeseen trend that may have saved capitalism from the fate of an ever higher organic composition of capital predicted by Marx.

15 Quoted in K. Robins and F. Webster, 'Broadcasting politics: communications and consumption', *Screen* 27 (1986), p. 36.

16 Kevin Wilson, *Technologies of Control: The New Interactive Media for the Home* (University of Wisconsin Press, Madison, 1988).

17 Anthony Giddens, *The Constitution of Society* (University of California Press, Berkeley, 1984), p. 148.

18 Daniel Nelson, *Frederick W. Taylor and the Rise of Scientific Management* (University of Wisconsin Press, Madison, 1980).

19 See R. Edwardes, *Contested Terrain: The Transformations of the Workplace in the Twentieth Century* (Heinemann, London, 1987).

20 K. Marx, *Grundrisee: Foundations of the Critique of Political Economy* (Penguin, Harmondsworth, 1974), p. 541.

21 Quoted in Murray, 'Fordism and socialist development', p. 9.

22 James Beniger, *The Control Revolution: Technological and Economic*

Origins of the Information Society (Harvard University Press, Cambridge Mass., 1986).

23   Quoted in Shoshanna Zuboff, *In the Age of the Smart Machine* (Basic Books, New York, 1988), p. 101.

24   H. A. Thomas, *Automation for Management* (Gower Press, London, 1969).

25   R. M. Bell, *Changing Technology and Manpower Requirements in the Engineering Industry* (Sussex University Press, London, 1972).

26   R. Kaplinsky, *Automation: The technology and Society* (Longman, London, 1984).

27   R. Kaplinsky, 'Electronics-based automation technologies and the onset of systemofacture: implications for Third World industrialisation', *World Development* 13 (1985), pp. 423–39.

28   N. Garnett and J. Dwyer, 'The factory of the future is at hand', *Financial Times*, 15 August 1989.

29   Larry Hirschhorn, *Beyond Mechanization* (MIT Press, Cambridge Mass., 1986).

30   Quoted in C. Freeman, 'The factory of the future: the productivity paradox, Japanese just-in-time and information technology'. *PICT Working Papers*, 3 (1988).

31   Richard H. Franke, 'Technological revolution and productivity decline: the case of US banks', *Technological Forecasting and Social Change* 31 (1987), pp. 143–54.

32   The work of Cristiano Antonelli has emphasized the importance of 'disembodied learning by using' in the spread of information technologies and associated social innovations: C. Antonelli (ed.), *New Information Technology and Industrial Change: The Italian Case* (Kluwer, Boston, 1988).

33   B. Baran and S. Teegarden, *Women's Labor in the Office of the Future* (BRIE, Berkeley, 1983), p. 13.

34   M. J. Earl and D. A. Ruge, 'Using telecommunications-based information systems for competitive advantage', Oxford Institute of Informational Management Research Discussion Paper (1987), p. 15.

35   Juan Rado, 'Information technology and services', in O. Giarini (ed.), *The Emerging Service Economy* (Pergamon, Oxford, 1982), p. 154.

36   See J. R. Galbraith, *Organization Design* (Addison-Wesley, Reading Mass., 1977).

Chapter 5   Network Technologies

1   Carl Snyder in 'The Review of Reviews', in 1902, quoted in 'Amateur Operators and American Broadcasting: Shaping the Future of Radio', in J. Corn (ed.), *Imagining Tomorrow* (MIT Press, Cambridge Mass., 1986).

2   More precisely a network for long-distance telegraphic writing.

3   Raymond Williams, *Television: Technology and Cultural Form* (Fontana, Glasgow, 1974).

4   In David Noble, *Forces of Production* (Knopf, New York, 1984).

5   Claude S. Fischer, '"Touch Someone": The Telephone Industry Discovers Sociability', *Technology and Culture* 29 (1988), p. 32.

6   Yves Stourdze, *Pour une poignée d'électrons* (Fayard, Paris, 1987), p. 271.

7   'Optical switches herald a new Age of Enlightenment', *Data Communications* (March 1988), pp. 81–90.

8   Peter Huber, *The Geodesic Network* (US Justice Department, Washington DC, 1987).

9   Anthony Rutkowski, *The Integrated Services Digital Network* (Artech, Dedham, 1985).

10   In *Communications News*, New York, April 1985.

11   R. T. Wigand, 'Integrated Services Digital Network: concepts, policies and emerging issues', *Journal of Communication* 38 (1988), pp. 29–50.

12   W. B. Allen, *Fibre Optics* (Oxford University Press, Oxford, 1980); S. Geckeler, *Optical Fiber Transmission Systems* (Artech House, Dedham, 1987).

13   Anthony Rutkowski in *Telecommunications* (New York) (February 1987).

14   Lorretta Anania and Richard Solomon, *The Flat-Rate Answer to ISDN Tariffing*, (MIT Research Program on Communications Policy, Cambridge Mass., 1987).

15   See, for example, Marvin Sirbu in *Proceedings of the MIT Symposium on World Telecommunications Policy* (MIT Research Program on Communications Policy, Cambridge Mass., 1988).

16   C. Lees, 'Intelligent networks: a convergence of views', *Telecommunications International Edition*, May (1989), pp. 26–8.

17   This need not be a single geographical place. Logical centralization is more important than spatial centralization.

18   Denis Gilhooly, 'Drawing the boundaries of network intelligence', *Communications Week International*, 26 February 1990, p. C2.

19   One result is that whereas early telephony was based on one circuit per line, at a cost of around £1,700 per channel kilometre, an equivalent, 565 mbs fibre-optic link in the 1990s has a comparable cost of around £0.20 per channel kilometre.

20   The UK's Personal Communications Networks, licensed in 1989, represent the first attempt to create a genuine mass market for mobile telephony.

21   Heinrich Armbruster, 'Worldwide approaches to broadband ISDN', *Telecommunications International Edition* (May 1989), pp. 49–54.

22   See G. J. Mulgan, *The New Holy Grail: Fibre Optic Grids and Industrial Strategies*, Working Paper (Centre for Communications and Information Studies, London, 1990).

23   H. T. Mouftah and C. H. Sauer, 'Computer-aided modeling, analysis and design of communication networks', *IEEE Journal on Selected Areas in Communications* 6 (1988), pp. 126–8.

24   Kenneth L. Phillips, 'Towards a universal broadband infrastructure for the US', paper presented to Bellcore/MIT Conference, Salt Lake City, 6–8 April 1988.

25   The approach is known as Code Division Multiplex and exploits both the time and the frequency domain. See D. M. Leakey, 'Integrated Services Digital Network: some possible ongoing evolutionary trends', *Computer Networks and ISDN* 15 (1988), pp. 303–13.

Chapter 6   The Limits of Free Flow: Commodities, Computers and Censorship

1   Sisella Bok, *Secrets* (Oxford University Press, Oxford, 1983), p. 11.

2   Quoted in E. Ploman and L. Clark Hamilton, *Copyright: Intellectual Property in the Information Age* (Routledge & Kegan Paul, London, 1980).

3   Elizabeth Eisenstein, 'Print culture and Enlightenment thought', *Réseaux* 31 (1988), 1987, p. 21.

4   W. Cornish, *Intellectual Property: Patents, Copyrights, Trade Marks and Allied Rights* (Sweet & Maxwell, London, 1981).

5   Vincent Porter, 'The New Protectionism', *Intermedia* 17 (1989), p. 10.

6   The neoclassical critique of copyright can be found in Arnold Plant's 'The economic aspects of copyright in books', *Economica*, May (1934), pp. 167–95; and Stephen Breyer, 'The uneasy case for copyright in books, photocopies and computer programs', *Harvard Law Review*, 84 (1970), pp. 281–351.

7   Although Sue Curry Jansen offers a convincing account of how censorship was transferred rather than abolished in *Censorship: The Knot that Binds Power and Knowledge* (Oxford University Press, New York, 1988).

8   See Nicholas Garnham, *Concepts of Culture* (Greater London Council Economic Policy Group, London, 1983).

9   Hans Magnus Enzensberger, 'The industrialisation of the mind', in *Dreamers of the Absolute* (Radius/Century Hutchinson, London, 1988).

10   J. Frow, 'Repetition and limitation: computer software and copyright law', *Screen* 29 (1988), p. 20.

11 See Barbara Ringer on copyright in *The International Encyclopedia of Communication* (Oxford University Press, New York, 1989).

12 Andy Lippman, *Electronic Pirates* (Routledge & Kegan Paul, London, 1988), p. 26.

13 Jeremy Tunstall, *Communications Deregulation: The Unleashing of America's Communications Industry* (Blackwell, Oxford, 1986), p. 175.

14 H. Croze and Y. Bismuth, *Droit de l'informatique* (Economica, Paris, 1986).

15 J. Gordon, 'The history and theory of modern cryptology', in *Data Privacy and Security* (Pergamon Infotech, Maidenhead, 1985).

16 David Hopkins, 'Ideas, their time has come: an argument and a proposal for copyrighting ideas', *Albany Law Review* 46 (1982), p. 453.

17 I. de Sola Pool and Richard Solomon, 'Intellectual property and transborder data flows', *Stanford Journal of International Law* (1980), p. 121.

Chapter 7   The Limits of State Control and Deregulation

1 M. Derthick and P. Quirk, *The Politics of Deregulation* (Brookings Institution, Washington DC, 1985).

2 Robert Britt Horwitz, *The Irony of Deregulation* (Oxford University Press, New York, 1989).

3 'Japan: the march towards competition', *Fintech 1 – Telecom Markets*, 23 February 1989, p. 6.

4 Henri Ergas, 'Telecoms 2000', presentation to International Institute of Communications Annual Conference, 3 September 1987. Though figures of this kind are widely cited they must be treated with caution; often they reflect definitional shifts, such that a PC moves from an office equipment to a telecommunications classification when it is linked into a network. As costs fall, there are equally strong grounds fo expecting a reduction in the proportion of GDP accounted for by telecommunications.

5 Commission of the European Communities, '*Towards a Competitive Community-wide Telecommunications Market in 1992: Implementing the Green Paper on the Development of the Common Market for Telecommunications Services and Equipment*', COM (88), 48 final, (CEC, Brussels, 1987).

6 Ergas, 'Telecoms 2000'.

7 See M. Beesley and B. Laidlaw, The Future of Telecommunications (Institute of Economic Affairs, London, 1989).

8 As Collingridge has shown, this kind of support for large-scale

projects has often, and inevitably, led to overinvestment and excess capacity as a way of coping with uncertainty. See D. Collingridge, *The Social Control of Technology* (Oxford University Press, Oxford, 1980).

9   M. Mann, *The Sources of Social Power* (Cambridge University Press, Cambridge, 1987).

10   Adam Smith, *The Wealth of Nations* (Penguin, Harmondsworth, 1982), p. 251.

11   Joseph Schumpeter, *Business Cycles* (McGraw-Hill, New York, 1939) and *The Theory of Economic Development* (Harvard University Press, Cambridge Mass., 1934).

12   J. Gershuny, *Social Innovation and the Division of Labour* (Oxford University Press, Oxford, 1983), p. 168.

13   There is an extensive recent literature on critical mass issues which is well summarized in David Allen, 'New telecommunications services: network externalities and critical mass', *Telecommunications Policy*, 12 (1988), pp. 257–72.

14   The ITU recently conducted an extensive survey of the relations between telecommunications and macroeconomic indicators in 76 countries; this suggested that as GNP increases the contribution of additional telephones decreases: *Telecommunications and the National Economy: A Quantitative Study Using a Macroeconomic Sectional Analysis* (ITU, Geneva, 1988).

15   For a thoughtful analysis of the impact of telecommunicatons on the economy, see Charles Jonscher, 'The economic role of telecommunications', in M. Moss (ed.), *Telecommunications and Productivity* (Addison-Wesley, Reading Mass., 1981).

16   Robert Fogel, 'A quantitative approach to the study of railroads in American economic growth', *Journal of Economic History*, June (1962).

17   Quoted in Vincent Mosco, *Computers, Communication and the Information Society* (Garramond, Toronto, 1989).

18   Defence Advanced Research Projects Agency, *Strategic Computing Program* (DARPA, Washington DC, 1983).

19   L. Siegel and J. Markoff, *The High Cost of High Tech* (Harper & Row, New York, 1985).

20   See Nicholas Garnham, 'Telecommunications policy in the United Kingdom', *Media, Culture and Society* 7 (1) (1985), pp. 7–29.

21   In particular in the Department of Trade and Industry 'MacDonald Committee' reports, *The Infrastructure for Tomorrow* and *The Evolution of the UK Communications Infrastructure* (HMSO, London, 1988).

22   'A clearer line to markets abroad', *Financial Times*, 6 March 1990, p. 18.

23 See Marcellus Snow (ed.), *Marketplace for Telecommunications: Regulation and Deregulation in Industrialised Democracies* (Longman, New York, 1986) for discussions of each of the major countries.

24 Simon Nora and Alain Minc, *The Computerization of Society* (MIT Press, Cambridge Mass., 1980).

25 In an early article on network externalities the American economist Jeffrey Rohlffs had argued that 'the most direct approach [to reaching critical mass] is to give the service free to a selected group of people for a limited time'; 'A theory of interdependent demand for a communication service', *Bell Journal of Economics and Management Science* 5 (1974), pp. 16–37.

26 ISDN was marketed under the name 'Numeris'.

27 Jean-Marie Charon and Jean-Paul Simon, 'Cable's infancy (1982–86), paper presented to the International Telecommunications Society at MIT, Cambridge Mass., 29 June 1988.

28 See Tessa Morris-Suzuki, *Beyond Computopia: Information, Automation and Democracy in Japan* (Routledge & Kegan Paul, London, 1988).

29 Jeremy Richardson, 'Policy, Politics and the Communications Revolution in Sweden', in K. Dyson and P. Humphreys (eds), *The Politics of the Communications Revolution in Western Europe* (Frank Cass, London, 1986).

30 E. Bohlin and O. Granstand, 'National monopolies in transition: illustrations from Sweden', paper presented to International Telecommunications Society, Budapest, August 1989.

31 'EC seeks to end parochialism in telecommunications', *Financial Times*, 11 July 1988.

32 See H. Ungerer and N. Costello, *Telecommunications in Europe* (European Perspectives/EC Publications, Brussels, 1988).

33 Karl Saurant, International Transactions in Services (UN CTC, New York, 1986).

34 F. D. Roosevelt, Inauguration Speech, Washington DC, January 1936.

35 International Institute of Communications, *Study of Telecoms Structures* (IIC, London, 1986).

36 Mike Hobday, *UK Telecommunications Policies in the 1980s: From Technology Push to Market Pull* (Science Policy Research Unit, University of Sussex, Falmer, 1989).

37 See Kevin Morgan, *Breaching the Monopoly: Telecommunications and the State in Britain*, Working Paper Series on Government–Industry Relations, 7 (University of Sussex, Falmer, 1987).

38 D. Charles, P. Monk and E. Sciberras, *Technology and Competition in the International Telecommunications Industry* (Pinter, London, 1989).

[39] J. L. McKenney and H. E. Nyce, 'The role of the large corporation in the communications market', paper presented to Symposium on Future Competition in Telecommunications, Harvard Business School, Cambridge Mass., 27–9 May 1987.

[40] See for example Anthony Oettinger, *The Formula is Everything: Costing and Pricing in the Telecommunications Industry* (Harvard Program on Information Resources Policy, Cambridge Mass., 1988).

[41] Harry Trebbing, 'A critique of economic deregulation in the context of emergent industry structures in the USA', paper for CPR Conference, Windsor, June 1988.

[42] See Jill Hills, *Deregulating Telecoms: Competition and Control in the United States, Japan and Britain* (Pinter, London, 1986).

[43] Jeremy Tunstall, *Communications Deregulation: The Unleashing of America's Communications Industry* (Blackwell, Oxford, 1986).

[44] The best account of AT&T divestiture is to be found in P. Temin, *The Fall of the Bell System* (Camridge University Press, Cambridge, 1988).

[45] According to Judge Greene, *Opinion and Order Regarding Modifications to the Modified Final Judgment*, United States Department of Justice, Washington DC, September 1987.

[46] For an account of the effects of deregulation in bypass and universal service, see Patricia Aufderheide, 'Telephone policy in the public interest', *Journal of Communication* 37 (1987), pp. 81–98.

[47] *The Infrastructure for Tomorrow* and *The Evolution of the UK Communications Infrastructure* (HMSO, London, 1988).

[48] The early British debate on natural monopoly is described in J. S. Foreman-Peck, 'Natural monopoly and railway policy in the nineteenth century', *Oxford Economic Papers* 39 (1987), pp. 699–718.

[49] See W. Baumol, J. Panzar and R. Willig, *Contestable Markets and the Theory of Industry Structure* (Harcourt Brace Jovanovich, New York, 1982), and the extensive literature which has followed.

[50] For an excellent analysis of German and US telecommunications policy and of some of the underlying economic issues, see C. B. Blankart and G. Knieps, 'Comparative institutional analysis, *Kyklos* 42 (1989).

[51] N. Curien and M. Gensollen, 'De la théorie des structures industrielles à l'économie des réseaux de communication', *Révue Economique* 38 (1987), p. 521.

[52] See B. Copeland and A. Severn, 'Price theory and telecommunication regulation: a dissenting view', *Yale Journal of Regulation* 13 (1988), p. 53.

[53] W. R. Ashby, 'Self-regulation and requisite variety', in *Systems Thinking*, vol. 1 (Penguin, Harmondsworth, 1969).

54 See Robert Bruce et al., *From Telecommunications to Electronic Services: A Global Spectrum of Definitions, Boundary Lines and Structure* (Butterworth, London and Boston, 1986).

55 J.-M. Charon, 'Videotex: from interaction to communication', *Media, Culture and Society* 9 (1987), pp. 301–30.

56 *Report of the Committee on Financing the BBC* (HMSO, London, 1986).

57 For an analysis of how common carriage rules might be imposed on broadband network operators, see M. Botein, 'Can fibre-optic broadband networks be regulated?', *Intermedia* 17 (1989), p. 35.

58 Quoted in Judge Greene, *Opinion and Order*.

59 For a general analysis of the regulatory issues surrounding new services, see Robin Mansell, 'Telecommunication network-based services: regulation and market structure in transition', *Telecommunications Policy* 12 (1988), pp. 243–57.

60 Commission of the European Communities, *The Development of the Common Market for Telecommunications Services and Equipment* (CEC, Brussels, 1987).

61 After lengthy negotiations ONP principles were agreed by the Council of Ministers at its meeting of 7 December 1989, with a series of directives to be issued during the course of 1990–2.

Chapter 8 Communicative Values

1 Claude E. Shannon, *The Mathematical Theory of Communication* (Urbana, Ill., 1949); Warren Weaver, 'The mathematics of communication, *Scientific American*, July (1949), p. 12.

2 Honourable recent exceptions include Norman Clark and Calestous Juma, *Long-run Economics* (Pinter, London, 1987); John Foster, *Evolutionary Economics* (Pergamon, London, 1988).

3 A useful recent collection of work on the economics of information in markets is to be found in Frank Hahn (ed.), *The Economics of Missing Markets, Information and Games* (Clarendon Press, Oxford, 1989).

4 S. Grossman and J. Stiglitz, 'On the impossibility of informationally efficient markets', *American Economic Review* 70 (1980), pp. 393–408.

5 George Stigler, 'The economics of information', *Journal of Political Economy* 69 (1969), pp. 213–25.

6 Herbert A. Simon, *Sciences of the Artificial* (MIT Press, Cambridge Mass., 1969).

7 Gary Becker, *Human Capital and the Personal Distribution of*

Income: An Analytical Approach (University of Michigan, Ann Arbor, 1967).

8 F. Machlup, *Knowledge: Its Creation, Distribution and Economic Significance* (Princeton University Press, Princeton NJ, 1980).

9 E. A. G. Robinson, *The Structure of Competitive Industry* (Nisbet, London, 1931).

10 R. H. Coase, 'The Nature of the Firm', *Economica* 4 (1937); O. E. Williamson, *Markets and Hierarchies: Analysis and Anti-trust Implications* (Free Press, New York, 1975).

11 A rare exception is to be found in F. R. FitzRoy, 'The modern corporation: efficiency, control and comparative organization', *Kyklos* 41 (1988), pp. 239–62.

12 Such as Machlup's seventeen-category classification, 'The economics of information; a new classification', *InterMedia* 11 (2) (1983).

13 Ibid.

14 Hans Magnus Enzensberger, 'The industrialization of the mind', in *Dreamers of the Absolute* (Radius, London, 1988).

15 Barbara Tuchman, *The Distant Mirror* (Penguin, Harmondsworth, 1978).

16 For one of the best accounts of the theory of telecommunications pricing, see Edward Zajac, *Fairness or Efficiency: An Introduction to Public Utility Pricing* (Ballinger, Cambridge Mass., 1978).

17 See, for example, Tessa Morris-Suzuki, 'Capitalism in the computer age', *New Left Review* (Nov./Dec. 1986), p. 81.

18 Klaus Krippendorf, 'Information, information society and some marxian propositions', ICA, San Francisco 1984 quoted in Sandra Braman, 'Defining information', *Telecommunications Policy* 13 (1989).

19 P. H. Richman, 'Telecommunications, matter and the formation of value', *IEEE Technology and Society Magazine* 7 (1988), p. 20.

20 W. J. Baumol and E. N. Woolf, 'Feedback models', in *Communication and Information Economics* (North-Holland, Amsterdam, 1984), pp. 73–94.

21 See Kenneth Phillips, 'ISDN in the year 2000', *Telecommunications Policy* 12 (1988).

22 Though of course the newspaper may become extremely valuable in future years. For an interesting analysis of the strange life-cycles of value, see Michael Thompson, *Rubbish Theory: The Creation and Destruction of Value* (Oxford University Press, Oxford, 1979).

23 For example Charles Jonscher, 'The economic causes of information growth', *Intermedia* 10 (1982), pp. 3–37.

24 In *Electronic Data Interchange: A Management Overview* (Digital Equipment Company, Boston Mass., 1988).

25 William Connolly, *Political Theory and Modernity* (Blackwell, Oxford, 1988).

26 Key writings on the role of networks in diffusing innovation into and within organizations include Everett Rogers, 'Information exchange and technological innovation', in Devendra Sahal (ed.), *The Transfer and Utilization of Technical Knowledge* (Lexington Books, Lexington Mass., 1982), pp. 105–23.

27 J. D. Bernal, *Science and Industry in the Nineteenth Century* (Routledge & Kegan Paul, London, 1955).

28 N. Danilian, *AT&T: Story of Industrial Conquest* (Vanguard, New York, 1939).

29 David Dickson, *The New Politics of Science* (University of Chicago Press, London, 1988), p. 74.

30 Stuart MacDonald and Dieter Kimbel, 'Telecommunications-based networks from an information perspective', paper based on report for OECD Information, Computer, Communications Policy Committee, 1989, p. 6.

31 A. Newstead, 'Future information cities: Japan's vision', *Futures* 21 (1989), p. 263.

32 K. J. Arrow, 'Economic welfare and the allocation of resources for invention', in D. M. Lamberton (ed.), *Economics of Information and Knowledge* (Penguin, Harmondsworth, 1971), pp. 155–6.

33 MacDonald and Kimbel, 'Telecommunications-based networks from an information perspective', p. 9.

34 Quoted in Dickson, *The New Politics of Science*, p. 60.

35 Michael Dertouzous in *Technology Review* (MIT, Cambridge Mass., 1986).

36 Mary Cheh, 'Government control of private ideas', in Harold Relyea (ed.), *Striking a Balance: National Security and Economic Freedom* (Committee on Scientific Freedom and Responsibility, American Association for the Advancement of Science, Washington DC, May 1985), p. 17.

37 Stuart MacDonald and Tom Mandeville, 'Innovation protection viewed from an information perspective', in W. Kingston (ed.), *Direct Provision of Innovation* (Kluwer Academic, Dordrecht, 1987), pp. 157–70.

38 The major text pursuing this argument is Pierre Bourdieu, *Distinction* (Routledge & Kegan Paul, London, 1984).

39 Karl Polanyi, *The Great Transformation* (Beacon Press, Boston, 1944), p. 50.

40 W. Haug, *Critique of Commodity Aesthetics: Appearance, Sexuality and Advertising in Capitalist Society* (University of Minnesota Press, Minneapolis, 1986).

41   R. Collins, N. Garnham and G. Locksley, *The Economics of Television: The UK Case* (Sage, London, 1988).

42   For a full account of the shifting allocation methods used in the US, see C. Weinhaus and A. Oettinger, *Behind the Telephone Debates* (Ablex, Norwood NJ, 1988).

43   See G. Mulgan, 'Costs and tariffs in ISDN and advanced networks: whatever you can get away with', in *European Telecommunications Policy Research* (IOS, Amsterdam, 1989), pp. 217–42.

44   M. Porat, *The Information Economy*, vol. 2 (Department of Commerce, Washington DC, 1977), p. 7.

45   Michael Walzer, *Spheres of Justice* (Basic Books, New York, 1983), p. 10.

46   Bourdieu, *Distinction*.

Chapter 9   Standardization and Flexibility

1   P. Samuelson, 'The pure theory of public expenditure', *Review of Economics and Statistics* 36 (1954), pp. 387–9.

2   Paul David, 'New Standards for the economics of standardization', in Dasgupta and Stoneman (eds), *Economic Theory and Technology Policy* (Cambridge University Press, Cambridge, 1987).

3   Charles P. Kindleberger, 'Standards as public, collective and private goods, *Kyklos* 36 (1983), p. 384.

4   David Teece, 'Capturing value from technological innovation', in B. R. Guile and H. Brooks (eds), *Technology and Global Industry: Companies and Nations in the World Economy* (National Academy Press, Washington DC, 1987), pp. 65–95.

5   Jeffrey Rohlffs, 'A theory of interdependent demand for a telecommunications service', *Bell Journal of Economics* 5 (1974); John Wenders, *The Economics of Telecommunications* (Ballinger, New York, 1987) draws a distinction between call externalities (the benefits of being able to receive calls) and subscriber externalities (the benefit of being able to initiate calls). Both contribute to the interdependent nature of demand growth for interactive services.

6   For an economic approach to the anti-competitive use of standards see W. Adams and J. Brock, 'Integrated monopoly and market power: system-making, compatible standards and market control', *Quarterly Review of Economics and Business* 22 (1982), pp. 27–42.

7   K. Hayashi, 'The economies of networking: implications for telecommunications liberalization', paper presented to the 7th International Telecommunications Society 29 June 1988; M. L. Katz and C. Shapiro, 'Technology adoption in the presence of network externalities', *Journal of Political Economy* 94 (1986).

8   M. Katz and C. Shapiro, 'Network externalities, competition and compatibility', *American Economic Review* (1985), pp. 424–40 further explains why in the case of network services and equipment the value for consumers depends on expectations of network size.

9   H. Leibenstein, 'Bandwagon, snob and Veblen effects in the theory of consumer's demand', *Quarterly Journal of Economics* 64 (1950).

10 Paul David argues that Qwerty offers a classic example of inappropriate and premature standards setting: Paul David, 'Clio and the economics of QWERTY', *American Economic Review Papers and Proceedings* 75 (1985), pp. 143–9.

11 S. Berg, 'Public policy and corporate strategies in the AM stereo market', in H. Landy Gabel (ed.), *Product Standardization as a Tool of Competitive Strategy* (North-Holland, Amsterdam, 1987), pp 149–70.

12 The argument can be found in 'Telecommunication survey', *The Economist*, 23 November 1985, and Eli Noam, 'Integrated digital networks: questions of cost and worth', *International Herald Tribune*, 20 May 1986.

13 Documented in Rhoda Crane, *The Politics of Standards* (Ablex, Norwood NJ, 1979).

14 Raymond Melwig, 'High-definition television', *Endeavour* NS 13 (1989), p. 63.

15 S. C. Neil, 'The politics of international standardisation revisited: the US and high-definition television', paper presented to the International Telecommunications Society, Cambridge, June 1988.

16 CCIR Draft Report XE/11, *Future Development of HDTV*, Conclusions of Extraordinary Meeting of CCIR Study Group 11 on HDTV, Geneva, May 1989.

17 'HDTV', *Transnational Data and Communication Report* 13 (February 1990), pp. 27–9.

18 For a full analysis of this issue in the early history of electricity supply, see P. David and S. Bunn, 'The economics of gateway technologies and network evolutions: lessons from the electric supply industry', *Information Economics and Policy* 3 (1988), pp. 165–202.

19 For an economic account of the role of standards committees, see J. Farrell and G. Saloner, 'Coordination through committees and markets', *Rand Journal of Economics* 19 (1988), pp. 235–52.

20 A. Codding and A. M. Rutkowski, *The ITU in a Changing World* (Artech House, Wesley Mass., 1982), pp. 103–4.

21 In *Telecommunications* (New York), October (1987), p. 80.

22 Lee McKnight, 'The international standardization of telecommunications services and equipment', in E. J. Mestmaecker (ed.), *Transborder Telecommunications Law and Economics* (Nomos, Baden-Baden, 1987).

23 ETSI was established in 1988 under the aegis of CEPT, the Conference of European Post and Telecommunications Administrations.
24 In *Le Monde*, 21 January 1984.
25 Tadao Saito, 'How interconnectivity may evolve', paper presented to USERCOM/ITU, Amsterdam, 15–17 March 1989.
26 George Gilder, 'Microcosm', *Harvard Business Review* 3 (1988), p. 53.

Chapter 10　Electromagnetic Spectrum and Electronic Enclosures

1 Quoted in A. Briggs, *History of Broadcasting in the UK*, vol. 1 (Oxford University Press, Oxford, 1961), p. 105.
2 Garrett Hardin, 'The tragedy of the Commons', *Science* 162 (1968), pp. 1243–48.
3 Congressman Wallace White (Maine), during Congressional hearings, quoted in E. Emery, *Broadcasting and Government* (Michigan State University Press, Lansing Mich., 1961).
4 Lloyd Espenschied, quoted in Eric Barnouw, *The Tube of Plenty* (Oxford University Press, New York, 1975), p. 43.
5 The best account of the economics of television is to be found in B. M. Owen, J. H. Beebe and W. G. Manning, *Television Economics* (Lexington Books, Lexington Mass., 1974).
6 R. H. Coase argued that centralized administration of spectrum inevitably leads to an overallocation to government and military users. R. H. Coase, 'The Interdepartmental Radio Advisory Committee', *Journal of Law and Economics* (1962).
7 Mark Fowler and D. L. Brenner, 'A marketplace approach to broadcast regulation, *Texas Law Review*, 60 (1982).
8 12 KHz is based on digital encoding at 8 kbs, together with guard bands, redundancy and control channels.
9 I. de Sola Pool, *Technologies of Freedom* (Harvard University Press, Cambridge Mass., 1984).
10 This argument has become widespread during the 1980s. See, for example, Samuel Brittan, 'The myth of spectrum shortage', *Financial Times*, 16 April 1987.
11 R. H. Coase, 'The FCC', *Journal of Law and Economics*, (1959).
12 A. S. De Vaney et al. in *Stanford Law Review* (1969); and *A Property System Approach to the Electromagnetic Spectrum* (Cato Institute, Washington DC, 1980).
13 A. Felker and K. Gordon, *A Framework for a Decentralized Radio Service* (Federal Communications Commission, Office of Plans and Policy, Washington DC, 1983).
14 D. W. Webbink, 'Setting FCC licence fees according to frequency

spectrum: a suggestion', *IEEE Trans. Broadcasting* BC 17 (1971), pp. 64–9.

15 William H. Melody, 'Radio spectrum allocation: the role of the market', *American Economic Review Papers and Proceedings* 70 (1980), pp. 393–7.

16 R. Wilson, 'A bidding model of perfect competition', *Review of Economic Studies* 44 (1977), pp. 511–19.

17 Docket 80-116 (FCC, Washington DC, 1980).

18 *Deregulation of the Radio Spectrum in the UK* (HMSO, London, 1987). This was the successor to the 'Merriman Report': J. Merriman, *Report of the Independent Review of the Radio Spectrum (30–960 MHz)* (HMSO, London, 1983).

19 *Management of the Radio Frequency Spectrum in New Zealand* (NERA, London, 1988).

20 Fowler and Brenner, 'A marketplace approach', p. 232.

21 Quoted in *Subscription Television* (HMSO, London, 1987).

Chapter 11 Transnational Corporate Networks

1 Quoted in M. Kidron and R. Segal, *Business, Money and Power* (Simon and Schuster/Touchstone, New York, 1987), p. 41.

2 Martha Buyer, 'Telecommunications and international banking', *Telecommunications* (New York), (1982).

3 Direct outward investment becomes more than the export of surplus capital: it can also be explained as an inevitable effect of evolving firm structures. See M. Jussawalla, 'International trade theory and communications', in M. Jussawalla and D. Lamberton (eds), *Communications Economics and Development* (Pergamon, New York, 1982), pp. 82–97.

4 Ithiel de Sola Pool, *Forecasting the Telephone: A Retrospective technology Assessment* (Ablex, Norwood NJ, 1983).

5 See Jorg Becker (ed.), *Transborder Data Flow and Development* (Friedrich Ebert Stiftung, Bonn, FRG, 1987).

6 M. Hepworth, 'The geography of technological change in the information economy', *Regional Studies* 20 (1987), pp. 407–24.

7 Mitchell Moss, 'Telecommunications and the future of cities', *Land Development Studies* 3 (1986), pp. 33–44.

8 From *Transnational Data Flows* (November 1986).

9 Walter Wriston quoted in P. Zurkowski, 'Liberalisation: The US experiment', *Intermedia* 15 (1987), p. 38.

10 Edward W. Ploman, *Space, Earth and Communication* (Westport Conn., 1984).

11 James Beniger, *The Control Revolution: Technological and Economic*

Origins of the Information Society (Harvard University Press, Cambridge Mass., 1986).

12 Raymond Vernon, *Storm over the Multinationals* (Macmillan, London, 1977), p. 2.

13 C. Bartlett and S. Ghoshal, *Managing across Borders* (Harvard Business School Press, Cambridge, Mass., 1989).

14 Vernon, *Storm over the Multinationals*, pp. 1–2.

15 See, for example, J. Cash and B. Konsynski, 'IS redraws competitive boundaries', *Harvard Business Review* (1985).

16 'Private Networks 1988', *Satellite Magazine*, July 1988, p. 32.

17 R. E. Mansell, 'The telecommunications bypass threat: real or imagined?', *Journal of Economic Issues* (1986).

18 See, for example, the OECD report in *Science/Technology/Industry Review* 5 (1989).

19 M. Kenney and R. Florida, 'Japan's Role in a Post-Fordist Age', *Futures* 21 (1989), p. 136.

20 Peter Drucker, 'The Coming of the New Organization', *Harvard Business Review* (1988).

21 Masahiko Aoki, 'Horizontal vs vertical information structure of the firm', *American Economic Review* (1986).

22 Theodor Levitt, *The Marketing Imagination* (Macmillan, London, 1983).

23 S. Douglas and Y. Wind, 'The myth of globalization', *Columbia Review of Business*, Winter (1987), p. 22.

24 M. Piore and C. Sabel, *The Second Industrial Divide* (Basic Books, New York, 1984).

25 Walter J. Ong, *Orality and Literacy: The Technologising of the Word* (Methuen, London, 1982).

26 Charles Sabel, 'The reemergence of regional economies', paper presented to Conference on 'Impresa rete', Camogli, 2–4 June 1988; C. Antonelli (ed.), *New Information Technology and Industrial Change: The Italian Case* (Kluwer, Bordrecht, 1988).

27 H. Thorelli, 'Networks: between markets and hierarchies', *Strategic Management Journal* 7 (1986), pp. 37–51.

28 Karl. P. Sauvant, *International Transactions in Services* (UN CTC, New York, 1986).

29 S. Milmo, *Business Marketing* (April 1983).

30 C. Antonelli, *FAST Report on Motor and Textile Industries* (CEC, Brussels, 1986).

31 For an account of why Ford chose to leave the Motornet system to build an exclusive network with its suppliers, see John Large, 'How networks net business', *Management Today* (February 1987), pp. 86–94.

32 Alain Lipietz, *Mirages and Miracles* (Verso, London, 1987).
33 Yves Doz, *Strategic Management in Multinational Companies* (Pergamon, Oxford, 1986).
34 Bartlett and Ghoshal, *Managing across Borders*.
35 'An outdated view of globalisation', *Financial Times*, 11 December 1988.

Chapter 12 Rethinking Public Control

1 In Neil Postman, *Amusing Ourselves to Death* (Penguin, Harmondsworth, 1986).
2 Quoted in Graham Murdock, 'Markets media and liberal democracy', unpublished paper, Leicester University, 1988.
3 Richard Sennett, *The Fall of Public Man* (Knopf, New York, 1977), p. 282.
4 See, for example, Josiane Jouet, *L'Ecran apprivoisé: télématique et informatique à domicile* (CNET, Paris, 1987).
5 Carolyn Marvin, *When Old Technologies Were New* (Oxford University Press, Oxford, 1988), p. 66.
6 Ibid., p. 68.
7 Anthony Smith, 'The public interest', in Markle Foundation, *New Directions in Telecommunications Policy*, vol. 1: *Regulatory Policy, Telephony in Mass Media* (Duke University Press, Durham NC, 1989).
8 Daniel Bell, *Cultural Contradictions of Capitalism* (Basic Books, New York, 1976), p. 223.
9 J. Habermas, in *New German Critique* Fall (1974).
10 Jürgen Habermas, *The Structural Transformation of the Public Sphere*, trans. T. Burger (MIT Press, Cambridge Mass., 1989).
11 W. A. Robson, 'The BBC as an institution', *Political Quarterly* 6 (1935), p. 473.
12 Both Canada and Spain have also had privately owned operators.
13 Raymond Williams, *Television: Technology and Cultural Form* (Fontana, Glasgow, 1974), p. 34.
14 Forsyth Hardy (ed.), *Grierson on Documentary* (Faber & Faber, London, 1966), p. 139.
15 As Martin Wiener argued, the tradition was also strongly anti-commercial: *English Culture and the Decline of the Industrial Spirit, 1850–1980* (Cambridge University Press, Cambridge, 1987).
16 Yves de la Haye and Bernard Miege, 'French Socialists and the question of the media: fundamental issues in social communication', *Media, Culture and Society* 5 (1983), pp. 326–8.
17 Theodor Vail, quoted in the AT&T Annual Report, 1910.

18   Ernest Gellner, *Nations and Nationalism* (Blackwell, Oxford, 1983).
19   Moreover, universal service only came to be defined in many instances in response to pressures of liberalization. See N. Garnham, 'Universal service in European telecommunications', in N. Garnham (ed.), *European Telecommunications Policy Research* (IOS, Amsterdam, 1989).
20   Gellner, *Nations and Nationalism*, p. 1.

Index